KAHALA

KAHALA

Growing Up In Hawaii

LAURIE AMES BIRNSTEEL

Contact the author at Lbirns99@bellsouth.net

ISBN 978-1-942262-00-8

Printed in the United States of America

Third Edition

First published in the United States
by McKenna Publishing Group

CONTENTS

DOROTHY-BELLE JOHNSTON
1915-1984

MY MOTHER WAS BY NO MEANS A BEAUTY. She knew it. It didn't bother her. Being beautiful is a chore and a chore would have tied her down.

She never fussed with her appearance; kept the same haircut until the day she died. A ring of auburn-red curls rode around her head like a wild yarmulke. Her eyes, like my sister Cynnie-Belle's and brother Bruce's, were hazel. She did pluck her eyebrows, although it really wasn't necessary as her thick cat-eye glasses obscured that part of her face. The glasses, like her hair style, remained the same except for an occasional change of color. She always wore a gold ankle bracelet with "Dorothy" etched on the small rectangular plate. She was named by her only sibling, Duke, who loved *The Wizard of Oz*.

Mother wasn't a large woman. Personality-wise, yes. She never met a stranger. But physically, no. She was always fighting weight, yet was not fat. She stood about 5'4" and had small feet. Her only make-up was lipstick. She did, however, keep her toes and fingernails polished red at all times.

Decisions were not a priority. When she found something she liked, Mother bought in bulk. Shoes and purses were a weakness. They ranked with funny greeting cards, which were purchased and forgotten as soon as she got home.

Mother had a passion for gems. Her jewelry box held rings,

necklaces, and pins of ruby, sapphire, diamond, and aquamarine. She also had lots of earrings. I was fascinated when she bought a pair that could hold live guppies.

The beauty of my mother lay in her sense of humor, the allure of her quick wit, and her ability to evoke laughter. Her mind absorbed everything. She could recall lyrics from poems and songs then recite them with a flair at the appropriate moment. She seemed never to worry and laughed at those who built bomb shelters.

My mother was brilliant. She skipped two grades and was out of high school at age fifteen. Her father had skyrocketed into the world of finance, prestige, and wealth. By the time my mother graduated, he'd made his way up the proverbial ladder and stood on top of a vast fortune. He'd settled his family in Montclair, New Jersey, a short commute to his offices in New York. He bought a large house on lots of land and filled it with servants and silver. It was a long way from his humble beginnings as a lamplighter in a small Kentucky town. My grandfather had power over everyone. Everyone except my mother.

"My father," she'd say, "wanted me to go to a small women's college in Virginia, wanted to instill me with 'class.' I wanted to go somewhere where I wasn't known, where I wasn't defined by being his daughter." I loved to hear her tell this story and how, instead, she went to Europe and attended the Sorbonne before going to the University of Munich.

"I almost married a man I met in Germany. His name was Peter Balls."

I was glad she hadn't. I don't think I'd like being named Laurie Balls.

The impending war sent my mother back to America where she took courses at Columbia University. A short time later she married her best friend's older brother, who had returned to Montclair after his divorce.

I have never seen a picture of the happy bride and groom. I've never heard one detail about the wedding nor seen a newspaper clipping, much less an announcement. I assume the union was another way of getting to my grandfather, doing the unaccepted and unexpected. It certainly got her out of making her debut.

Kahala is a true story recreated through the use of Mother's day-by-day diaries. When I wrote the first draft, I thought it was about her. When I finished, I realized it was about me and my life with her and without her.

March 2000.

KAHALA

IN THE BEGINNING

MOTHER NEVER DID ANYTHING SIMPLY. My brother was born in a room which straddled a county line. He has two birth certificates. I was lucky to get even one.

I never took it as a rejection, the events surrounding my birth. I found it humorous when my mother referred to me as an accident. I was not expected. "A mistake," she'd say to whomever hadn't heard the tale. She had lost two babies, one to a miscarriage and the other, named Noel, to a lung problem two days after her birth. The losses had given my mother a devil-may-care attitude, at least that's what I thought. She described how she rode horses and I'd picture her bouncing along while I held on for dear life, a womb warrior. Obviously her attempts at dislodgment didn't work. When she accepted my reality, she settled on my being born the seventeenth of July, her birthday.

I was five days late. Labor started around 4:30 a.m. She attributed the discomfort to a batch of mint juleps she'd drunk the night before. She finally called her mother and the doctor. The ambulance didn't make it in time, but Grandmother did, and she delivered me amidst the imploring whines of my sister and brother, who stood outside the bedroom door wanting to know why their mother was breathing so hard. My father's attempts to quiet them fell on deaf ears.

I was wrapped in blue towels and whisked away in an ambulance which had gone to the wrong town. I spent the next ten days in isolation.

Contamination never set in. Nor, I believe, did bonding.

—

We moved to Hawaii in 1948. Montclair had been impossible in January. The new year was ushered in by a wild snow storm that rendered roads impassable. No trains ran. No electricity pulsed through wires. A state of emergency was called while Mother frantically stoked logs in the fireplace to keep warm. My father was out of town. It took five days to get power restored. By then Mother had had it. "We're going to Hawaii. We're going to visit Duke!" she declared. And we did. We visited for two months. Then we moved. Joined Uncle Duke, his wife Cecily, and their five children for a life in Aloha Land.

"We liked it so much, we moved," Mother always said, and I believed her. I used the same answer myself over the years. People weren't used to those who just up and moved so far away. I never questioned Mother's decision to locate in the middle of the Pacific. Had no reason to.

My mother didn't drive, blamed it on poor eyesight and a run-in with a truck the day she got her license. It made her sort of helpless. So when the move was made to Honolulu, she sent distress signals to her parents in Montclair. She referred to them as "God-sent" when Elsie and Watts, cook and chauffeur respectively, arrived from New Jersey. I watched in silence as they moved into the three rooms above the garage.

I disliked them immediately. Elsie smelled like whiskey. Her eyes were bloodshot and watery and reminded me of spaghetti and meatballs. Watts just smelled. I rebelled as best I could, often refusing to cooperate or doing so on a delayed basis. Witnessing my reluctance one afternoon, Mother pulled me into the bathroom and shut the door. "If you keep this up," she said as she bent down and leaned into my face, "I will cut off your head with a pair of dull manicure scissors, throw it in the garbage can, and put the lid on." I had no earthly idea what she was talking about, but beheading? I understood. I behaved. When she used that tone of voice, we all behaved.

Eventually, Elsie and Watts left. I don't think they were actually fired, because Mother booked them passage on a luxury liner named "Lurline." I waited five days for it to sail by our house. Mother referred to it as "Boat Week." Something was wrong with the engines. Mom lost her patience. "I don't care if they are afraid to fly," she said, then put them on a plane to New Jersey. Elsie and Watts became history which was okay. By then, Mom had Ellen to take their place.

The first time I laid eyes on Ellen, I was sitting at the kitchen table licking the remains of egg salad from a metal bowl. The bowl was so shiny I could see my reflection. Behind me Mother was washing dishes. I could hear the thunk and thud of plates. "This is getting real old," Mother muttered.

I was expecting the milkman with his bottles capped with waxed lids, lids to keep the cream from oozing out, but it was Ellen who made her way down the sidewalk toward our house.

"Is this the Ames residence?" she asked through the screened window.

Mother came rushing up behind me. "You must be Ellen. Thank God you're here. Cooking, cleaning, and taking care of these kids is for the birds," she said. Then added, "Myna birds."

In the beginning, it was all so simple. A space between World War II and McCarthyism. Pleasure was found in acts such as harvesting phosphorous at night. We'd start at dusk when the sun had departed, its afterglow still visible. As the orange and crimson skies melted into darkness, patches of phosphorus would start to appear in the shallows. We'd rush gleefully down the beach, the wet sand oozing between our toes, our silhouettes looking as if Tinkerbell were leading us to a treasure trove.

Finding a dense patch glowing a bright clear green, we'd squat down and carefully gather a cupped handful. There was an art to the harvest. You had to get under the patch in a way where it wouldn't break apart in your hand. It was like getting the first wedge of pie out of a pan. Once successful, Cynnie-Belle, Bruce, and I would carry the glow home, giggling and trying not to spill the sand. We sought the downstairs closet, the one full of medicines, towels, and smells of soap. We entered, one at a time, taking turns to watch the phosphorous in our created darkness. Sometimes we'd try to slide the sandy beds onto plates to carry upstairs for the night. Most often we'd dump the sand and wonder, the next morning, why it seemed such a big to-do the night before.

We lived between Kahala Avenue and the Pacific on the island of Oahu. Alleyways connected us with the sea. The avenue itself paralleled the ocean for almost two miles. It began at Black Point, which lay on the slopes of Diamond Head, a dormant volcano, and ended in a field of sugar cane just past the Waialae Country Club. About a fourth of a mile before it reached the club, the road traversed the first canal. It was a nice name for a drainage ditch. The second canal bordered the club itself.

The homes along the beach looked out on a bay complete with coral reefs. Almost in the middle there was a channel big enough to worry the military during World War II. Afraid of mini-subs beaching, they dumped a lot of old cars to block any passage into shallow waters. At low tide you could see the cars lying in their watery grave, automobiles made in the days of just black, inhabited by thousands of colorful fish, eels, and crabs.

The beach along the bay began as jagged rocks at Black Point. Retaining walls held back erosion. We rarely ventured to Black Point. The beach was under water at high tide. Low tide and certain conditions caused an influx of slimy green seaweed.

Walking on it was like walking on phlegm, and it smelled like rotten eggs in hot weather. The only reason for ever going there was to search for the likes of a lost dog. We lived far from it on the nicest stretch of the beach, just to the left of the channel.

Each alley connected to Kahala Avenue had its own particular ambiance. Those near the cane field were full of shanties; born-and-bred islanders whose heritage preceded the missionaries, lived in them. The most grandiose alley on the avenue led to Uncle Duke's home. His lawn was manicured by a slew of gardeners. Thick, plush foliage concealed his tennis court and swimming pool. I used to beg Mother for a pool of our own. "You have the entire Pacific Ocean to swim in!" she'd reply in not-too-friendly tones.

Our alley was raw and cluttered, full of carports. Most held one or two houses tucked neatly between the beachfront homes and the avenue. Ours had nine. All the homes were rented except the Buscher's, and they owned their own property. Fourteen children, all within five years of each other, commanded the territory. We ran wild along the beach, through each other's yards, and up and down the alley wearing no shoes and very little clothing. Sand was a constant on our bodies, in our hair. More often than not, knees were scraped and toes were stubbed on the dried tar that paved our paths.

The pivotal point in our alley, the place where it came to a tee, was a beach gate made of huge, heavy metal bars, much like those found in prisons. When slammed shut, it creaked and clanked. Behind the gate were the garbage cans. The place smelled like a dead bird, but it never bothered us. We'd tie rope to the bars and spend hours carving arcs and chanting songs hoping to throw skippers and jumpers off balance. Behind the gates, beside the trash cans, the boys drew circles in the dirty brown sand and played marbles.

Our home was the largest. The Buschers lived on one side, the Hueys on the other. Behind us were the Hanebergs. The

Hueys were bird people. They kept chickens and a rooster in a coop that bordered our back yard. Inside their house they had what seemed like a thousand parakeets. Although there were two large cages, the doors were opened wide. The birds flew freely, shedding feathers of all colors. Bird seed and droppings splattered everywhere. I thought it all wonderful. Their rooster was another story. The cock could only reach the crescendo of "a-doodle." Early in the mornings, I'd lie and listen to the surf pounding against the reef, my windows gently vibrating in the soft breezes, and the tides shifting sand. I could hear the rustle of coconut leaves, the incessant cooing of doves, and myna birds scolding and squawking at each other. It was all rather serene until the rooster began his repeated attempts to bring forth the day. I'd listen for the second half of his greetings, but the down side of "doo" was never realized. At least not to my knowledge.

We belonged to the Outrigger Canoe Club, a little fortress for the elite, in the heart of Waikiki. The club had room for canoes, catamarans, and surfboards. Three sand volleyball courts provided a release of energy when the men and women tired of water sports. The snack bar served food for those in wet bathing suits. It was always loaded with kids dripping in ice cream or slugging down a drink called "Green River," dispensed from a large, transparent glass bottle.

The Outrigger, located between the Royal Hawaiian and Moana Surfrider hotels, was not my mother's favorite place. We kids liked it, so she took us once in a while. She'd sit on the beach, towels spread between canoes, and watch us play in the ocean. It was there, on the beach at Waikiki, that Mother befriended the beachboys. She liked the beachboys, men devoted to the sea and having fun. They were a lovable group of guys who were quick to offer surfing lessons and canoe rides to visitors. They seemed to live laughing. I guess that's why they had funny names like Turkey, Steamboat, Blue, and Rabbit.

—

Soupy wasn't a beachboy. When he was not driving Mother around, he was a bartender at The Spare Room, a bar and bowling alley next door to my father's office. That's where she met him and found out he could drive. He replaced Watts as her chauffeur. Lucky for Soupy. He would never have made it as a beachboy. He was afraid of the water. Most beachboys didn't drive. They didn't need to. Their world revolved around the mile-or-so stretch of Waikiki Beach. They could walk to any of the hotels in a matter of minutes. Who needed a car? Beachboys seemed to have wings as they soared from land to sea.

One afternoon Soupy dropped Mother off. I watched her trot across the lawn as he backed out of the driveway. Cynnie-Belle, Bruce, and I were into a game of War. I was feeling happy and contented being with the two of them.

"Wait till you see what I got," Mother announced as she came through the door.

"Now what?" asked Cynnie-Belle, the disruption not to her liking. She was winning the game of cards, as usual.

"Beauty marks!" declared Mother.

I recoiled, frightened by the thought of her buying beauty. My mind raced. If she got beautiful, she might be gone even more, maybe for good. Cynnie-Belle and Bruce grabbed the sack and spilled its contents onto the dining room table, obviously not sharing my thoughts. They poked through tiny pieces of adhesive black silk, sliced into stars, quarter moons, top hats, and dots. It looked to me as if someone had cut up the black edges used to secure pictures in our photograph albums.

"Beauty marks," laughed Mother as she licked her index finger and stuck it onto a quarter moon. It adhered, she raised it toward her cheek bone and, with a quick swift stab, stuck it in place.

"See any difference?" she asked, smiling.

As the decade neared its end, Mother hired a photographer to document our claim to island life. We looked like a fine family. Mother had totally replaced her love of great danes in New Jersey with dachshunds in Hawaii. Pele, who belonged to the Hanebergs, and our Siegfried appeared in some of the pictures.

The photographer captured us in black and white—Mother and we girls in muumuus, Bruce and Father in aloha shirts. All our outfits matched. Children planted in the sand aimed Pele and Siggy at the camera. In one photograph, my sister's unruly mop of white hair is swept across her face by the wind. I have one eye shut, like a wink. My brother grins into the lens. His smile shows two missing front teeth at a time when a song on that subject was a hit.

There were also pictures taken of our living room, dining room, and lanai. A shot of the driveway includes my parents standing next to their latest two cars. We children aren't in it, but Pele and Siggy are.

Mother chose one taken under the tree in our front yard for the yearly Christmas card. We were leaning against an outrigger canoe. "Mele Kalikimaka," it says. "Aloha from the Ameses."

1950

As a new-decade present to each other, Mother and Father had the bar built. It faced out to sea, on the lanai, next to the base of the two steps that led to the living room door. The bar was quite elaborate. Its sides were inlaid with woven mats framed by two strips of bamboo. Its surface was a rich, deep mahogany, lacquered to a shiny perfection. It was well-made. Never ever got a water spot. Within the bar were an ice box; a sink with running water; drawers for utensils and towels; and enough space for bottles, glasses, and a work area. It also held a Victrola for the heavy 78-rpm records Mother brought with her from New Jersey. When the bar was finished, they hung a couple of coconut hats and pictures on the walls above it. Two signs were also put up. One read "Bartender on Duty." The other asked on one line, "Do you serve women here?" On another, "No, you have to bring your own."

I guess it was pretty funny to them.

I liked to play bar. I suppose I could have called it playing "room," another term for "bar" as in the Spare Room by Father's office and the Sky Room at the airport. Room sounded better than Spare Bar or Sky Bar. I settled for bar. It didn't matter what I called it, the rules were the same. I'd color water and funnel it into empty bottles, take orders from whomever was around, mix and serve. Ellen, who had settled into the quarters above the garage, didn't drink. I served her "real" water or soda pop.

I played bar in the kitchen a lot. The real bar on the lanai was too high. No one could see me when I stood behind it, so I played bar in the kitchen. There was a recessed corner to the right of the sink where a second set of supplies was kept. I assume there was a bar area in the kitchen because it was easier than going outdoors. Maybe that's not right; maybe they just wanted the house covered at both ends. At any rate, I'd play away, mixing and serving fake concoctions to whomever would pay attention. Mother was a great customer. "Make me a sidecar," she'd say. She would take a sip, smack her lips together, and praise my talent. I usually offered to make something else, too, but she rarely had the time. Once, to prove I was a true bartender, I slipped into pidgin English for authenticity.

"Hey, Dottie," I yelled as she came through the front door. "You like one drink?" I was decked out in an apron and mopping the kitchen counter with a damp cheese cloth.

"What?"

"You like one drink, me make one, den you go jump in da watta, swim."

"Don't you dare talk like that," she said, looking me straight in the eye. "But Mom, bartenders talk like that."

"But you are not a real bartender." She turned and walked off.

I watched her leave in confusion. "Mom," I called, "I was just pretending." But she was gone. Maybe she just didn't hear me. Maybe she had that thing she called the curse. I took off my apron and threw the cheese cloth back into the bucket full of water and Ivory soap.

I got sick a lot, no big deal. As a matter of fact, I liked the attention, mostly from Ellen. For awhile, life seemed like one continuous cold.

"Her tonsils need to come out," Dr. Lam said. He was holding a mirrored instrument to the back of my throat, showing my mother the inflammation.

"That's fine," she said as he withdrew the object of torture. "These trips to your office aren't easy . . . ."

"Mom, guess what. My throat doesn't hurt. I feel great." I had hopes of thwarting the operation from the start.

"Don't be a worry wart, there's nothing to it. You go to sleep, and you wake up."

The thought of being cut scared me. I decided not to think about it. Maybe something would come up and it would be forgotten.

When nothing came up, I was taken to a small hospital. I was not happy. When they tried to lift me onto the moving table, I fought tooth and nail. I won. A nurse had to carry me to the operating room. It took two to hold me down while a third placed a strainer-like basket over my face.

"Breathe," said a voice. What a dumb thing to say. The smell was the last thing I remembered.

I was very thirsty when I awoke and was also very indignant. They had me in a crib! My mother and Soupy came in. Mother carried a cup of ice cubes.

"I don't want ice cubes, I want water," I whispered as she sat down by my crib.

"Water will make you sick. You're to take liquids a little at a time, so here, take an ice cube." She plucked one from the cup.

"I want water and I want out of this baby bed!"

"The crib is for your safety, so you won't fall out. And I said no water. It's the doctor's orders."

I wanted to ask if I could lick her hand as I watched a few drops fall to the floor, but I didn't. It hurt to talk.

"Look, I'll leave this cup here, take a few sips at a time. Get some sleep, I'll be back later."

Then she was gone.

My father came after work. He brought me a dish of ice cream and stayed with me while I ate it.

The next morning I felt much better. So did the little boy

in the crib across the floor. We started jumping up and down trying to outdo each other in the obscenities department.

"Wee-wee," I'd yell.

"Doo-doo," he'd say, and we'd fall onto our beds laughing hysterically. It didn't take long for the nurses to arrive and put a stop to our game.

A few months earlier, my mother had had an operation to shrink the varicose veins in her legs. She'd brought a glass straw home from the hospital. "Here," she'd said, "a present." It didn't take long for it to break. They didn't give me a glass straw when I left the hospital that afternoon. In fact, the nurses seemed somewhat astounded by my request.

My mother always wore a bathing cap. Its rubber strap, fastened tightly to a snap under her left ear, sucked the skin beneath her chin. I never understood why she wore such a thing. By the time the swim was swum, normal leakage, coupled with a sweaty scalp, left her curls a plastered-down rendition of what had been.

Nevertheless, cap on head, she'd plunge blindly into the Pacific. Eyeglasses to see and a shot glass filled with brandy to fortify body and soul were left on a towel in our front yard.

Mother swam in slow motion. I always thought the rubber cap with its dense, embossed floral design helped slow her down. It was quite heavy. Off she'd go, without warning, practicing her sidestroke and frog kick as she headed off shore. I'd try to keep up with her. I'd plunge in and race after her, once I realized she'd left.

"Mom. Wait for me," I'd shout as I dog paddled toward her.

"Don't come too far," she'd yell.

Although she swam in slow motion, she was always beyond my reach.

Once in a while I would catch her. Sometimes I was able to throw myself into her arms before she'd make her break. I could feel the cool dampness of her skin—skin like the lizards that lived on our screened windows. In no time, she would tense, extract herself from my grip, and swim away.

Sufficiently exercised, she'd pull herself out of the water, stroll back to the grass, pat herself dry, and pull the cap from her soaked curls. If she decided to sunbathe, she'd go behind the bar, select some loud blues music, and lie down with a wash rag over her face.

"The Tennessee Waltz," sung by Patti Page, pulsed from the jukebox. It was late. Earlier that day we'd gone on a picnic, a rare event for our whole family. Mother went on lots of picnics with Soupy, but not with us. This time not only did we get to go, but so did Father.

We left home before noon and made the winding trip along the cliff-lined coast that jutted high above the sea. We arrived in the rustic town of Waimanalo an hour later. It was the usual flawless, deep-blue sky, puffy clouds, gentle breezes, crystal-clear kind of day. Waimanalo Bay had a calm, gentle beach with lots of white sand around and under the sea.

We waded in the ocean with glass-bottom boxes that allowed us to see beneath the surface. We played tag with the waves, following them as they receded, then scurrying to dry safety before the next set lapped the shore. We ate tuna fish sand-wiches and deviled eggs with sandy hands. We drank Coca-Cola from glass bottles.

"Let's go kids, let's pack it up."

"Oh Mom," said Cynnie-Belle. "We just got here, can't we stay longer? We never do things together like this."

"What do you mean?" she asked. She sounded a little angry. "We do all sorts of things together. Besides, we want to get home before dark."

"It's early," said Cynnie-Belle. "It won't be dark for hours."

Bruce and I stayed out of it. If anyone were to win an argument, it would be Cynnie-Belle.

"Look, we'll do this again."

"When?" asked Cynnie-Belle.

"Soon," she replied. "Now scoot."

Father stood there, watching, saying nothing in our defense. A word on our behalf might have helped.

We packed up and piled into the car for the trip home. We weren't ten minutes into the journey before Mother suggested stopping to have "one for the road." Hours later, we once again headed for home. We drove into the sunset, past the shacks, Quonset huts, ice houses, tents, and small wooden cottages that sprinkled the coastline. By then, the fruit and vegetable stands along the unlit cliffs had closed.

My parents celebrated their thirteenth wedding anniversary by taking us all to The Willows for lunch. The Willows was a wonderful restaurant. It was built around a pond, its floors so low you could stick your toes in the water. The pond was covered with lily pads; tons of fish swam among them. There were ordinary little fish and large multi-colored carp. We'd feed the fish while waiting for our meals and scamper around the different levels of the restaurant. In one area there was a small waterfall created by a drop in the terrain.

"Barbara Buscher fell in once," warned Mother.

"The Barbara who lives next door?" I asked.

"The same," she said. "Be careful."

The Willows had waitresses who wore jumpers with large ruffles at the shoulders. I was enchanted with their uniforms and wished I were older so that I, too, could be a waitress. They were so kind to everyone, especially children. They knew what we would order and had the Shirley Temples delivered before we could ask. The Willows specialized in pies with at least a three-inch cloud of meringue. Never once did I see a topping slide off.

—

Christmas arrived. We all piled into the family car in search of the perfect tree. They weren't much to look at as they were shipped to the islands on anything except luxury liners that crossed the ocean. Once they arrived, they stood on dry docks until distribution points were selected.

"These are awful, too," said Cynnie-Belle, mad. "Let's go!"

"No more," said Mother. "This is the third and final lot we're going to look at. It's obvious they're all going to be scrawny."

"These are terrible," Cynnie-Belle continued.

"Let's get a white one," I said, pointing to a man who was spray painting a tree with white foam.

"No," Mother said. "They look fake."

"But Mom, these trees have been painted green," I argued, proud of holding my own in front of Cynnie-Belle and Bruce. I pulled out a branch for her inspection.

"So, they've had a long trip and needed a goose," she said, reaching to pinch my fanny. I scooted ahead of her.

"Hey, we're getting a green tree," she called to me. "It doesn't snow here, snow looks fake."

I really didn't care about the color of the tree. I thought they were all gorgeous. To ease my sister's anger, my mother bought a can of white foam which Cynnie-Belle promptly took over. She used most of it to write "Merry Christmas" on the side of the wash-house.

On Christmas Eve we left our stockings for Santa draped on the backs of chairs, as we had no chimney. "He'll come through the kitchen door," said Mother as we headed out with water for the reindeer.

"What about the oleander bushes?" I asked as I set the bowl down on the grass. Oleander bushes separated us from our neighbors. Mom told us never to eat its leaves. "Poison!" she warned.

"What about the oleander bushes? What if the reindeer decide to nibble on them?"

"Don't worry, reindeer are real smart. They won't."

I was absolutely positive I heard hooves on the roof before I fell asleep.

The next morning, we came down the stairs as the sun rose. We always opened our stockings first. I was halfway through opening presents when I came upon the box . . . . A nightgown or bathrobe, I thought. I could always tell clothes, clothes made no noise. Not one for great enthusiasm and gushing over gifts, I opened the package with nonchalance.

I was stunned as I pushed the tissue aside and pulled out the content. My heart started pounding, I couldn't speak. My hands rested on the most beautiful dress I'd ever seen, much less hoped to own. It was a pure white pinafore with smocking to the waist. Its shoulders were engulfed in a wide arch of ruffles. It looked like a Willow's bridal gown. I was beside myself and ran to hug my mother.

"It's just like a Willow's waitress dress but better."

She smiled; she should have. She had outdone herself. The rest of the presents didn't matter. I had the best gift in the world. The thought that Mother might prefer my playing waitress flitted briefly through my mind.

Later that day, Mother prepared for the first of her eggnog parties. She had an old recipe from her mother's family. It required an in-order method of preparation. She let us help. We were allowed to crack and beat eggs, pour in the cream, sugar, and finally add the liquor. "Slowly," my mother would say. "Pour it in slowly, we don't want to bruise the bourbon." I wasn't sure what she meant by bruising the bourbon, but pour slowly we did with delight.

Late in the afternoon, after the bourbon had had time to "cook" the other ingredients, the neighbors came over. They drank the eggnog from silver goblets served from a petaled silver punch bowl. It was quite an impressive production. I dispensed napkins, standing back far enough to keep from getting splashes on my brand new dress. Everyone liked it, I know. They told me. I was happy. I was in seventh heaven.

We left for Maui. Bruce and I went; Cynnie-Belle stayed home with Ellen. Father had a meeting to attend. He couldn't go, but Soupy could. My brother was seething. "I'm sick of that guy hanging around Mom," he told me in secret.

After we arrived, Mother deposited us in the Maui Grand Hotel. She left for a golfing tournament, or some such thing, with friends. "I'll check on you tomorrow," she said as she kissed me. "Be good to her," she warned Bruce. Then she was gone.

I had worn my new white dress on the plane but had changed into shorts so as not to get the dress dirty. It was lying on the back of a chair, sort of like an unfilled stocking at Christmas, when Bruce grabbed it and started taunting me.

Bruce had hopes of going fishing and brought his new bamboo fishing pole with him. Before I realized what was happening, he hooked my dress to the line and cast it out the second story window.

Horrified, I raced down the stairs and dashed outside to retrieve my prized possession. As soon as I got near, he reeled it back into the room.

This went on for some time. I'd run back up; he'd fling it out the window; back down I'd go, enraged.

Bruce ultimately got bored with the situation and pitched my dress on a chair before I raced into the room for the last time. I was on the attack when he knocked the bottle off the desk. I heard a cracking sound, glass skidding on glass then saw the bottle fall to the floor.

It fell in slow motion.

The liquid, loosened in flight, joined the rest of the mess on the carpet. We stared in horror as the puddle of blue ink grew.

It was then that he grabbed my dress, fell to his knees and began rubbing and mopping up the spreading stain. I was stunned by the enormity of his actions.

"Stop it." I screamed, "You'll ruin my dress."

Bruce never looked up. When an area of white became blue, he'd pick a clean place on the dress and go at it again. I watched, crushed. Realizing the hopelessness of it all, I started to cry. I started and I couldn't stop. Bruce hurled threats to no avail. I was finally forced to quit when I developed a fierce nosebleed and couldn't breathe.

"You can't go to dinner," Bruce told me. "They won't let you looking that way. You'll make people sick."

I spent a miserable evening alone in the room. The next morning Mother arrived. When she realized what had happened, she bawled out Bruce. "You are seven years old! Laurie's only four. Shame on you," I heard her say. "Tonight, you'll go without dinner."

I knew he'd stuff himself all day, and I resented his punishment.

"We'll find you another dress, Laurie," Mother said.

"I don't want another dress," I told her, then muttered, "I'm going to stick to tending bar."

"What did you say?" she asked.

"Nothing."

We returned home on New Year's Eve only to realize we had no fireworks. A frantic search ensued. Soupy carted us to Kailua, a small town on the other side of the island. No luck. We finally found some at K. Okada's, a tiny mom-and-pop grocery complete with wooden floors and live chickens roaming around the establishment. Okada's was located a little inward from Kahala Avenue. You could cut through the pig farms and get there in no time.

I wasn't fond of New Year's Eve. I didn't mind the firecrackers or sparklers that started early in the afternoon. I was fascinated by a new type my father had brought home. He'd light it, and as it burned, it evolved into what looked like a brown snake or a pile of doo-doo. It made no noise, which I liked. It also put permanent stains on the floor of the lanai, which we didn't realize until too late.

New Year's Eve was too noisy. I hated the cherry bombs that people went berserk over near midnight. They ascended into heaven whistling shrilly before exploding and lighting up the entire sky. I'd stay inside when they started and cup my ears when the whistles began. For comfort, I'd hold Siggy, who had been trembling since the first burst of firecrackers earlier in the day.

At midnight, residents all over Kahala and back into the mountains would string rows of firecrackers into trees and light them. Some people could get the lines going for twenty to thirty minutes. The incessant popping annoyed me, as did the smells of gun powder and smoke. By one o'clock it was almost over. I crawled into bed anticipating a silence, but the silence was broken by isolated bangs for a few more hours. Finally, I slept, a sleep interrupted too soon by the feeble sound of the Huey's rooster at dawn.

1951

I DON'T KNOW WHOSE IDEA IT WAS, but it sounded like a nifty one. We'd start the New Year with a neighborhood picnic and burn our Christmas trees on the beach, all together, in unison. If by rare chance it got out of control, the trees could be pitched into the ocean.

We met at four. We had spent the earlier part of the day dismantling our creations. My task in the process had been to remove the ornaments from the lowest limbs of the tree. It required a lot of bending and crawling around. I emerged a little scratched and covered with what few pine needles were left. While we dismantled the tree, my mother made deviled eggs for the festivities. Ellen was off for a few days.

Soon, the trees began to arrive from all directions. Up and down the beach they came from as far away as Uncle Duke's. Neighbors near the avenue brought them down the alleys. Some were carried, others dragged, but they all got there and were heaped into a pile on the sand.

We began eating hot dogs and eggs and drinking soft drinks. All the children were congenial, no fights, no gang-ups occurred. It was fun, sort of mellow, until the trees were torched. The moment the match touched, the grown-ups realized they had made a tremendous mistake. Flames licked the air with wild abandon, climbing higher as each successive tree caught fire. The heat was intense and everyone backed off in a hurry. Pitching the trees into the sea seemed a dumb idea.

Parents started screaming for us to return home. We pretended we couldn't hear them over the roar.

Mr. Buscher ran for his hose. It was too short. Other adults took off to find their hoses, hoping to have enough to attach together to reach the incipient inferno. Someone finally had sense enough to call the fire department. They arrived, but not before a large patch of grass was burned in the Buscher's yard.

"You folks lucky," I heard a fireman say. "If wind come up, your houses woulda burn down."

Shortly thereafter, an ordinance was passed banning the burning of Christmas trees on all beaches.

"You're going to nursery school," Mother announced .

"I don't want to go to nursery school," I said. It would cut into what little time I spent with her.

"Sure you do," she replied. "You'll go off in the mornings just like Cynnie-Belle and Bruce."

"I don't want to go off like them. I want to stay home."

"You're going to nursery school and you will love it."

I thought about crying but decided it would do no good. She seemed pretty firm on the subject. I hoped, however, to wear her down, like Bruce had the month before when she sent him to camp.

Bruce did not want to go to camp. A counselor had to hold him back when we left. The following weekend we went to visit. Soupy drove. "He put on a disgraceful exhibition," my mother said to Father when we got home. "He chased after the car then threw himself onto a thorny bush as we sped away."

I had watched the disgraceful exhibition through the rear window. His actions scared me, but they worked. He came home a few days later. Armed with the knowledge of his success, I had every intention of wearing my mother down.

"Mom," I said a few days later, "why can't I stay home with the maids?" It wasn't as if the house were empty during the day.

Faye came two days a week for heavier cleaning. Stella, Ellen's sister, came once a week to iron. "Why can't I stay with them?"

"Because they are busy doing their jobs. They're not baby-sitters."

"I'll be good, I'll help them, like I do now for Ellen. I need to stay home, Mom," I pleaded. My pleas fell on deaf ears.

I began to worry. I still had no intention of leaving Ellen. I needed to be there when the milkman arrived. Who would add the bluing to the wash to keep it white? Who would carry the bird cages out for their daily dose of sun. "Who?" I asked my mother.

"I don't want to hear it," she said.

When I got particularly obnoxious, she'd threaten to cut my head off with a pair of dull manicure scissors.

I did not give in with ease. To be in school required a doctor's exam. I disliked the doctor's office as much as the thought of school. When the morning of my appointment came, I made like Siggy, and I took off for parts unknown.

I could hear Mother calling me as I fled across the Buscher's front yard. When I reached the alley, I took a left and headed toward the avenue. Mrs. Haneberg, with a sack full of trash, spotted me from the garbage cans. I mumbled something to her, turned, and headed back out toward the beach.

Mother's shouts were getting closer. Her tone told me she was truly ticked off. I saw her before she saw me and dove into the oleander bushes which bordered the alley.

I can't see how she missed seeing me curled into the hedges. I stared at her red toenails as she called to Mrs. Haneberg.

"Have you seen Laurie?" she yelled down the path.

"She was just here," came the reply.

It was then Mother looked down.

"I can't believe this of you," she snarled as she dragged me up and out by the arm. "You've always been my good child, how could you?" she continued as she hauled me into the kitchen and dumped me onto a chair, strapped my sandals on in silence, and pulled me out and into Soupy's car. Off we roared to acknowledge my fitness to belong to the real world.

Mother and I sat in Doctor Lam's office waiting to hear his report. He had a stuffed pheasant on his desk. It was a real ratty old bird, but I wanted it. It made such a statement in his office, up there in the coolness of Manoa Valley. It symbolized all I did not want to be just then . . . dry, mounted on someone's desk, looking like a pheasant that had been shot down before it could ask questions, fend for itself, talk back, fly.

"Mom, could you ask Dr. Lam if I could have that bird?"

"No," she said.

So I did when he came in. "Do you think I could have that bird?" I asked, pointing to the pheasant as Dr. Lam came into the room.

"Sure," he told me. "It's seen better days, in fact it's falling to pieces." He reached over to pick it up. A few feathers dislodged and floated to the floor. My room could be a Huey room, I thought.

"Laurie, no," Mother growled between clenched teeth.

I passed the physical, failed to bring home the pheasant, and was escorted to nursery school. Father drove, dropped off my mother and me, and left to take Cynnie-Belle and Bruce to school at Punahou a few blocks up the street. As we walked on the sidewalk that separated the two classrooms in silence, I still hoped she'd abandon the idea. We entered the door of the inner building.

Children were playing all around the room. Some were dressing in grown-up clothes pulled from a trunk; others were cooking in a make-believe kitchen on a make-believe stove; still others sat silent and watched the activities. It was foreign to me. I didn't like seeing so many kids my own age, and the prospect of playing with them made me want to weep. I am not going to stay here, I told myself.

The teacher approached. She was large, elderly, with gray hair. She smiled.

"This is Laurie," said Mother. "She sure is looking forward to nursery school."

"Good morning, Laurie," The large lady said. "You're going to have a wonderful time here." She reached out to touch me, but before she could, I leaned over and spit on her foot.

My mother and father spent a lot of time on the island of Maui. They were building a vacation home. A place for the family to go on holidays. "We're going to name it "Hale Ola," she told us. "That means 'House of Happiness' in Hawaiian. It's on the ocean, and Laurie, there's a stable down the street."

I loved horses. My pre-birth gallops might have had something to do with this love, adoration, and esteem I held for the animal. My first horse, made of wood, lived in our back yard. It consisted of a head attached to a seat by a strip of wood and was short enough for my hands to grip its pegged ears. The saddle was on a spring that pitched back and forth when rocked. I'd ride that black and white chunk of wood for hours while belting out tunes at the top of my lungs. By the time it disintegrated, Cynnie-Belle had given me Gilly. Gilly was made of metal. He stood about three feet tall. I rode him by pushing down then releasing his pedal stirrups. Gilly was easier to pull around than ride. Made a lot of noise either way.

"Actually, the stable is about a mile away, but you can walk. Saddle Road is a safe street. Only one way in and out," Mother continued. "Beach houses on one side and a barbed-wire fence on the other. The barbed wire was put up to keep people off the railroad track."

I really wasn't interested in the road. The horses were another story. I waited for her to continue about the stables.

"Of course, the barbed wire and railroad tracks make it hard to run inland if there's a tidal wave. But the real estate agent assured me one hasn't hit the area in over forty years." Then she left in a taxi for the airport.

"Pele's getting fat," I told Mother as I watched the dog waddle across the driveway.

"Siggy and Pele got married," she said.

When? I wondered. Siggy was running off at least once or twice a week. Sometimes he was gone for days. "Marriage makes a dog fat?" I asked.

"Pele's going to have puppies," she said.

Puppies, I thought. That is interesting! Siggy was around about as much as my father was. But maybe that's what marriage was all about, being separated all the time. I didn't buy the reasoning, of course. All the neighbors were married and the fathers were always home except during the day. Even the neighborhood dogs stayed around. Curly, the Buscher's cocker, stayed home. As if the rooster weren't enough, Curly stayed home, slept all day, and barked all night. And Uncle Duke's dog, Blackie. He'd come down the beach to visit, but not without a human at his side. Siggy must have his reasons . . . .

Pele had her puppies.

Siggy joined the Salvation Army.

At least that's what Mom told us when she came home with a puppy tucked under either arm. "Salvation Army's going to love him, I mean Siggy joining an organization for the homeless? It's a natural."

The puppies were adorable but gone in a few weeks. One got lost. Another was found down the beach with a spear through its head. Mrs. Haneberg gave us the last of the litter. Mom named her Frauline. I watched Frau like a hawk. I wasn't about to let this one go. I thought my constant vigil would make Frau devoted to me. It didn't. She loved my mother most, like me, in spite of her absence.

Soupy left like Siggy. It might have had something to do with Cynnie-Belle and Bruce cutting up his clothes. They discovered his suitcase in the train room, thought he had plans to move in with us, and they weren't going to let it happen. Cynnie-Belle scrounged up the scissors and the two spent a few hours cutting the contents of his suitcase to shreds.

The train room took up the entire left side of our garage. My father had it filled with Lionels. They buzzed through tunnels, stopped at depots, crossed drawbridges, and had passenger cars that lit up inside. The engine belched smelly white smoke when the whistles blew.

My father controlled his trains. No one was to touch them, and he kept the door to the room shut. Cynnie-Belle and Bruce had found the suitcase in an area already off-limits. Being discovered in the act of sabotage was unlikely.

My mother found the suitcase the next day. Not being a participant, I watched her anger fall on Cynnie-Belle and Bruce. She scolded, told them how disappointed she was, and how it hurt her. The lecture fell on deaf ears. Cynnie-Belle and Bruce were nonchalant. They stood, arms folded, and waited until she was finished. Before the punishment could be doled out, Cynnie-Belle announced that they were going to run away.

"Fine," said Mother, "stay right there."

She came back shortly with two bundles of their clothes, each attached to a branch of panax hedge. I was so enthralled with the procedures for their departure I failed to get upset.

"Farewell," my mother yelled, waving a white handkerchief for effect. Not to be outdone, I picked up Frau and, flapping her paw, yelled goodbye to their backs.

Secretly, I believe my mother was ready for Soupy to leave our lives. As Bruce and Cynnie-Belle disappeared around the corner, she turned to me with a slight smile on her lips and a definite twinkle in her eyes.

Cynnie-Belle and Bruce weren't gone long nor did they make it very far down the avenue. Mrs. Buscher saw them. "They said they were going to seek their fortunes," she later told my mother.

"It's a letter from your teacher," said Bruce, waving a white sheet of paper in front of my nose. "It was on Mom's desk. Want to know what it says?"

I eyed my brother, not sure of his intentions. The day before he'd tricked me into taking a sip of 7-Up from a bottle he'd peed into. I'd been had, and I wasn't going to be had again. I looked at him for any signs, signs I might have been missing. Chuckling clues like the ones he suppressed as he handed me the green bottle of soda. This was after he came out carrying it from the bathroom.

"Why would she write to me?"

"It's not to you, it's about you. You never listen! The letter's to Mom and Dad. See? It's got Mr. and Mrs. on the envelope."

I couldn't read, but stared at it as if I could.

"Why is it about me?"

"Chicken-why-why," he replied.

"Not funny," I said, starting toward him.

"Chicken-why-why," he repeated. "Chicken-why-why."

"I'm not chicken," I snapped, tasting the anger. "I am not a chicken, you jerk," I yelled. "I drank your piss, didn't I? I knew what you'd done; I faked it, though. You thought I drank from that bottle. Well, let me tell you, I faked it."

"Yeah?" Bruce said with a snarl. "You faked it as well as you pretended to read this envelope?"

Once more he waved the white sheet of paper in front of me.

"I hate your guts," I screamed as I hurled misdirected punches in his direction. Bruce danced backward, holding the paper beyond my reach.

"I hate you," I repeated . . . again and again and again.

But I didn't. Later, the two of us settled into the space between his twin beds. Holding a flashlight, Bruce read to me under a tent of blankets the words typed on the white sheet of paper.

"Laurie seems more interested in herself than others. She seemed quite moody when first enrolled and would cry to herself on the church steps before coming into the room."

"You cried?" asked Bruce. "Why?"

"Chicken-why-why," I told him. What I was really thinking was, "Who is he to ask me why?"

I could feel my brother's eyes boring into me. "Hey, drop the chicken bit," his voice was steady. "Why did you cry? What was wrong?"

"Dunno," I told him. "Didn't want to be there. Wanted to stay home with Ellen."

He continued reading. "She always seems to need love and attention. We make an effort to give her this security, and she responds well. The fact that she's the youngest of three in a very busy family may account for her distress."

"Busy family? Do you think we have a busy family?" Bruce asked. He turned and looked me in the face.

"Well, if busy means not home, yeah, I guess."

"Well, you probably cry because you are the youngest," he said emphasizing you are.

Bruce glanced back down at the page. He seemed uncomfortable. "Says you climb well and handle large blocks with ease. You are a good talker and crave attention from adults. That means grown-ups," he clarified as he folded the letter. "I better put this back before Mom comes home."

"Don't worry, Bruce. She's still on Maui. She called earlier, won't be back for a few days."

Mrs. Buscher and Mrs. Haneberg had baby boys. Both were so precious. Too precious. They'd crawl around clutching baby bottles in their chubby little hands. I'm not sure who thought of it first, but we older kids decided that we could be just as cute if we, too, had baby bottles of our own. All mothers were begged to the point of relenting. For awhile, most children could be seen clutching baby bottles. Mom let us pour Coca-Cola into ours. The other kids were jealous, said their mothers swore Cokes caused our teeth to rot. When Bruce lost a tooth, we placed it in a bowl of Coke for weeks. Nothing happened. Mom said she'd keep buying Cokes after our experiment, said she didn't trust rumors anyway. Sometimes we'd drink apple juice or milk from our bottles. Orange or guava juice required biting a bigger hole into the nipple. The baby bottle phase ended around the time we got sewers.

"Make way for King Iolee," we chanted as we pranced around Calley Haneberg. She was pushing her brother in his stroller. The baby, as always, was standing up, holding the tray for support. "Make way for King Iolee," we chorused, pausing to mute our giggles. We were sure the grown-ups, who stood discussing the boxes of dried human bones that lined the alley, were not aware of the few times we slipped in the word "okole," the Hawaiian word for fanny.

The smell of salty, wet sand came from the trenches dug straight down the alley. Kahala Avenue was also dug up. There were pits with pipes to take waste out to sea. Septic tanks were being replaced, sewers were being installed. More than once ours had backed up, usually after a bad rain had saturated the ground to sea level. The waste had no alternative but to surface. Our tank was located outside the washhouse, under the lines where Ellen hung our clothes. When it overflowed, the stench was terrible.

Piles of dug-up sand lined the ditches. Behind the piles lay the boxes of bones. Pieces of skeletons, leg bones, arm bones, fingers, feet, and heads, disconnected and placed in boxes strewn up and down the alley. The bones were discolored, off-white with patches of brown in places. They were somewhat eroded by their salty graves. Many of the skulls had teeth. Those that did not looked up from the cardboard containers with gaping sockets that once held eyes and noses and tongues. The bones smelled funny. Those by the alley gate smelled like musty dead birds.

Authorities from the Bishop Museum came to see the bones. A Hawaiian burial ground or battle ground? No one was sure. It didn't matter to us. We marched among the boxes until they were blessed and taken to yet another final resting place. We were babies; we had bottles to suck; death meant nothing to us. When the sewers were installed in all of Kahala and all bones were removed to other locations, we gave up our baby bottles.

Mother gave me a gold St. Christopher medal for my birthday. What I really wanted was an ankle bracelet, but she put her foot down and I got the St. Christopher medal instead. "Laurie Madelyn Ames" was etched on the back. It hung on a chain long enough for me to gnaw its grooved edges. The medal was as beautiful as the story of St. Christopher's protective reputation. It felt good to know that I had a saint watching over me. I also got a whistle, the kind teachers used to call children in from play. And, best of all, I got my own phonograph.

The record player was somewhat of a surprise, but it meant I could listen to "Mockingbird Hill" alone in my room. I loved that song. I really loved that song. Mom bought the record. I'd play it on the Victrola in the bar, slide the repeat lever to the left, and let go, over and over again, all day if I could. The "Twiddle-de-de" melted me. I was so enchanted with those lines, I often ignored the rest of the melody. "You're driving everyone to distraction," Mother said. "Knock it off!"

"Please, please, pretty please? Just one more time?" Secretly, I liked driving everyone to distraction.

"No!"

"Oaky-doky, Mom," I'd say as I turned off the machine. The record would stop, but not I. I'd skip out to the beach, flap my arms like wings, throw my head back, and, delirious, belt out my rendition of bird twills. I was just sorry we didn't have mockingbirds in Hawaii, I could have sung with them. We would have been great together!

The whistle, also, was cause for distraction. Cynnie-Belle and Bruce started complaining bitterly. When no one in authority was around, I'd blow it and take off. I got good at surprise and loved to see them jump when ambushed. At night I'd hide the whistle to keep Cynnie-Belle and Bruce from stealing it.

In retaliation, they glared. At meals, they'd prop their elbows on the kitchen table, hold their heads between clenched fists, and stare evil stares full of hate.

I'd wolf down my food and ask to be excused before they'd finished eating. As I walked out of the kitchen, I'd pull the whistle from my pocket and blow a blast. Not always, but often enough to cause surprise.

Their stares eventually got to me, or maybe it was just Mother. She moved me into the dining room where I ate alone.

"Here," I said to Cynnie-Belle one day, "take this," and I handed her the whistle.

"You're lucky we didn't kill you," she said.

"I know," I replied, thinking St. Christopher probably had a lot to do with it.

I was allowed back into the kitchen for meals when Mother realized that this, too, had passed.

1952

MY MOTHER'S PARENTS, PAPPY AND BEY, came for a visit. Liked it so much they stayed for the entire year. Uncle Duke found them a house two doors up the beach from his, six from ours. They bought the house and Mom said she figured they were there to stay.

Pappy wasn't well and he had a hard time getting around. He was a big man. Kalakaua, even bigger, was hired as help. Daily they took walks, back and forth across the yard. Kalakaua was added to the entourage of servants. Servants, that's what Pappy called them, but Kalakaua wasn't like the rest of what Mom referred to as "the help." He did not deal in household affairs, children, or my mother's need to be driven someplace. He was nothing like the staff at Uncle Duke's. Kalakaua was a gentle giant.

Pappy could be found, almost all the time, sitting in his front yard watching the ocean for whales. At his side sat a red wagon "Flyer." It was for the kukui nuts that fell off the tree under which he sat. He expected all visitors to participate in this unofficial clean-yard campaign. Bruce? He got into it, pulling the wagon through the grass as he scooped up the fallen nuts. I didn't like picking up the flat circles that oozed a gummy sap. I didn't like the picking up and I didn't like Grandfather. And I know that he did not like me. Nevertheless, gathering the kukui nuts was expected. Rewards came in the form of sticks of Juicy-

Fruit gum that were kept in a large glass jar shelved on a ledge in the dining room. He also distributed cigar bands which we used as rings. Once in awhile he'd give out an empty cigar box to some fortunate grandchild.

I spent a lot of time at my grandparents' despite the fact that I felt my grandfather's hostility. I blamed his aloofness on his age and health. My grandmother? She made everything all right. She loved me and I knew it. We'd do things together, like scrub the stairs and the lanai. "What can I do?" I'd ask as I walked in. "Here, you can help . . . ." and she'd finish her sentence with the chore to be completed.

My grandparents began to do everything for Cynnie-Belle, Bruce, and me. They took us for haircuts, shopped for our clothes, motored us to various appointments, and kept us, even on school nights. When I wasn't with them, I was with Ellen. Like Mom, Ellen didn't drive. But unlike Mom, Ellen and I took the bus everywhere—to movies, the zoo, the aquarium, downtown, anywhere we wanted to go. When home, Ellen and I caught rats and sand crabs, tried to save wounded birds, and watched for whales in winter.

My grandparents took us to Hana, Maui for Easter. When Mother announced the family trip, she added, "We'll be going to a ranch." I was thrilled . . . horses!

We documented the departure with pictures, all of us once more in matching attire, sitting on laps, arms draped around each other. We were all smiles in varying stages of growth. Some wore sandals, others were barefoot. Another windswept scene was photographed to freeze the moment in time, which it succeeded in doing.

We took up the entire two-engine plane. To Hana on a gift! We did, indeed, ride horses everyday. I rode with cousin Diane because I was too small and young to handle a beast of my own.

One afternoon a horse ran away with Mother. It bolted and

there she went, over the horizon and into the Pacific for all we knew. I was concerned, but the older children thought it was a riot. They soothed me and we plodded along without her, leaving the rescuing to the guide who had dug in his heels and taken off in her wake.

The day after we returned, I was diagnosed with having pink-eye. "I bet you caught it in the swimming pool," Mother said. "It wasn't very clean."

Now you tell me, I thought.

Hale Ola neared completion. My parents made elaborate plans for a housewarming party. I asked Ellen about the house-warming idea. I was still a little uneasy after the burning of our Christmas trees on the beach. She assured me it was just the term for a type of party, a luau in this case. "There will be hula dancers, a pig will be roasted in a dirt pit, and they'll grill fresh fish. Lots of singing and dancing to Hawaiian music."

"Sounds like a lot of fun," I said. "I can't wait to go, especially to see the stables."

"We'll take you later. This is a party for grown-ups only. We'll have a party just for you guys later," Mom promised. "Be fun, you'll see, just we five, together in our new home away from home."

Right!

My grandparents gave me a party for my sixth birthday. All cousins and children from our alley came, including Marilyn, the new kid. Her family moved into the cottage behind the Buscher's garage. Marilyn was an only child, and her parents doted on her. We became inseparable, which pushed Calley Haneberg a little out of the picture. Calley was two years older than I, Marilyn, one. The newness of our friendship helped the summer pass. That and the riding lessons I took, a birthday gift from my absentee parents.

I lived and breathed horses and couldn't wait to begin my first lesson. Pretending with my collection of miniatures and with Gilly was not enough. Even the time spent prancing and snorting around the yard was beginning to bore me. I got good at whinnying, though, and could send the Huey's chickens into a tailspin when I managed one particularly loud snort. Sometimes I could even get the dogs barking, and that pleased me, verifying my talent. But, in all, it wasn't enough. I was ready for the real thing.

Mrs. Rich taught riding. She lived nearby. She was portly and wore her white hair in a tight bun at the top of her head. She sported jodhpurs and carried a riding crop. Her accent was English. Mrs. Rich also terrified me. She was so cold and so strict. One morning she drove me to the stables for my first lesson. I got to her car way before the time of departure. I didn't want to be late. I didn't want to anger her. I waited in fear and apprehension.

We arrived at the stables, a dilapidated ring of stalls on the Waikiki side of Diamond Head. A road separated it from Kapiolani Park. It did have a small beginners' ring, but most of the riding was done in the park where there was a field for playing polo. The polo ponies were the stars of the stables. Within the ring of stalls was a circular hitching post. Attached to it were beautiful privately owned horses and those that were for rent. I got one of the ones for rent.

When Mrs. Rich said I'd ride Shorty, she meant it. My heart fell as she led me over to what was obviously a pitiful specimen not much larger than Gilly. I managed to keep my disappointment to myself and kept my mouth shut. But to make matters worse, once I mounted, Mrs. Rich led me around the circle the entire time. I held the reins in the correct position, but she pulled on the halter. "I want you to get the feel of the horse," she told me. I was humiliated and hoped the situation would soon improve. It did.

—

The week after my party, we were taken to Hale Ola. The house was situated on a beach within another bay. It was built on bunkers left over from the war. My mother showed me where they leveled mounds of sand before building. In the pine forest behind and to the side, there were still signs of local defenses. One bunker had a ladder descending into its depths. We were sure the space contained the bones of a dead soldier.

The Maui house bored me. There were no neighbors near. Huge, slippery rocks lined the sea wall, there was no beach, just small areas of sand that lay under water at high tides. The stables were the biggest disappointment. The horses were privately owned. You couldn't ride them. After making the mile journey from and to our house, I stopped going just to look at the animals. We did belong to the Maui Country Club and would swim while the adults played golf all day. The best things about the Club were their steak sandwiches and orange soda-pop.

I couldn't wait to get back to Honolulu. I was even looking forward to first grade. Being in the same school as my sister and brother was exciting. No more of this baby stuff at Central Union.

Mother had her hair done at Dael's. His shop was located in the heart of Waikiki. Mother took me to Dael's for my first beauty parlor appointment. He cut my hair real short. I loved it.

Located next to Dael's was The House of Music. While waiting for Mother to finish, I went into the store. They let clients listen to records in one of their three booths. The House of Music was packed with albums and 78s stored in paper jackets. There was a huge section reserved for sheet music. Guitars and ukuleles sat on shelves. In one corner there was a xylophone and a set of drums for sale. In another, a piano. On the front desk sat a large book that held information on every song ever published, rather like a Bible. The owners didn't mind my being there, no matter how long my mother's appointment lasted. They knew she'd buy me a record or two.

Behind Dael's was a local bar called Chapman's. I was a bit surprised when Mother announced we'd lunch at Chapman's. Since I was being treated to a grown-up hair cut, I assumed I'd be treated to a grown-up lunch at The Broiler. The Broiler was a steak house. It had waterfalls, torches, and pools that separated the reservation area from the dining room. You crossed on stepping stones made of lava rock. Exotic plants were everywhere, the atmosphere was dark and elegant, and the tables had tablecloths. Checks were presented inside folded napkins along with wrapped pieces of coffee candy, a few cigarettes and matches. We ate there on special occasions.

Chapman's was a bar and grill. The building looked like a trailer—at least that's how people described it. I'd never been in a trailer home on wheels. Living in a trailer sounded wonderful, driving around in your own bedroom. "Neat!" I said, before asking if we could buy one.

"Where would we go?" Mother said. "You can drive around the entire island and be back before dark." I couldn't answer her but going to Chapman's sounded interesting.

"Chapman's it is!" I exclaimed, as we left the House of Music. By then, I was eager to see its insides.

"Hey Larry," she yelled to the bartender as we walked in.

"How's it, Dottie?" he said. "What a nice surprise!"

I looked around. Formica-topped tables with metal containers for napkins were placed around the room. In the corner were a jukebox and a shuffle board. The bar ran the width of the establishment.

"Larry, this is my youngest, Laurie."

"How's it?" he asked, as he came through the bar door. He was small, like Soupy, with dark eyes and wavy hair.

"Laurie, this is Larry Vincente. He's Italian."

I wasn't sure what being Italian meant, but I didn't mull over the information. I was too busy trying to figure out why he looked so familiar. Later, while listening to "Kiss of Fire," the new record I bought after our hair cuts, I remembered. Larry was in almost every picture taken at the Hale Ola housewarming and his eyes were always on my mother.

First grade was located on the lower campus of Punahou School and situated in some Army barracks erected during World War II. There were three buildings, two classes in each, with fenced-in back yards. In the front was a long, wide stretch of land called the Lower Field. In our given space were sandboxes, teeter-totters, and swings.

I learned to read. Fast. I'd pay close attention to the lessons and tuck Dick and Jane under my arm to take home every night. We were allowed to read other books for extra credit. I took those home, too. I read constantly, no longer content listening to records like "Bozo Under the Sea" gurgling "Turn the page, turn the page. Please, please help me, turn the page." I replaced picture books with those with real words. Where once I sat, fingers poised between pages, ready to keep Bozo from drowning, I now sat reading out loud.

"Mom," I'd say, "listen to this, will you?" and I'd proceed to recite lines about Spot and Sally as if I were giving a news report. I'd read aloud to anyone who would listen. Ellen was my most consistent audience, but everyone was encouraging. They were tired of my renditions of talking record books.

A boy named Sammy chased me daily. He never let up, not even when I complained to the teacher. I couldn't stand him until he gave me this pin. It was a plastic yellow traffic light. When you pulled its string, it would change from red to yellow to green. Sammy was okay after that.

Linda Katsuki painted pictures of horses for me during art. They were fantastic replicas of the real thing. I'd take her drawings home, carefully rolled and secured with a rubber band, and hang them on my walls.

I wanted to kill for the triangle during music and would sulk when I got the strap with bells. Susan Crosby became my best friend in school. I took trampoline lessons one day a week and ballet on another.

I was pretty good on the trampoline and got to somersaults before I realized I could hurt myself. My mother came for my one exhibition. She watched me spin around within the safety of a halter attached to ropes held by the instructors. I could see her on the other side of a ceiling-high chain link fence. Parents stood outside for safety reasons. Punahou didn't want anyone hurt by a flying child.

I began ballet again. Ballet was safer than trampoline. I'd make the long walk to the fringes of the Upper Campus to take lessons from Mrs. Flanders. I took lessons when I was younger but wasn't coordinated enough. At least, that's what I was told. We had one recital. I spent more time banging on a tambourine than dancing. It was okay because I got to wear make-up. Three days after the performance, Mother made me wash my face.

Ballet might have been safe but it was more confusing than the trampoline. There were mirrors around the entire room. When a position was called, I had a hard time distinguishing my left foot from my right. I had a big scar on my left ankle. I'd gotten my foot caught in the spokes as I rode on the back of Calley Haneberg's bike. Usually the scar helped me tell my left from my right, but I was so busy fixed on my image in the mirrors, I'd end up in a position backwards. When Mrs. Flanders corrected me, I'd frantically lift up each leg looking for my scar. To be sure I had the right foot, I'd do it again which evoked groans and sighs from fellow ballerinas. It took a long time before I could get into a position without looking at my ankle.

—

Larry started coming over to cook steaks. Unlike Soupy, Larry hung around the house. Steaks were his specialty. I liked Larry. Even Cynnie-Belle and Bruce seemed a little more tolerant of him. Larry wasn't a beach boy, he wasn't even a cab driver, just a bartender. Mom was using a man named Herman to take her places. She said Herman talked funny because he was from the Philippines. Funny or not, he was hard to understand. Herman's car had a meter and he kept the flag up while he drove us around. It embarrassed me. Although Herman's car looked like a family car, the meter, which could be seen from within and without, screamed taxi.

Almost everyone had a boat anchored in front of his house except for us. We had the dumb outrigger canoe that was never used, because no one knew how to steer it. Of course it didn't matter, as we had no paddles.

I liked to go out in the Hueys' boat. Mrs. Huey would sink the oars into the oar locks and off we'd row to the channel to fish around the sunken cars. Mrs. Huey was in charge of transportation and Dorothy baited the hooks attached to our bamboo poles. Forgiving my squeamishness, they were content to just let me fish. I'd dangle the fishing line into the sea and wait . . . a complete angler.

We always went fishing on beautiful days with calm seas and crystal-clear waters. Mrs. Huey would guide the boat around the coral beds, the movement leaving a little wake in our path. When we found a good spot, Dorothy would throw the anchor. We'd fish and listen to the surf break upon the reef. Our only efforts were soaking up the sun and licking salt spray from our lips. After a couple of hours, tired and toasted, we returned to shore. I'd carry the pail of catch onto Hueys' front lawn while someone tied the boat. Conveniently, I'd go home to change while Mrs. Huey cleaned the fish. Later I'd return for dinner. Stuffed and happy, I'd usually leave with a small keepsake given to me by Dorothy. My favorites were her empty perfume bottles.

On November 4, Election Day, the first tidal wave in forty years hit the "House of Happiness" on Maui. Mom and Larry flew out that afternoon. "We're off to repair the damage," she said before kissing me goodbye. After they left, I wondered where they'd stay. That night I fell out of bed and split my chin open. I had to have six stitches. My grandmother drove me to the hospital. Ellen, who was staying with us, had called her.

"Where's Roger?" Bey asked when she brought me home.

"He's out of town," Ellen said.

"Funny, I didn't know he wasn't in town."

Neither did I, I thought.

Mom returned a few days later. "The house is still standing," she said. "But all the windows were smashed by the force of the wave. We found some furniture on Saddle Road. Other pieces washed out to sea. Our icebox was almost a mile down the beach! The house is full of mud and sand and dead fish. Got it all cleaned up, though. Larry was a prince," she said, looking at him and smiling.

"What about the horses?" I asked her.

"Oh, they're fine. It didn't go that far inland. Larry stopped and got us all steaks for dinner."

Great, I thought, and wondered why she hadn't asked me about the bandage on my chin.

1953

"IT'S HERE, IT'S HERE," yelled Mother from the lanai. Father's whistle cut through the air and into our senses. We were poised, immobile, silent, our eyes fastened to the television set in the Buscher's living room. What we watched made absolutely no difference to us. The impact came from the delicious feelings we got watching the black and white images on the screen. It was January and television had arrived in the islands.

The calls and whistles continued. Legs untangled, bodies rose from the floor, and out the door we went, falling over each other in our haste to beat it home. We left so fast no one complained of blocking their view. Our excitement heightened as we flew onto the lanai and through the door held open by Mother. Cynnie-Belle, Bruce, and I stopped.

There it stood, in the middle of the living room, between the two windows that looked onto the Hueys' house: an oval screen embedded in wood. Our very own television set. It was a brand name I'd never heard of, a Bendix, and to our consternation the screen displayed an elusive image dotted by static that looked like snow. A snowy television.

"It's not working," said Cynnie-Belle.

"It doesn't look right," said Bruce. And out the door they went, me hot on their heels, beating a track back to the Buschers.

"What's wrong?" asked Barbara when we arrived.

"They bought some kind of television called a Bendix and it doesn't work," said Cynnie-Belle.

Later, the television worked fine. They had to hook it up to an antenna bought and placed on our roof for reception. It looked like a giant clothes line, a 50s version of radar tracking down images, and not those of the enemy. Our parents were back in our good graces.

Television changed our lives. It made us want to acquire. Chlorophyll was discovered to make things refreshing. The ads on TV enticed us to buy toothpaste with chlorophyll.

"Ninety-nine percent of a goat's diet is chlorophyll and they still stink," said Mother. She bought the toothpaste anyway.

Visual images replaced the mental images of radio. Before I learned to read, I'd go upstairs to Bruce's bedroom and listen to the radio. We'd make our tented fort and listen to the detective tales of "Boston Blackie" or be petrified by the squeaking doors of "Inner Sanctum." Television changed us. We took on a whole new lifestyle.

My favorite show was "Your Hit Parade." I loved to watch the leggy packs of Lucky Strikes tap dance during commercials. Each week the same cast would sing and act out the most popular songs. Since it took awhile for programs to reach the island, the shows weren't up-to-date, but nobody minded. I never tired of watching and listening to them sing, particularly Snooky Lansing. He was cute. "Doggie in the Window" was number one for thirteen weeks. They managed a different routine each time. True stars, I thought to myself.

My mother loved wrestling matches. I did not share her enthusiasm. I didn't like the stomping, punching, and pulling. Mother liked to root for certain characters like Gorgeous George. I found him ridiculous with his long blond hair and tiny underpants.

Mother also loved the Roller Derby, which I considered no better than the wrestling, but I did admire the agility of the skaters. I could barely get my foot clamped and keyed into a pair of skates much less glide across the lanai with ease. Time after time I'd try to go solo, but I couldn't relinquish my strong hold on the backs of chairs as I edged forward. I finally gave up, thinking I was still too young.

My mother adored movies. She started taking me to the ones she thought I could sit through. "The Million Dollar Mermaid" did me in. I was determined to be a mermaid!

I would don a face mask and watch the fish, fish that lived around abandoned anchors, scooting back and forth in fish frenzies. My favorite anchor was in the shape of a horse shoe. It was embedded in sand in front of the Buschers'. I'd hold my breath and submerge into the liquid lifestyle of the ocean. There lay forests of seaweed, mountains of coral, and lands of sand. The colorful schools of fish would dart back and forth. Once in awhile, I'd scoop-net a few into a can to take home. But I'd always worry about their well-being and I'd throw them back a short time later.

After "The Million Dollar Mermaid," fish became my royal subjects. It was a pretend world I wished would come true. I couldn't wait to go see them, and I spent hours dunking myself, watching and holding imaginary conversations under water. Sometimes, I'd let the current carry me down to the Hueys', all the while attuned to the ocean floor.

When I was tired, I'd drag myself onto the shore with my arms-legs stiff and crossed at the ankles, true to the mermaid form. Then reclining, head balanced on the palm of my hand, elbow dug into the sand for support, I'd wait for someone to walk by and say, "Oh, look, a mermaid."

No one ever did, but I came close once. Aunt Cecily, on her way to visit Mrs. Buscher, stopped to ask if I was all right. Before I could answer, her dog Blackie, peed on me.

My mother tore up the beach one morning in April. The word had spread that he was here, staying in the house next door to my Uncle Duke's. The "he" was The Lone Ranger. I was ready to die before accompanying Mother to see him.

"Let's go," she yelled at me.

"You can't go like that," I said. It was early morning. She was wearing a bathrobe.

"Why not? These are the islands, nobody cares how you dress."

"Well, I do, and I am not going with you in your pajamas."

Mother turned tail and tore up the beach to meet The Lone Ranger. I watched her, coffee in hand, her housecoat flapping wildly in the wind.

After awhile, she came home holding high a fake silver coin with his name embossed around its edges. It came from one of those machines intended as time killers in airports and hotel lobbies. You could spin the wheel to the letter or number you wanted, point the clock-type hand, and pull a lever. This was done until you spelled out what you wanted: "I love you," "Have a Good Trip," or simply your name and address if the space allowed. Why a middle-aged cowboy found them enticing souvenirs I would never know. I wondered about the person who must have sat for days making the coins over and over again. I wondered if it was Tonto. If it had been Hopalong Cassidy, I thought, I might have gone with Mom, bathrobe or no bathrobe.

A few days after Mom's visit to The Lone Ranger, the second tidal wave in forty years hit "The House of Happiness" on Maui.

"Shit," Mother said when she heard the news.

We made our first trip back to Montclair in June. Ellen came with us, my father did not. The journey took forever.

"We've reached the point of no return," announced a voice. Just like that, out of nowhere, a voice told us we'd reached the point of no return.

"What does that mean?" I asked Ellen.

"I'm not sure," she replied.

I wasn't sure that she wasn't sure. Point of no return, I mused. Sounds scary.

After landing in San Francisco, Mother explained. "When it's an overseas flight, it means passing the halfway mark. Once that happens, there's no going back, not enough fuel to get there."

"Great!" I said.

We left San Francisco for Chicago. The airport was closed due to bad weather. We circled for over an hour. I thought we'd never stop going around and around. Water or no water, I waited for a voice to announce the point of no return. Cynnie-Belle got sick and threw up in a paper bag. In a foul humor, she laid the blame on us for the lousy flight.

"I never had this trouble when I flew by myself last summer!" she wailed before diving back into her vomit bag. We missed the connection to New York, and twenty-seven hours after we left Honolulu, we arrived in New Jersey.

My grandparents' estate was large. Barns, pastures, woods, and two cottages surrounded the stately white brick house. It had pillars holding it up. "They're called columns," my mother said. There were also two good-size playhouses for children. The house had a basement. We didn't have basements in Hawaii. It was dark and cool, its walls dark rich wood, the floors slate. That part of the basement we used. Another part held laundry facilities and an enormous storage cellar for food, cooking utensils, wine, liquor, and jars of every shape and size.

The attic was the third floor. Trunks of old clothes, photographs, doll furniture, magazines, playbills from theaters, and programs from the opera sat among the extra beds made up for spill-over company. It smelled old and comforting. I loved the attic and spent hours playing with my mother's old dolls and her tea set.

I shared the first-floor bedroom with Ellen, but I followed Madge around constantly. Madge had been my mother's nursemaid. After Duke and my mother left for Honolulu, Madge was made cook. "I'd much rather take care of you children," she told me. And it showed.

Madge poured a cup of coffee for me every morning, filled it full of milk and sugar. As she stirred, bubbles grew and popped and spread across the top. She'd spoon up some of the bubbles and say to me, "Honey, each one of these bubbles stands for how much money you're going to make when you grow up." Each morning we would go through the same routine before digging into the fresh cantaloupe, strawberries, or honeydews she prepared.

The only bubbles I managed to create during the visit were ones which came out of my nose. "Smell this," Ellen said, holding up a jar of soap powder. I got too close and inhaled two nostrils full. Thinking water would help, she cupped her hands under the faucet and told me to sniff the water. For a good ten minutes, I sneezed my kind of bubbles. I never have been able to recreate bubbles in coffee like Madge, all that froth and foam. Maybe she used real cream and sugar. Maybe she used magic.

We saw all the sights in New York. We went to the musical "Porgy and Bess" and saw the Rockettes at Radio City Music Hall. The dinosaurs at the Museum of Natural History were my favorite. Coming in a close second was the movie "Beast from 20,000 Fathoms." A block or so before the theater, someone had drawn giant reptilian footprints on the sidewalk. A man with a sign picturing the monster paced back and forth yelling, "Watch out, the beast is coming, the beast is coming." I clutched my mother's hand, not sure if I really wanted to see the film.

"The story was about a prehistoric dinosaur that got thawed by the heat from an atomic blast," I told Madge. "Mad at being disturbed, he stomped all over the city. Made a mess, he did."

I was glad I went. There were dinosaurs once and now there

was an atomic bomb. It could happen again, I thought. Mother assured me it could not.

While I followed Madge around, Bruce followed Emery. Emery was my grandfather's driver and overseer of the estate. He lived on the property, next door to the barn. Emery had a daughter who was my age. We played during the day and caught fireflies in the early evening. Fireflies were as magical as Madge. I'd never seen such an insect. Cynnie-Belle, having spent every summer in Montclair since we left, spent days with her friends. Something was always going on at my grandparents' house. There were games of croquet, elaborate lunches, and a constant flow of visitors.

We motored up to Cape Cod to visit my father's sister and his dad, whom we called Father Ames. My grandmother drove. Cynnie-Belle and Bruce returned with her a few days later. I remained with Mother and Ellen. We stayed in an old inn overlooking a body of water that was not the ocean. It was quite slimy, so I dug for clams rather than swim. I spent a lot of time watching a chipmunk and being in awe of Allen H. Good, our waiter. I'd never seen a chipmunk and I thought Allen H. Good was as handsome as a movie star. He gave me his autograph twice. The first time he wrote in script that I couldn't read. The second, he printed just for me.

Father Ames ran a bed-and-breakfast. His backyard contained a huge chicken coop, totally unlike the primitive one in the Hueys' yard. He sold fresh eggs to the people in town. He also grew all the fruits used in his homemade jellies. His lifestyle was far different from my other grandparents'. It was simple.

My Aunt Mad lived in Chatham, a quaint town. On the Fourth of July, we went to an Independence Day parade. The band came marching down the street and passed in front of a white lattice gazebo that held the town's dignitaries. The troops, resplendent in their starched white pants and red jackets with gold tassels falling from their epaulets, looked so fine. Young women led the way, batons twirling and whirling in the air, deftly caught only to be tossed once more. This was a parade, I said to myself. This was real, with marching tunes of songs I understood. Balloons occasionally broke from some child's grasp and ascended slowly into the heavens. I wanted to stay here, in this town, forever and be like these families.

Parades in the islands were different, somewhat savage depending on the ethnic celebration. Often, twelve foot dragons slithered along the street, dragons on human legs, bobbing up and down in an atmosphere alive with exploding fireworks. The air was smoky with the smells of strong sulfuric gun powder. Participants carried banners with words depicted by unrecognizable symbols. Many parades were full of paper lanterns and fish.

The Hawaiian parades were not noisy. Marchers filed down Kalakaua Avenue on foot, on horses, or on floats, dressed in hula skirts and sarongs, both men and women. Those descended from royalty wore white uniforms. Garlands of flowers were draped over everyone and everything, even the animals. There were chants and songs and dancers who undulated their hips while making hand and arm motions to convey their stories.

I didn't understand the parades in Hawaii; I didn't know what was being celebrated or why. Once in a while, Ellen took me to Bon Dances where I'd bob up and down and weave in and out of the circle of festivities honoring the dead . . . the dancers richly attired in kimonos, I barefoot and in shorts.

It was okay, but I wanted to live this type of life. I wanted a mainland existence. I didn't want to live in the middle of an ocean surrounded by people who didn't look like me or talk like me. I always felt uncomfortable when they taught the hula in school. I couldn't make the moves fluid. I felt foolish and out of place trying to follow the traditions of a culture to which I didn't belong. A seed was planted that sunny afternoon on the Fourth of July in Chatham. I wanted out, and I tucked that information deep inside of me.

Mother and I took the train back to New York. I had never been on a train. I scrutinized each town we passed, looking for other Chathams. Emery picked us up at the station. He dropped off mother at the Blackstone Hotel before taking me to Montclair.

"I'll be back shortly," she said as she closed the car door. "I'm going to meet a few friends."

She was gone a week. When she returned, Larry was by her side. We left Montclair the next day. It was time to go home.

My second grade teacher was Miss Davidson. She was pretty and patient. She listened and cared. Miss Davidson was like Dorothy Huey. I adored her.

"I want to tell you a story," she announced the day before Thanksgiving vacation. Eager to listen to anything she said, we gathered around in a circle. She pulled up a chair, sat down, and began. "There was a young woman who came to Hawaii on the Lurline," she said. "During the five-day crossing, she met a man and fell in love. He returned to California and she stayed to teach a class of the most wonderful second graders on the face of the earth. All of them were smart, creative, and very understanding."

I began to get suspicious when I heard the word understanding. Mother used the term when she was about to tell me she couldn't do something.

"After he returned, the two wrote to each other every day," she continued. "He asked her to marry him, and she said yes." She paused, her eyes swept over us. "That woman," she said slowly, "is me."

Two weeks later, Miss Davidson departed. I was devastated.

I couldn't believe she'd leave in the middle of the school year. Leave me? I was her best helper. "I can always count on you," she'd tell me in confidence.

On her last day of class, she wrote her new name and address on the blackboard. Each one of us copied it as we sat at our desks. When done, we taped the information to the backs of our cubbyholes. There were lots of tears, hugs, and promises to keep in touch. I wrote her almost immediately, told her about the new teacher, how awful she was, how no teacher could take her place. She never wrote back.

"Maybe you got the address wrong," Mother said.

"Mom, no one could get the address wrong. It's in everyone's cubby-hole. Cubby-holes don't have doors. You can't miss seeing it even if someone's writing is terrible."

"Then it just must have gotten lost."

Lost? Right. I guessed. But I never wrote to her again.

The Hanebergs left too. They moved into a home of their own. It was inevitable. Another boy was born and their rental house was too small. There were new homes to buy. Progress was wiping out pastures, pig and produce farms. We tried to stop the development of Waialae-Kahala. Children from up and down the avenue, on bikes and bare feet, spent hours dragging limbs and brush across the plowed places for roads. The hours spent were wasted, our efforts destroyed by the time we returned. It was a losing battle. We finally gave up, started crawling around and exploring the tracts of houses.

They were advertised as Cinderella Homes. I guess that meant the happily-ever-after part of the fairy tale. Advertisements showed smiling couples with grinning children, neighbors chatting over fences and sharing hot dogs on outdoor grills. I began to relish the thought of living in a Cinderella Home with pink kitchen appliances and windows that didn't rattle. When models were opened to the public, I'd spend hours admiring and pretending I lived in them. I tried to get my mother to take a look, hoping to lure her from the beach and all the relatives. "Don't be silly," she'd say. "We're staying right here! I have no intention of living in suburbia." Shortly after the houses were started, plans for a large shopping center were revealed. It was announced that a big grocery store, called "Piggly Wiggly," was going to be built. I honestly thought Piggly Wiggly was in honor of the pig farms being replaced.

Whiz Buscher, Barbara's brother, was a terror. When unexplained fires occurred in the alley, Whiz was the number-one-resident pyromaniac-suspect. At least as far as my mom was concerned and as far as my family was concerned. Whiz was nasty, surly, whinny, and a slob. He was very spoiled. My mother referred to him as "the slug who walked like a little boy."

Whiz was the one who told me Santa Claus was a fake. "There is no such person as Santa Claus!" he said. We were on his living room couch.

"What do you mean?" I was stunned.

"I mean what I said. There is no Santa. No tooth fairy either. It's just our parents. Santa and the tooth fairy are our parents. Boy, you're dumber than I thought," he sneered.

What he said made sense. I had figured the Easter Bunny stuff out a long time ago. What made me mad was his making a fool of me. Whiz was younger. How dare he dish out this awful information, and in such smug tones! The Bunny and tooth fairy were one thing, but Santa? I believed in Santa. Santa was a man, not a giant bunny.

Revenge, well a kind of revenge, came Christmas day. Whiz had gotten an extravagant battleship. It shot eight bullets from various points on the boat. We decided to play war. He bombarded my camp on the beach. I spent a considerable time packing cups of moist sand and turning them over to make my mighty fortress. After a half hour or so of attacking my territory, he decided he was hungry. He didn't declare a truce or time out as he trotted up onto the grass and disappeared into his house. Dismissed by that bratty brat, I sat on the shore and surveyed the scene. The eight bullets stuck silently into my fort. I pulled them all out and ran down the beach, dug eight holes and deposited a bullet in each one before covering them up.

The screams and wails began shortly thereafter. I could hear him from our kitchen. He was livid. "My bullets, where are my bullets?" he yelled. Reluctantly, I went outside. I was sorry to have to give in but I was afraid the commotion would alert both our families who were basking in the serenity of a Christmas afternoon. Actually, my mother was busy preparing for the annual eggnog party scheduled to start at four o'clock. I joined Whiz and down the beach we went to where I thought I had hidden the bullets. I pointed to the area.

"Dig," he said, eyes brimming with tears, nose red and running.

And dig I did for the rest of the afternoon, though I never recovered a single one.

As punishment, Whiz started biting me, grabbing my arm or leg when I least expected it and chomping down. I tried to tell everyone what he was doing, but no one listened. One day, Mom caught him in the act. She laid him out on the floor of the guest room and had at it, biting him hard enough to show marks. He went home howling. I don't know whether he told his parents or not, but he never bit me again.

1954

I BECAME AN EPISCOPALIAN. It took awhile. I first tried to be a
Mormon with the Hanebergs. The grape juice served at commu-
nion in tiny paper cups was wonderful, but Mom put a stop to my
going when I started talking about tithing. I think it might have
been over-reaction on her part. I had no idea what tithing meant.

Marilyn was a Catholic. After I finally learned to ride a bike,
we'd peddle up to Star of the Sea for Sunday Mass. I loved the
gift shop with its beads and rosaries. I memorized Hail Mary.
I even got the chest rapping ritual down pat. I didn't understand one word of the service. I was never even sure of the
proper knee to bend before entering the pew. It caused a little
paranoia. I was positive the entire congregation was watching
my arrivals. "Look, that child is not a Catholic," I could hear
them say as I walked in.

I went to a few Lutheran services with a kid up the street, but
that fizzled out as did our friendship.

By the time I talked to Mother about it, I had exhausted my
resources. The Christian Scientists didn't believe in medicine,
the Seventh Day Adventists went to services on Saturdays, and
Buddha was just too fat to pray to. Besides that, his religion
called for binding of women's feet. I knew that for a fact. We
visited a shrine on a field trip. I saw, with my own eyes, a lady
whose feet were no larger than a baby's clenched fist. No way,
I thought, as they carried her out the door while I and my
classmates watched, dumbfounded.

"Why don't you try the Episcopal church?" Mother asked. "You can go with Aunt Libby, Uncle Jim, and Madelyn; Holy Nativity is almost in their back yard." My Aunt Libby and Uncle Jim moved to Hawaii with their only child, Madelyn, shortly after their initial visit.

"Good idea, Mom," I said. "Real good idea."

Our summer trip was still fresh in my mind. Aunt Libby's family was an awful lot like Aunt Mad's in Chatham. The kind of family I wanted.

I liked the Episcopal church. I enjoyed the Sunday School classes we attended before we got to join the grown-ups. We sang "Jesus Wants Me for a Sunbeam," and a whole lot of other songs. I heard lots of Bible stories and told them all to Ellen. When we prayed, I thanked Mother for suggesting the Episcopalians. It was a lot more fun than having to learn Latin like Marilyn. I did wish we had those prayer beads, though. I would have bought them in every color. After awhile, I'd spend almost every Saturday night at Aunt Libby's happily anticipating the walks together the next morning. After church, they'd take me home. I'd change and trot up the beach to have lunch with my grandparents. It all seemed so normal!

Mother became consumed by her volunteer job at the International Institute. I was crazy about her involvement. She was a volunteer, like a lot of other mothers. She still spent too much time with Larry, but she was working with a known and respected organization.

"My mom volunteers for the International Institute. It's a YWCA program," I told my friends and teachers.

Every week, they held a luncheon in honor of an ethnic group. The Institute was located in a small house on the fringe of downtown Honolulu. Tuesdays the menus were planned, Thursdays the food was cooked, and on Friday the food was served. That left only Mondays and Wednesdays free for

Mother. Of course there were the weekends, so I didn't mind. She was involved, and that was all I could hope for, a mother with a cause.

The International Institute was a support group for brides brought to the states after World War II. They offered classes to teach the English language and provided space for nationalities, alike and different, to get together. The building wasn't much, but I loved waiting there for Mother. I'd wander around, sit at desks, and chat with the volunteers. I never met any of the war brides, but then, I never went to a luncheon.

"What happened here?" I asked one day, examining a water color on the wall of an office.

"Cockroaches," the secretary replied. "They like to nibble on the paint, particularly certain colors."

"What colors?"

"Look at the painting, you tell me what's missing."

I looked. I looked hard. "They like every color in it," I replied. I was anxious to get home and pitch my narrow tin of paints. I pictured cockroaches lurking in my bedroom, waiting to get a lick of yellow or red. I hated cockroaches. They were huge, big as baby dachshunds, Mother said. Some even flew. They came out at night. Light a darkened room and see bugs all over the place.

"I'm good at killing cockroaches," I told the secretary. "I deliberately surprise them, then go for the kill."

"Deliberately?" she asked.

"Yeah, it takes cunning, speed, and power to get them," I continued, pumped up by her interest in what I had to say. "Cunning in the surprise, speed in getting into a murderous position, and power in the blow. One chance is all you get."

"My, my," the secretary said, shaking her head. "You sure know your stuff."

"Yeah, pretty much." I didn't tell her that most of the time I'd wind up hearing the thud of a shoe on bare floor or rug, long after the roach was gone. Roach crunches were rare. No wonder they're the oldest creatures on earth.

Well, the Institute did keep Mother out of trouble and respectable for awhile. In the midst of the most successful luncheon, they decided to publish a cookbook to raise money for the program. Mom offered to put it together and volunteered my father to do the illustrations. I was beside myself, a double dose of normalcy. I watched, all spring, while they discussed appropriate pictures for the various countries, my father at his draft table in the guest bedroom. It was heaven. I thought that everything would be all right. *Menus Around the World* was published. My mother was made Chairman of the Board. Maybe, I thought, it has something to do with my going to church, something to do with St. Christopher even.

My father came home with a tape recorder, one of those reel to reels. He placed it alongside our Victrola. The big buttons to make it work were explained. After the novelty wore off and we all had denied even remotely sounding as the tapes suggested, I started to play with it alone. Judy Garland's version of "The Man that Got Away" was my favorite. I'd play and sing with the record as the tape captured my most sexy, prepuberty, sultry voice. It was a thrill to think my mother was right. She said I was destined for a career as a singer. My only fear was that this new style called "rock and roll" would put the Judy Garlands and Patti Pages out of business. My mother said not to worry, but I wasn't sure. "Shake Rattle and Roll" was climbing the charts at record speed.

Now that I was eight, I was old enough to catch the bus by myself so I spent hours at the stables. Bruce spent more and more time with the beachboys. He also paddled canoes for an Outrigger Canoe Club team. We went to almost every race, to cheer him on to victory.

We continued to make the usual rounds of movies, wrestling matches, roller derbies, and, because of me, rodeos.

Cynnie-Belle had a boyfriend. She didn't bother much with us, which was fine. She was mostly moody. Mother said she could take her moods to her boyfriend's parents. "She'll get over it. She's just at that age," said Dad.

Things were great, couldn't be better! Mother was home. She often attended church with me, and her devotion to the YWCA continued. Since I had been gone the summer before, I made big plans for my birthday, a store-bought cake from Leonard's bakery and movies. I invited kids from the alley and relatives close to my age. I also asked Susan Crosby, my best friend at school. I'd never had a friend from school visit . . . I was excited.

The day arrived. The cake was in the shape of a horse and I received lots of attention for such a clever idea. We played a few games, like statue. The "it" would twirl each person around and the one landing in the best pose won. We had outgrown pin-the-tail-on-the-donkey. We were, to use a new word, cool.

Inside the house, my father set up a projector and screen. Uncle Duke was out of town so we were spared the inevitable magic show.

I was excited, but a little apprehensive when my brother and cousin Stephen, home from a series of boarding schools and military academies, appeared. They had been getting into trouble lately. The most recent episode was their breaking a case of empty coke bottles in a neighbor's garage. The neighbors, who lived in Duke's alley, had been out of town and Bruce and Stephen were caught in the act from the noise of all that smashing glass. Disgusted, Mom made them clean up the entire mess with their bare hands. Bruce, twelve, adored Stephen who was fifteen. I consoled myself with the fact that on this occasion both my parents were present. Nothing bad could happen.

The 16-millimeter projector, threaded and ready to go,

whirred into action. Cowboys raced across the screen in pursuit of Indians. I grabbed my Davy Crockett coonskin cap, a present from my grandparents, and stuck it on my head. Great, I thought, we weren't going to watch dumb cartoons.

After a few minutes, squaws appeared on the screen, feathers tucked into their headbands. They carried bows. Each one had a pouch filled with arrows, slung across a shoulder. We watched, anticipating intrigue, as they crept between boulders. When they finally came into full view they were stark naked.

It took Mother a moment for the scene to sink in. "Stop that projector," she yelled. "Stop it this instant!"

"No, don't, leave it," Stephen yelped.

"Aw come on, leave it, let us watch," whined Bruce.

I was red, flushed with embarrassment. I looked around. All eyes were firmly fixed on the screen, mouths in various stages of grins, even Susan Crosby's.

Stephen jumped up and started hopping around in a circle, first one foot then the other. Bruce followed. Howls and war cries filled the air. My father stopped the projector but forgot to turn off the bulb. We watched the frozen frame disintegrate.

"How could you do this?" Mother demanded.

"I'm sorry," Father said. "The title was 'Indians Whoop It Up.' I assumed it was a western."

It was a western all right, but I'm not sure the mix-up was an accident. I'm almost positive Stephen and Bruce had something to do with it. Anyway, my party became famous. Hoping to be invited next year, strangers became friends, and I dug the attention.

Mother became a celebrity when *Menus Around the World* was published. It was a smashing success. Her picture and recipes were featured in both newspapers. She talked on radio and appeared on television programs to demonstrate her cooking skills. She practiced making the dishes at home and, since I was around the most, tested them on me. Three meals a day some-times became four or five. Just a little extra was added to my girth. I neither noticed nor cared, just proud to be of help. Larry tasted, too. The luncheons at the Institute swelled in attendance.

Sometimes I'd ride with Mother and Larry to watch her talk on radio. On our way, we had to pass a T.B. hospital. I'd take deep gulps of air then hold my breath. Once in a while, I'd miss the approach, being too busy thumping and singing to myself in the back seat. Realizing my mistake, I'd panic, shut down my intake of air, and hope to make the endless drive past the windows of the sick and infirm. No matter what the circum-stances, cars seemed to pass the hospital in slow motion. I'd watch the signs. Signs that read "No Honking of Horns" crept by. Holding my breath worked. I didn't get the disease, and I only came close to suffocating a few times.

Dorothy Huey got married. I was her flower girl, which helped take the edge off her moving to the mainland. She took me shopping and we found the perfect dress. It was white chiffon over stiff, starched crinoline petticoats. A headband, attached with baby red roses, framed the Mamie Eisenhower bangs cut straight across my forehead and I was allowed a little lipstick. I scattered petals down the aisle. Later Bruce and I had our picture taken together. He looked so handsome in a coat and pink polka-dotted tie, his hair slicked and held fast with Brylcreem. Arm-in-arm we posed with the Pacific ocean behind us. We looked so happy, framed in time. Despite the circum-stances, it had been a swell year. So what if my father stopped coming home.

1955

MOTHER APPEARED REGULARLY on the "Napua Stevens Show." It aired once a week on television. Once Mom got me out of class to demonstrate an Osterizer blender. Well, not the blender; actually I was asked to demonstrate the gift one would receive if he or she purchased the mixer. I was asked to show how the little plastic battery blender worked.

While Mother and Napua prepared for the show, I tried to cajole them into letting me make some comment about the weather. The kitchen window, on the set, depicted a small mountainous terrain with snow capped peaks.

"Can't I just say, 'Oh what a beautiful day?'" I asked. "Oklahoma," which I'd seen some months earlier, was stuck in my brain.

"Laurie, the scene has nothing to do with the islands," said Mother.

"It doesn't matter."

"Yes, it does."

I'd just learned about poetic license in school so I tried that argument and lost.

"Stop! Laurie. Stop it!"

I had to content myself with the demonstration alone. I stood in front of the little plastic mixer, showed how it operated on batteries. Next, I poured in a half cup of milk and a half cup of ice cream. To that I added chocolate sauce, and, making sure to address the camera with the red light on, I flipped the metal switch, smiling at an unseen audience.

The first glob of shake hit Mother's eyeglasses. The remainder splattered all three of us, rendering the rest of the demonstration impossible.

"Cut to commercial," a voice said.

I had forgotten to put the top on.

I was always at the dentist. My mother bought me hamburgers and vanilla milk shakes at the Gou-Goy Room in the Alexander Young Hotel. The name of the restaurant was actually the Hob-Nob Room, but read upside down on their cocktail napkins, it looked like Gou-Goy. It was our inside joke. I ate a lot of lunches there before dental appointments. It became a ritual, a bite of juicy hamburger dripping in tomatoes, lettuce, and loads of ketchup, savored in my mouth before a straw's sip of milkshake joined it—wonderful. I had my mother all to myself on those afternoons, just the two of us. During those moments, I felt blessed.

After lunch, we'd get into one of two heavy elevators, the ones with massive metal gates that had to be pulled shut before the second set of doors was closed. You couldn't see through that second set. Up we'd go, serenaded by the clanging chains hoisting us to the third floor. Every elevator had an operator, and, if you frequented buildings as much as I did the Alexander Young, you were on a first-name basis.

The Alexander Young Hotel building had been converted into doctor's offices. We'd ride up to the third floor and step out into a wide marbled corridor with beveled-glass half doors, the kind of doors you could almost see through. Our dentist, Henry Freitas, was one of Aunt Cecily's two brothers. His office was at the very end of the hall. The walk from the elevator took forever.

"Her teeth are like chalk," he'd tell my mother. "I drill and they crumble."

I had loads of cavities all the time. I was always in the dentist chair waiting for the Novocain to work, the drilling to stop, and the mercury to be mixed. It took forever to fill a tooth. Sometimes Dr. Freitas let me take a few beads of mercury home to brighten once-silver coins. I left, jaw sore, with a tea bag or something like that clenched between my teeth.

The dentist was one thing. Other facial functions were another. When the teacher made the announcement: "Boys and girls line up. We're going to have our eyes and ears tested," I panicked. I knew I couldn't see, not like normal people. If something were too far away, I'd round my mouth into an O, which caused a slight tug on my nostrils, place my middle finger at the corner of my right eye and gently pull the world into focus. So far, I'd gotten away with my blindness. No one noticed that I'd read with my nose buried in the crack of a book. I could pull out in an instant and assume the proper reading position. This seeing and hearing test, I knew, was going to be my downfall.

We lined up and took the short walk to the nurses' station in Castle Hall. Castle Hall was also the girls' dormitory for those who attended Punahou from other islands. I hung back at the end of the line, hoping they'd run out of time before everyone could be tested. No such luck. We entered a long hallway. Situated at one end was the hearing equipment. Half of the class, my half, was deposited there. The others were taken to eye testing.

The hearing part was easy. I lifted the proper hand to signal what side the sound was coming from, relieved that I wasn't asked right or left. I was so apprehensive about the eye business, I would have had to revert to lifting my ankles before answering.

It seemed too soon when I found myself facing a chart on the wall. A piece of tape was pulled across the floor. "Stand behind the line," a voice said. "Now, cover your right eye and read the letters." I stood there, flushed, staring at a white and black blur.

"Well?" the voice said.

"I'm reading them," I replied.

"Read them out loud," said the voice, shattering my last hope of getting out of the mess. If I could have willed myself to throw up, I would have.

"I can't see the chart," I said in a small voice hoping no one would hear.

"Then try covering your left eye." I did, but nothing came clear. "OK," continued the voice, "let's walk up to this line closer to the chart." I repeated my performance, humiliated. Sensing my extreme discomfort, the voice released me. I was sure all my classmates were snickering. I turned around. Everyone was watching just as I expected, but the looks were looks of pity. I thought it was worse than being laughed at or taunted.

I was taken to Dr. Gordon's in the Alexander Young Hotel the next day. "Not the dentist this time," Mother told the elevator operator. "This time it's eyes."

I shrank into a corner.

Dr. Gordon didn't hurt. He just took forever. Drops were given and when he finally returned, he seated me behind a big machine that looked like something out of a science fiction movie. He placed the machine in front of my face and ran glass back and forth in front of each eye. "Now? Or now?" he'd ask in an accent I thought was German. "Can you see better with this one, or this one?" His voice and the clicking changes were the only sounds in the darkened room.

Later, Mother helped me pick out cat-eyed frames like hers. At first the glasses bothered me, gave me a headache. There was so much to see. I felt so tall when I looked down—tall and unbalanced. I was amazed! I could differentiate each leaf on mango trees in my grandparents backyard. Glasses offered a whole new world to me which I had to catch in intervals. I was embarrassed to be seen with the glasses on outside the confines of family or after lessons in class. My eye tugging continued to pull the world into focus. I probably would have looked more appealing had I left my glasses on and not opted for distortion, but it was a way of asserting my independence. "Don't need no glasses no how," I told myself. Bad teeth, bad eyes, and a little too porky for cinch belts and crinolines, but I was not about to give in, no siree!

I loved my crinolines that Ellen starched to cardboard stiffness. I wore them under skirts, my favorite being one with a felt poodle appliquéd on the front. I got that far, but the cinch belts defeated me. Moments after clasping the wide band around my waist, it shriveled into something resembling a tube or thick twine. I'd try to fix it. I'd stick my thumbs under the elastic in an effort to flatten the belt to normal size, but I wasn't normal size which made my attempts futile. By the end of the day, the skin around my waist was dented with belt impressions.

I was a little more successful with my ponytail than my clothes. My hair was long and thick. I kept it tied with a rubber band, high on top of my head. The little tufts of newer hair bothered me. Like the boys with their Duck Ass haircuts, I'd slick the worrisome hairs in place with Brylcreem. It looked great on the guys, so I figured it looked great on me. No one said anything to the contrary.

"Oh, goody," said Mother one afternoon. "Here he comes."

"Who?" I asked, peering out the kitchen window with her.

"The salesman," she said. "I'm getting a Relax-a-cizor. It's the end of dieting. It's going to melt pounds of flesh off me, and make me a new person."

Sounds great, I thought.

In came the salesman, toting a huge black case as big as the toter himself.

"Let's take it into my room," Mother said, and off she went. I was right on her heels. When I got inside her room, she shooed me off and shut the door. I sat on the stairs outside and waited, anticipating the miracle. When Cynnie-Belle and Bruce got home, they joined me.

We waited awhile. The door finally opened and we stepped in to see what looked more like a magic show. "Uncle Duke should be here," I whispered to Bruce. "Him and his magic tricks." Uncle Duke's magic tricks for birthday parties were legendary. He'd pull stuff out of noses and ears. He dazzled us with his skills all the time. But we were getting older and magic was disappearing from our list of likes.

"Now this," I said, whispering into Bruce's ear, "truly looks magical."

There she lay, flat on her back. She was wearing a two piece bathing suit. Wires cascaded from all exposed parts of her body. They fed into a machine that emitted small buzzing noises that sounded like flies being fried by hot lights. We stood there staring, rendered speechless by the scene.

"You're right," Bruce said and left the room in disgust.

As I watched, visions of a slender me danced in my head. Maybe I, too, could become as thin as my sister.

"Here, feel this," said my mother as she detached a padded wire from her upper arm and placed it on mine. I jumped when I felt a tiny shock. The feeling however, wasn't unbearable. It was something I could live with. Images of a new me began to grow stronger.

Cynnie-Belle slipped out of the room; diets never did interest her. I stayed and stared lovingly at the wires. "By the way, you're not to touch this machine," Mother said.

"Oh, Mom," I started to whine. She knew what I was thinking! The machine was magic!

"No," she said and that was that.

I left, saddened to think the Relax-a-cizer and I were not to be. It wasn't fair. Osterizers and Relax-a-cizers. "Fat and Skinny had a race," I sang softly to myself, "Fat fell down and

Skinny won the race." If she only knew how much I needed to be skinny.

Three days later, Mother cooked fifty pounds of chicken cacciatore for an Italian luncheon at the Institute. That night she took us to an Italian restaurant with Larry. So much for weight loss.

Uncle Duke built a house. He named it "Pale Hua" which meant fertile slopes or something like that. The house was located in a range southwest of Honolulu. The main road, which ran along the circumference of the island, skirted miles of cane fields. My uncle said he built Pale Hua as a retreat. It took over an hour to get to the spot where we'd begin the half-hour ascent. We crossed numerous cattle guards and had to unlock three property gates before arriving. It was pretty slow going, but it was worth it.

We started going to Pale Hua on Sundays. We'd pack two cars full of children and food and head out about eleven. I'd ride with my grandparents, my grandmother at the wheel. We'd sing hymns and play "Riddlemeree" or "Twenty Questions" to while away the time. Mom came sometimes, but not often.

"That place is too damp and cold," she told me. "Reminds me of the mainland, damp fall days. I'd rather go to Makaha Beach. I mean, if I'm going to come this far from home, I might as well enjoy Makaha."

Makaha was pretty remote, about an hour up the road from the turn-off to Pale Hua. "Does Larry have family living there?" I asked.

"Something like that," Mother replied.

We went to Pale Hua a lot. The wooden structure was a walk-out ranch. Upstairs, the living and dining rooms were combined into one. There was a large fireplace. Through the picture window, you could see the battleships at Pearl Harbor. Diamond Head looked minute in the distance.

The driveway ran along the lower level of the house. It began on a steep hill and ended at a small outbuilding at the bottom of a pretty deep slope. To the side of the driveway was a small pasture. The entire site was surrounded by brittle bushes. Barbed wire marked the demarcation line between safe and unsafe territory. Wild boar, my cousin Stanton assured me, lurked on the other side. Of course, I believed him.

While waiting for steaks to be cooked and the rest of lunch prepared, Stanton and I would take his red wagon, and after a running start, jump in and fly down the driveway using the handle to steer. It was another world up there in the mountains. The cool, often misty atmosphere smelling of burning logs and woods reminded me of the setting in "Seven Brides for Seven Brothers," my current most-favorite movie. Awaiting my turn for a solo flight down the drive, I'd sing "Lonesome Polecat" while stalking and swinging at imaginary trunks of trees.

I loved Pale Hua. It was kind of western. The times we all went, parents and children, I felt as if I'd died and gone to heaven. There were no intruders, no tourists to entertain. I enjoyed the life Pale Hua afforded, if only for a few hours.

We were on our way home from Pale Hua when I decided I wanted a horse of my own. I was tired of the riding lessons and taking care of animals that weren't mine. Cynnie-Belle had her own horse in Montclair at my age, why not me? We'd been winding down the mountain. I had forgotten to pee before we left and was already feeling the effects. Mother was in the back seat with me, my grandmother at the wheel. To divert myself, I played with a miniature horse that I galloped up and down the seat. It was brown with a white blaze down its forehead.

"I've got to pee," I said. We had reached the main road and were speeding toward the little town of Waipahu. "Please, can we stop?" I asked.

"There's no place to stop until Pearl City," said my mother

as we zoomed past Arakawa's, an everything-you-would-need warehouse store.

"What about Arakawa's?"

But it was too late, and Mother said, "You can hold it,"

"I suppose I'll have to." She shot me one of her looks.

We ultimately reached a gas station. If it hadn't been for the miniature horse diverting me, I probably would have wet my pants. I decided to wait, until the time was right, to ask for a horse of my own.

In March Mauna Kea erupted. Mother took us to see it. We flew over on a Sunday night. Rivers of lava oozed slowly down the slopes, looking like pictures I'd seen of molten steel. Trees caught fire like struck matches chain reacting, tossing balls of flame high into the air. Orange molten rock cut through the blackness of the night, its light reflecting on our faces staring out the windows of the plane.

We flew back and forth a few times before the rocks spit too high and pelted the metal around us. The beauty and terror of it all left me speechless.

A few days later we had another tidal wave alert, but it was a no-show and the "House of Happiness" was spared.

I decided to ask for a horse in April. My father had just returned from a trip to the mainland. His arrival was delayed a day because two engines on his plane caught fire and they had to turn back. I wanted to know where the plane was in relation to "the point of no return." If it had happened at the point of no return, would they have gone forward or back to the mainland? But I wanted the horse more than I wanted to hear his answer.

"Can I get a horse?" We were seated at the dining room table. Dinner was over, Bruce and Cynnie-Belle had gone to their rooms. I was on my second bowl of ice cream, enjoying my good fortune of having both my mother and father home, together.

"A horse?" said Mother. "I don't know, you're awfully young."

"Cynnie-Belle got a horse when she was my age," I pointed out.

"That was different," said Mother. "She had people to take care of it."

"I'll take care of it, promise," I said, angry at myself for not having a better argument.

"We'll discuss it," said Mother. Father said nothing.

I took refuge in the downstairs bathtub. I splashed and soaked and rolled around in apprehension. When my fingers started to look like prunes, I decided I'd given them enough time. I got out, dried off, and slipped my nightgown over my head. I approached the dining room cautiously. This is it, I thought. In a few moments I'll know.

They were still at the table. Mother looked at me and smiled. "All right, you can have a horse, but you'd better take care of it," she warned.

"Yay, thank you!" I cried and hugged them before leaving the room on a cloud.

I wondered if my father consented because he was happy to survive a burning plane. But then, I thought, he probably had nothing to do with the decision.

It took a few tries to find the right horse. Larry drove us to the other side of the island to look at one.

"Perfect," I said, "Let's buy it."

"Wait a minute," said Mother, and marched off with the owner. I could see her asking questions as she walked around the animal. They went at it awhile before she returned to the car.

"Let's go," she said. "We aren't buying that one."

"Why not?" I wanted to know.

"Because I said so."

We looked at a few others before she turned the search over to Mr. Causey. Mr. Causey ran the stables. He was a wonderful man. It didn't take long for him to find Dickie. Terrible, I thought, but he came with the name. He was a nice looking horse, brown with a black mane. Dickie, however, had a rotten temper. He was soon called "Dickie the Devil." I had big problems with the horse. I couldn't stay on him. Every time I'd climb aboard, he'd throw me off. Sometimes he got rid of me in an instant; other times it was a surprise. Mother screamed foul play when I got dumped in the middle of a busy street while crossing over to Kapiolani Park. Mr. Causey towed Dickie away with his jeep and returned with Pepper.

Talk about safe. Pepper personified the term "plug." He was so bow legged I could walk right through his hind legs and never touch horse flesh. This was no mean feat. I no longer was getting fat, I was fat. But I loved the horse and taking care of him. Nothing felt better than cleaning a stall. I got good at filling the wheel barrow with manure and taking a running start up the ramp to the dump truck. I got good at lifting buckets of fresh water, giving Pepper a bath, pitching hay, and polishing tack. I practically lived at the stables. I became close friends with Diane and Denby, both my sister's age. By now, Cynnie-Belle had totally abandoned horses for boys. The camaraderie among all at the stables was wonderful. Age didn't matter and the friendships continued after we went home.

"Cattle Call" blasted forth from Freddy's small radio. Freddy shod horses on a slightly raised wooden platform that kept sand off the horses' hooves. Hoots and howls, in imitation of Eddie Arnold's rounding up the herds, echoed from various parts of the stables. I was watching Freddy at work. He'd wedge the horse's leg between his while he trimmed the smelly edges, fitted the iron, and pounded in nails he held between his teeth. Freddy, of no discernible origin, was good at his job. He was a man of few words made fewer by his mouth being stuffed with tobacco along with the nails. He and Tuna helped Mr. Causey run the place.

True to his name Tuna resembled a fish. He had dark greasy hair and black eyebrows that made his deep blue eyes seem more so. He was in his early twenties and despite the description, not bad looking. He liked to show off his muscles by rolling up a pack of cigarettes in the sleeve of his T-shirt. The gesture also displayed his tattoo, a heart with an arrow through it, not too original but the only tattoo I'd ever seen up close.

Tuna owned his version of a hot rod. It was decorated with flames and decals, but it was also wired to shock anything that touched it, horses included. I kept my distance from the man, but the older girls thought Tuna was wonderful. Andy, a lithe tomboy who had the only blond ponytail at the stables, won his affections.

I spotted Diane and Denby coming up the drive from the lower pasture. They were deep in conversation.

"What's up?" I asked when I reached them.

"We're thinking of taking our horses home for the night."

"Great, can I come with you?"

"If it's okay with your parents."

It was okay. They were so preoccupied when I asked, I don't even think they listened to the request. "Fine, be careful," was the reply.

We set off early. Our route took us around the backside of Diamond Head which was safer than the busy road along the coast. We rode through Fort Ruger and into Waialae-Kahala. It gave us time to see the tremendous impact of encroaching civilization. Houses in various stages of completion filled the once rugged terrain. There were so many—where would the people come from? The three of us grumbled over the destruction. We felt uneasy and helpless. Our safe world was changing and we weren't sure what that meant. But these thoughts were soon forgotten when we hit the already established streets and received smiles and attention from passing motorists and residents.

Ellen fixed us lunch after the crisis over where to tie the horses. We settled on a water spigot in the front yard and ate sandwiches while the alley kids trickled in to see the horses and beg for rides.

The afternoon was spent riding between Black Point and the First Canal. Diane and Denby cantered far ahead of me. I hadn't figured out how to get Pepper to even trot. I faked this minor detail as best I could, hopping off for drinks of water or pretending concern with a twisted rein or saddle blanket. "Pepper's tired," I'd say to those who actually asked why we were only walking around and hoped they would get bored and leave. Whiz, however, never did let up. "You can't make him run," he'd chant. "You can't make him run." I could have killed him!

Late in the afternoon Diane and Denby went to their respective homes. I tied Pepper to the side of the house. There was a small corridor that separated us from the Hueys' hedges, and I thought the confines resembled a kind of natural stall. The space was big enough for two banana trees as well as a horse. I was pleased.

The worry began almost immediately. What if he came untied in the night? How am I going to ride back by myself in the morning? What if a strange dog attacks? You name it, I worried about it.

By dinner I was sick with dread. I couldn't even choke down my favorite supper of mashed potatoes, fried chicken, and peas. Ellen, the only one home, tried to calm me down. It didn't work. Ellen, I realized, would be no help in a crisis. She was deathly afraid of horses.

I stationed myself in the chair next to the window under which Pepper was tied. I spent most of the night jumping up and peering out with every little noise. My total lack of appetite, even for my usual bowls of ice cream, was a first for me. I tucked the reaction away to ponder at a later date.

Pepper and I survived the night. The next morning we set

off early, making our way over back roads and dirt paths. The opposite approach looked so different from the day before, but Pepper seemed to know where he was going, so I let him lead. Horse sense, I thought.

There was a funeral going on as we crossed Diamond Head Cemetery on our way up to Fort Ruger. A woman was screaming, "Papa, Papa, come back. What will I do without you, Papa?" My first confrontation with death and grief. Papa was not going to come back, and there I was, riding under blue skies, tired and trying to look invisible.

The overnight adventure had an impact on me. I realized the importance of the security at the stables. Familiar felt comfortable.

What gets me is the incredible ease with which Mother approached the divorce. It was June and my father had left for the mainland again.

She told us individually, in the bathroom. She liked to do that, break news while seated on the side of the tub.

I was the last informed. It took me by surprise. I knew Dad wasn't home much and that she spent more time with other men than she did with him. Nevertheless, I was shocked. I only remembered one argument between them. I was asleep in his bed when he came home in the middle of the night. Half asleep, I heard her hiss, "You're gone so much, I didn't know when you'd be back. Go sleep in her room."

Sure, I knew we weren't not like a lot of families, but divorce? The news devastated me. When I broke down in tears, Mother became a little hostile. "What difference does it make?" she asked defensively. "He's never here." It made a great deal of difference to me. Her marriage gave credibility to our lives. I lost all hope of having a mother, a life style, and an ideal home like those portrayed in magazines, on radio, or on the still-embryonic television shows. I knew that day in June that we'd never live like others. I'd never see Chatham or live in a Cinderella house. The next day, I heard her say to Larry on the telephone, "Stayed home, got to know the kids, built their character."

Mr. Causey, a family man with four sons one of whom I adored from afar sensed my sadness. The divorce became common knowledge quickly, as did everything on the island.

"There's a rodeo in Kailua," he told me. "How about me taking you and Pepper?"

And he did.

We loaded our horses into a tiny trailer attached to his jeep and headed for the other side of the Pali. The narrow two-lane road that threaded through the mountain was terrifying. Most people avoided the route. The hairpin turns and strong winds were treacherous. True tales of cars being blown off the cliffs abounded. The road was so narrow in places that drivers had to stop and honk their horns to avoid head-on collisions. At one particular turn, it was better to get out and walk before driving around. But the day was calm, the visibility unhampered by rain showers, and we made it to Kailua without a hitch.

Mr. Causey parked the car. We unloaded the horses and saddled up. He then left for the arena with instructions on where he could be found. I watched him trot away. "Let's go," I said to Pepper, as I perched on his back. I cut a dashing figure, blue jeans with cuffs rolled up to my calves, black flats, white socks, my hair in a pony tail, still slicked back with a light touch of Brylcreem, glasses cleaned so I could see. To really be in the swing of things, I had tied a coil of rope to the side of the saddle. I thought it looked very much like a lasso. I thought I looked very much like a cowgirl!

"Come on, Pepper," I said and kicked him.

Pepper didn't move.

"Pepper," I whined, "let's go." I kicked harder.

He still didn't move. Not a muscle.

I looked around to see if anyone were watching. Those leaving their parked cars were headed across the field toward the arena. No one seemed to notice my foiled attempt at being a buckaroo. I started kicking continuously, my legs rising higher with each kick. Still nothing.

I can't believe this, I said to myself. In desperation, I pulled some of the rope off the saddle, enough to clobber the poor horse. But one swift swat on the neck was all it took. Off we went at a canter. It was the first time since I got Pepper that he did more than walk. I was absolutely elated and blessed my luck in finding the motivation.

I had a great day and didn't even get scared when Mr. Causey's jeep started rolling in reverse on a particularly steep grade of the Pali on our way home. My hero could do no wrong. I knew he wouldn't let us catapult down the mountain. The truth be known: I was so happy, I didn't even care.

My father called from my grandparents' in Montclair to announce the divorce was final. My mother danced around the house singing, "I'm free, I'm free."

The day Dad returned to Honolulu, he came over. It was July 17, Mother's 40th birthday.

She noticed his car pulling into the driveway before I did. "Christ," she said. I could tell she was desperately thinking of what to do. Suddenly, out the lanai door she went. "I'm going to the Buscher's, tell him I'm not home!" I stood there in the middle of the living room, totally confused. He came in, all smiles, waving a record in the air. "Where's Dot?" he asked, "I've brought her a birthday present."

"I don't know," I said. "I'll be right back," as I, too, slipped out the door and sped across the front yard to the Buschers. I found her sitting in their living room. There they were, Mr. and Mrs. Buscher and my mother, on the couch in front of the TV. Whiz, propped up on a bunch of pillows, lay on the floor. He looked at me as if to say, "How are you going to handle this, smarty pants?" I ignored him as best I could.

"Mom, he's brought you a present, it's your birthday." I thought the gesture heroic considering the circumstances.

"I told you to tell him I wasn't home," she said, angry. "Go back, tell him you don't know where I am."

But I did know where she was and to say I didn't was a lie. I was furious and hurt. I could feel Whiz's eyes on my back as I left.

"Um, Dad, I thought Mom was at the Buscher's. It seems she's not there," I stammered. I pictured my cheeks getting red, my nose growing longer.

"Well, I'll wait awhile," he said. "Here, I brought her a record, let's play it." It was some dumb song about popcorn. We listened to it quite a few times. Too many times.

"Great song Dad," I repeated as I bobbed and weaved around the lanai. Keeping rhythm to the music was pretty easy considering the circumstances. So was being able to lie for the second time in a matter of minutes.

After the divorce, Mother had our house professionally decorated. It was so out of character, the choices she made. My room was pink and white. Pink walls, pink venetian blinds, pink desk, and a pink dresser. Every night, I'd have to pull the bed out from under pink shelves. The designer's idea for more floor space. Two stark-white throw rugs partially covered the wood floor.

In Cynnie-Belle's room, heavy curtains engulfed the four windows. They were of the same material and color as the purple bedspread. Everything else was as white as the wall-to-wall carpet.

Bruce got black-and-red-checked bedspreads. Plaids and plain colors replaced the floral prints on the chairs and the couches downstairs. Outside, the lanai furniture was covered in material that could withstand wet bathing suits. Another of the designer's helpful hints. Although the new decor didn't fit Mother's personality, it did reflect the styles of the day. Well, at least we could look like a Cinderella Home.

It was on a bus that Cynnie-Belle met Buzzy. He taught her how to play the ukulele. When she found out he lived in the last alley near the cane fields, the lessons continued at his house. She could walk there in a few minutes.

Buzzy's father was a musician, an accomplished writer of Hawaiian songs. His mother was an alcoholic. He was five years older than Cynnie-Belle, a high school dropout. Buzzy was quiet and shy, which endeared him to her. They became friends, sharing similar frustrations and anger over absentee parents.

Buzzy had an older brother named Mickey. Unlike Buzzy, Mickey was boisterous, chubby and full of humor. He'd laugh at anything, particularly himself. The brothers complemented each other. Cynnie-Belle became friends with Mickey, and through the two brothers, she met Bernard. Bernard, a high school senior, was a lot like Mickey. He was a big teddy bear with a flat top, who also loved to laugh.

Cynnie-Belle kept her new friends a secret for quite a while. She might have thought the maids, the big house, Herman, or just our style of living might be too overwhelming for them. Lord knows those boys were notches above the company Mother kept. Whatever my sister's reasons, we only heard about Bernard and Mickey and Buzzy. Finally she brought them home, and there they stayed, usually on the lanai playing cards or music, and always laughing. You couldn't help but love the group. Slowly, even more friends joined and it didn't take long for everyone to learn to love "Dottie." They all were treated like adults; which, age wise, they were. At the same time, Dottie pampered and cooked for them.

Bernard was a Catholic and Cynnie-Belle started going to church. When things got hectic after the divorce, she converted to Catholicism and made plans to join Barbara Buscher at Dominican for her freshman year. Dominican was a Catholic school for girls outside of San Francisco.

"Feed Buzzy every once in awhile; he has a horrible home life," she told Mother before she left.

The day after Cynnie-Belle's departure, Mother moved Buzzy into the downstairs guest room.

Now I had two brothers. Neat, I thought.

To my relief, Mother stayed involved with the Institute after her divorce. The luncheons continued. There were also weekly gatherings of The Friendship Club at our house. The club consisted of Chinese ladies who played mahjong on the lanai, gossiped and giggled. Mother didn't participate in the game, but kept busy serving refreshments. They'd stay a few hours, then disappear. I never bothered with the group, nor they with me. I'm not sure if they even spoke English.

Ellen was off on Wednesdays, so Mother was usually home. She cooked elaborate meals for Larry which she also served to us. Bruce and I persevered, and Buzzy, ecstatic over being a part of our lives, couldn't have cared less what he ate. He'd sit there, eyes sparkling, with a crooked grin, and he'd watch with the intensity of a nineteen year old given a new lease on life. Bruce and I were more interested in a pot of chili than a nine-course Chinese meal. But Chinese was nothing compared to the concoctions from the Philippines. Products of new recipes began to appear in front of us with regularity. Many of the meals included chicken. Bruce said chickens were popular because so many of the roosters got killed in cock fights.

"So, what?" I asked him.

"Too many chickens left for the remaining roosters to handle."

"Handle?"

"You know, take care of. Population control."

"Oh, that," I said. I had no idea what he was talking about, but I wasn't going to let on.

Chicken dishes were, for the most part, not bad. Problems began when Mother decided to get creative and daring.

"What is this? It looks dreadful!" Pushing my salad around, I peered between the folds of lettuce.

"Well, the salad has fresh oranges and mashed white radishes in it. The meal is Lumpia with Ocho Sauce."

"And just what is that?" I had to know.

"Lumpia's a mixture of fresh and dried shrimp, garlic, garbanzo beans, Chinese peas, chestnuts, cabbage, lettuce, potatoes, and string beans."

"Sounds yummy," I said, blanching.

"Eat it and don't forget there are a lot of starving children in China."

I didn't eat it, merely shoved a few loads into my mouth before spitting them back into my napkin. To further the illusion of consumption, I spread the remains around the plate. Before we were excused, I wedged the napkin into a space beneath the table. Later, when everyone was gone, I sneaked back and retrieved the junk to flush down the toilet.

One night Mother tried to serve an inedible flank steak. It was topped with ground pork, pimiento, raisins, hard boiled eggs, and onions.

"Mom," I said, sniffing the mixture in front of me. "I'm not eating something that smells this terrible."

"Hush," she replied. "You'll hurt Larry's feelings."

"Larry's feelings? Larry's not even here tonight."

"Well, if he were, you would."

"Why?"

"Because he's part Filipino."

"Part Filipino? I thought you said he was Italian."

"He's both, part both."

"An Italian Filipino? Never heard of such a thing."

"Hawaii's a melting pot, you know that, anything can happen in the islands."

"Well, what about us? How about some American food?"

"American foods are boring."

I got a fish bowl to put on the pink dresser in my room. It was a simple aquarium, one not cluttered with pumps and filters. I selected two mollies from the pet store to be the occupants. I thought the pink and black combination would look jazzy, as my mother would say. Lo and behold, they had some babies. Actually, it wasn't really lo and behold. I asked for a male and female and that's what I got. I'd watch him stabbing her, wondering at the connection. I didn't understand it all, but I was impressed by the relationship. Only one baby survived. I named him Herman after our cab driver.

I don't know what possessed me to use his name. As I got older, Herman got to be a true source of embarrassment. He'd cart me home from school when I couldn't find a ride with someone's mother or an older sibling. I made him park far from the Winnie Units so no one would see me in a taxi cab. He insisted on jumping out of the car to open my door, giggling all the while and nodding up and down.

I guess I liked him more than I thought, to name a fish after him and all.

One afternoon I decided to clean the tank. I placed the fish, seaweed, and snails in a mixing bowl while the new water reached room temperature, and left for a football game. It was dark when I got home. Remembering the fish, I trotted upstairs and flipped on the lights in my bedroom. There, on my white rug, lay the three mollies. I started screaming. By the time my mother got to me, I was crying, inconsolable. I was devastated for days, horrified by my lack of responsibility. It was my fault they died. I murdered something I helped create. The fish were replaced, but it was never the same. Some mermaid I would have made.

My fish dreams began after that. I'd have nightmares of fish trapped in flumes used to irrigate the cane fields. Maybe that was because Herman, like Larry, was Filipino, and Filipino's worked in the cane fields. Perhaps it was just coincidence. In the dreams, I was never able to free the fish. I tried to catch them, to take them to the sea, but I couldn't. They slipped through my fingers, and I stood there feeling hopeless and helpless.

Cynnie-Belle came home for Christmas vacation acting nicer than ever towards Bruce and me. To Mother, however, Cynnie-Belle was quite different. "I told you to feed him once in a while," she hissed. "You didn't need to move him in, Dorothy."

Wow, I thought. This Catholic school's given her even more guts. Geez, I was expecting her to return wearing some sort of habit or frock, something sort of holy. She made me feel like I did, indeed, have a sister!

We got into making like Patience and Prudence and harmonized all their songs. We'd sing upstairs in her purple and white room. Sometimes, late at night, she'd awaken me to go for a treat with her friends. The Jolly Roger was my favorite. Located in the heart of Waikiki, I'd scarf down hot fudge sundaes late into the night.

Cynnie-Belle didn't stay around much during the day. She was often with Bernard or one of her many girl friends. "I can't stand to watch the way Mother treats Buzzy," she told me. "Doesn't it make you mad? I mean he's more of a son to her than Bruce. It's disgusting!"

I thought no, but I didn't want to lie. Instead, I said "I guess." Buzzy didn't bother me. He was kind and I liked him a lot.

1956

FOR SOMEONE WHO DIDN'T DRIVE, my mother sure bought a lot of cars. The day my sister returned to Dominican, Mom purchased a hot rod for Buzzy. "It's a fabulous '37 Ford coupe with floor shift," she proudly announced as she walked in the front door. She had sense enough to wait until Cynnie-Belle was in the air before letting Buzzy bring it home. Cynnie-Belle's disapproval of Buzzy was ever-present. Her relationship with Bernard helped smooth out some of the situations, but Cynnie-Belle let it be known she wanted Buzzy out of the house. Of course, Mother ignored her complaints.

I thought the car was wonderful. It had a rumble seat that pulled out, sort of like my beds. Buzzy would take me for rides. I delighted in waving to all we passed. This is what it's like to be a star, I thought, everyone looking at you. I pretended it was me being admired, not the car.

Everyone vied for Mother's attention. She mediated altercations between Buzzy and Bruce, Buzzy and Bernard, Bernard and Bruce. Of course, Larry wanted in on her attentions, too. Buzzy's friends were different, like orphans. My mother looked after them. She took Bernard to the hospital when he came down with acute gastritis, brought him back to our house the next day, then bought him a car. Nothing fancy, but a car, nonetheless.

Buzzy got sick and Larry came over to cook soup for Mother. Larry got sick and Buzzy took her out to dinner. If Bruce or I got sick, we were left with Ellen.

I stayed out of it by being at the stables, at friends' houses or at my father's. He moved into an apartment directly across the park from the stables. Mary, one of my mother's girl friends, helped him get settled.

"You bring your pals here anytime," he told me.

I did. It was fun. I'd let myself in through the trash door, push aside the rubber waste basket, push open the cabinet, and be in his kitchen. Then I'd let my friends in the front door. We were there almost every day for lunch. Fried spam for sandwiches was the meal of choice. We got so full of ourselves that we formed a club and called ourselves "The Sly Ones." Mary typed up an exclusive membership card for each of us. Diane, Denby, and I made the membership decisions. A small initiation was required, but it wasn't hard to pass. In fact, no one ever flunked. One of the requirements was having a horse. B.J. Filoni didn't own a horse, but everyone loved her, so we let her join.

Mary was always with my dad. They took me out to dinner every weekend, sometimes even during the week. I loved the attention. Mary took me on errands and to market to shop for "The Sly Ones." She loved buying Dad little goodies to eat. When I could, I'd spend Friday or Saturday nights with them so I could be at the stables before dawn.

My father resumed his interest in art and created pictures just for me. One was a comical head of a horse. It was bright blue and had a yellow mane. It was painted onto a background of shocking pink. Another was of two floppy-eared dogs. Both paintings looked terrific in my room. Especially the horse with its yellow mane painted on pink. Mary and I, "us girls," spent hours pleasing Dad with surprises. We'd bake cookies and fudge and bring home little gifts. It made him very happy. He was the center of attention. He deserved it. "You're my sweet Dad," I'd tell him. I never questioned why the attention now, but not when he was married to Mother.

Bruce spent more and more time at the Outrigger with the beachboys or in detention after school. He was getting into trouble with his teachers. Dr. Johnson called our home on a regular basis.

"Mom," I said, the first time he called. "It's someone named Dr. Johnson."

"Shit," she said. "That's Bruce's principal."

Horrified, I clamped my hand over the receiver. After that, I made sure the mouthpiece was covered before I told her who it was.

My brother surrounded himself with his own friends who lived nearby. I didn't worry about my brother's pals. Their parents were married. They ate dinner with their families. They also attended Punahou.

When Mom started to talk about being involved with a "World Brotherhood" organization, I became very concerned.

"World Brotherhood?"

"Yes, World Brotherhood, where everyone meets in the middle."

"Middle of what?" I asked.

"Middle of everything, life."

"Middle of life? What's the middle of life?" I had to know. The definition of middle of life was important. Did it mean age or being among the living? My question stumped her for a few minutes.

"Brotherhood is where everyone is related through being human. It disregards nationality or wealth. Everyone is an equal, that's all."

So that's why she allowed all these people here. And that's what Madge meant in Montclair. I remembered Madge scratching her arm. The scratches turned white.

"Why don't you scratch all over and look like me?" I asked.

"Color doesn't matter," Madge had said. "We're all the same inside."

I didn't know about that, had to think about it. I found it hard to believe her friends, uneducated and poor, were on our level. But, as usual, I was receiving mixed messages. I was confused, caught between the social worlds of my grandparents and Uncle Duke and my mother's world filled with what? I wasn't sure. Where did we stand? Where did I stand? Did we belong among the rich, when my mother cavorted with beach boys and bartenders? Why were we attending exclusive private schools when Mother's friends were uneducated. Somehow, I wasn't ready to buy the idea of "World Brotherhood." Yes, we were all human beings, but we were not the same. I knew what I wanted and it didn't include her lifestyle. I didn't need any more brothers. There were already too many men.

In March, Mother bought another hot rod for Buzzy. It was a brilliant pink with shiny chrome everywhere. The pink was pinker than my room, pinker than the background in my blue horse painting, pinker than the Royal Hawaiian Hotel. The rod was spectacular, square and low to the ground. It was unbelievable and brought gasps when it hit the streets. This incredible car was one to stand back and admire for an hour! A car you could pull a chair up to and watch. It was definitely not one to race.

Even though the National Association of Police Chiefs and The Safety Council condemned the practice, my mother allowed Buzzy to become a stock car and drag race driver. Maybe she thought it would make him feel good about himself. I don't know, but from then on, Saturdays she spent at the track with the pit crew from Island Fender Body Shop. Buzzy used his new rod for pleasure rides. He wasn't about to wreck it on a track or drag strip.

The car was so fantastic, my mother purchased a green Chevrolet station wagon for everyday errands.

"He hasn't lived here seven months and he has three cars," Bruce complained.

The wagon was all right. Even though it didn't have a suburban father poised behind the wheel, it did accommodate Bruce's surfboard. It wasn't long before Mother bought Larry a station wagon, too.

"Hope she's not thinking of making Larry the father behind the wheel," I said out loud. As usual, no one was around to hear me.

"Your Mother's been blackballed from the Outrigger," Whiz stated. He'd asked me why we never went anymore.

"What does that mean, blackballed?" I asked.

"Me to know and you to find out," he replied.

"You dip stick," I growled.

"What did you call me?"

"A dip stick."

"What's a dip stick?" he asked before realizing his mistake.

"That's for me to know and you to find out," I told him.

"Your Mother was blackballed because of her morals," he screeched and ran off.

I went looking for Ellen. "Morals are the way people behave," she told me.

Mom behaves just fine, I thought. Whiz must have his facts wrong.

The Surf Club, located down the beach toward Diamond Head, was the locals' answer to the Outrigger. There were facilities for surfboards and canoes, but no clubhouse. Members just hung around under a big old tree at the edge of the beach. A bar across the street was all they needed for a clubhouse. Mother began rooting for Surf Club teams. The Surf Club was made up of beachboys whose heritage scanned the gambit of nationalities. Most spoke pidgin English. I think my mother was the only Haole, or Caucasian, in the Club. They made her an honorary member after she managed to get blackballed from the Outrigger.

Mother's involvement with the Surf Club was a little embarrassing. Bruce's team paddled against Surf Club's team. Although Mom cheered him on during the races, she gave her support to Surf Club at all other times. It worked out okay, until Cynnie-Belle arrived home from boarding school.

Mom was having a victory party. "Surf Club scooped up most of the ribbons," she explained to Cynnie-Belle. "That's why I had Roger fetch you. Glad you're back, honey. Did you have a nice semester?"

I watched the scene. My sister was livid. "Where's Bruce?" she asked, her voice controlled.

"Bruce is at the Outrigger. His team was one of the few that won their division, great huh?"

Cynnie-Belle turned, gesturing toward the front yard. "Who are all these people? Why are they at our house?"

"These folks belong to the Surf Club."

"Why are they here, I'm asking you why are they here?" she reiterated.

"Because I'm a new member, an honorary member, no less."

"Well, you're a member of the Outrigger, too."

"Not anymore, honey, not anymore."

"Dorothy, get these creeps out of here."

"Miss Cynthia-Belle, I do not approve of that kind of attitude in teenagers. You're my first born, the oldest, I depend on you."

"Yeah? For what? Car approvals?"

—

Two days later Cynnie-Belle and her friend Kehau stole Buzzy's '37 Ford coupe and drove it over the Pali to visit a friend. Cynnie-Belle was arrested for driving without a permit or license.

"I can't believe we got caught," she told Bruce and me when she returned. "We made the hairpin turn on the Pali without any problems. But, seems this damn policeman thought we looked suspicious as we drove through Kailua."

Guess so, I thought, two fifteen-year-old girls, one white, the other Hawaiian, driving a hot rod with a rumble seat.

No charges were filed; my mother's wrath was mild. A week later my sister got her permit. I was so happy to have Cynnie-Belle home to do battle for us, I could have wept.

I was very excited to be going to another island. School was out and the Hanebergs asked me to spend two weeks in Hana, Maui. Of course, I said yes. I loved the Hanebergs, they were my home away from home.

I was late getting to the airport. The plane was about to leave and I was running lickity-split toward the ramp when I fell. Terribly embarrassed, I rose and hobbled up the stairs and into the plane. The stewardess was so nice. Dismayed by my much-scraped knee, she brought out her first aid kit and dabbed a bit of this and a bit of that on my wound. Soothed, I thanked her and fastened my seat belt for take off.

The Hanebergs house was located on a rustic road that dead-ended in a pasture. The house itself was plain and primitive. A wooden bungalow with a kitchen, two bedrooms, a bath, and a living room that all flowed together in the floor plan. To get to a bedroom you had to go through the kitchen or the living room. It was so uncomplicated, so symbolic of our oneness as a family. I really did feel a part of the brood, until some mysterious pimples appeared on my scraped knee.

"What's that?" yelled Jon, pointing to the infested area. Too late to hide the sores, all eyes were upon my leg.

"Let me see," said Mrs. Haneberg, scrutinizing what was now beginning to itch like mad.

"Let me break them open with a needle and put peroxide on them," she said. And she did, every night. It felt wonderful when she operated on me. The sores were so itchy that I couldn't wait for her attention. Because she didn't know what the infection was, I had to sleep by myself and not share towels. There went any hope of my playing normal family life. The kids played with me, all right, but they kept their distance and never let me forget my disease.

The only joy I derived during that vacation was the nightly ritual of taking that needle and stabbing the sacs on my leg. They multiplied daily, but I didn't care. Relieving the itch was almost a religious experience.

When I got home, Mother took me to Dr. Lam. "Impetigo," he pronounced. "Lancing the sores made it spread." He gave me a shot and some salve and it was gone in a few days.

First pink-eye, now impetigo. What is it with Hana, I asked myself.

When Cynnie-Belle passed her driver's test, she got a car. It was a blue '49 Ford a cousin owned before she went off to college. Cynnie-Belle was the next in line to inherit the blue bombshell, as it was called, but she went to work on being allowed to drive Buzzy's pink rod. She didn't mean to be a pest. She'd already driven his coupe. But my sister was ready for bigger and better experiences. She didn't give a twit about what she drove over the Pali. Cynnie-Belle told Mom, "I don't need to drive the coupe. I've already done that." Mother, at a loss for words, threatened to have Cynnie-Belle arrested if she stole the car again.

"I want to drive his pink hot rod," she whispered to Mother. We'd been to dinner at Canlis Broiler and were walking across the street to the Kuhio Theater to see "Friendly Persuasion." Gary Cooper and Dorothy McGuire were the stars.

"You can't," said Mother.

"Why not?"

"Because it's too much for you to handle."

"I drove the coupe over the Pali perfectly," Cynnie-Belle replied.

"I don't care, you might have an accident and wreck it."

"I've never had an accident."

"Cynthia-Belle," said Mother, "you've only had your license a few days, now hush!"

"You're my mother and you won't let your own daughter drive a car you bought for someone who is not even related to us?"

"Don't speak like that to me. Buzzy's part of this family, now drop it!"

Tony Perkins was in the middle of his "I wanna see Ohio, Momma," scene. Chills were crawling all over me as I listened to his intentions. I had no idea where Ohio was, but I rolled the "I wanna see Ohio, Momma," words around in my head. I thought the way he said it was wonderful.

Cynnie-Belle broke my attention.

"Move your legs," she said as she climbed over me and headed toward the aisle. I knew she had been arguing with Mother, but they argued a lot since Cynnie-Belle got home from school. I didn't pay much attention to her departure, figured she'd gone to get something to eat. But she did not return. When the movie was over, we walked back to Canlis where Cynnie-Belle's car was parked.

"I wanna see Ohio, Momma," I blurted out. It sounded pretty good.

"What?" said Mother.

Great, I thought, I can do it again!

"I wanna see Ohio, Momma!"

This time it was even better.

"What are you talking about?"

It occurred to me she may have missed the scene.

"Never mind."

I didn't feel like explaining. There was no sign of Cynnie-Belle nor her car when we reached the parking lot.

"Shit," said Mother.

Luckily a cab was there and we got in. "Kahala," she told the driver.

When we pulled up at the house, the pink rod was parked, as usual, in the middle of the back yard. Too many cars pulled in and out, and it was less apt to be scratched there. The station wagon was in the driveway. There was no sign of Cynnie-Belle's Ford. Mother paid the fare and out we climbed.

"What's that on the rod?" I asked as we neared the house.

"My God!" Mother exclaimed.

The fabulous hot rod was covered with raw eggs, a couple of dozen at least. Yellow ooze and chips of shell reflected off its body. I thought the pink and yellow looked better in Dad's painting, but admired Cynnie-Belle's choice of weapons.

"Ugh," I said and ran inside.

Mother referred to Cynnie-Belle's egg throwing as, "A disgraceful episode."

A few days later, my sister had surgery for a hemorrhoid and spent five days in the hospital.

"Probably explains her evil temper," Mother told Ellen. The night Cynnie-Belle returned home, Mother went to watch Buzzy race.

Things weren't good at home so I sought solace at the stables. But that, too, had changed. Mr. Causey left. Just like that, he was gone. A Chinese man had purchased the circle of stalls and the surrounding pastures. His name was Mr. Ling.

Mr. Ling was evil. He carried a bull whip that he'd snap at

us, and he'd giggle idiotically. He had a particular fondness for doing this when we were on horseback. It scared us and the horses.

Mr. Ling was dangerous. He had a mistress, a Swedish woman named Ursula. I think she was a maid. At least, she always wore a white uniform. I wasn't sure what a mistress did, but Diane and Denby assured me it was naughty. They "did it" everyday at noon, proof being that everyday at lunch time, Ursula would drive up and they would disappear into his small house located off the bridle path. I'd watch them go inside.

Mr. Ling wore jodhpurs, boots that came up to his knees, and white shirts that ill concealed his large stomach. He constantly said, "You see, you know, you see, you see, you know," when he spoke. It drove us to distraction, but we all became experts at imitating him.

When I wasn't at the stables, I'd try for a friend's house. There was a terrible infestation of army worms that completely ruined the local lawns. Beedie, who had moved into a new home on the same circle as the Hanebergs, had acquired a needle and syringe. We'd flood each other's yards, plucking the worms as they rose to the surface and then we'd inject them with various colors of dye. They would turn the same shade. Beedie not only had the injection equipment, she also had a jewelry box with tons of drawers. We would color-code the victims and file them away, pretending to be mad scientists. Horror films and comic books were all the rage. It was our way of taking part in the madness. Not a bad time. I was happy. I had a horse, places to go, and friends. So what if my family fell apart? I had a life of my own.

It was all over by the time Cynnie-Belle and Bruce got home. Bruce had gone surfing and had decided not to go dove hunting with the older boys. Often he'd follow them into KoKo Head Crater to assault the birds. But Bruce didn't own a 22 rifle. He was too young, and he was tired of being an observer even though he liked being with the guys. The waves were up and that seemed more appealing that certain Monday in July. Cynnie-Belle had taken her car and had driven to Kailua to see Kuulei. Both had returned home in time for dinner.

I was there. I saw it all happen. Bernard, Mickey, Buzzy, and Nicky, a fairly new fixture on our lanai, returned early in the afternoon, happy with the number of doves felled and very full of themselves. Norman, a friend of Bruce's, dropped by looking for Bruce. I stayed to watch the cleaning of the guns and birds.

Drinking Cokes and sprawled on various sofas and chairs, the boys chatted among themselves as barrels were unloaded, oiled, and snapped back into place. Nicky was in the yard washing his hands under the water faucet when Norman jumped up, grabbed a rifle and laughingly cried, "Look, a lion!"

There was a cracking sound. Down went Nicky, onto the grass, his head shaded by the spider lilies that bordered the lanai.

At first we thought he was kidding. Shouts of "Get up Nicky," filled the air as the boys punched each other playfully. But Nicky didn't move. Norman stood there silently as the others approached the stilled body. I stood frozen. Buzzy started shouting, "Nicky's been shot, Nicky's been shot." I turned and tore into the house to find my mother, vocalizing the horrible reality. "Nicky's been shot, Mom, Nicky's been shot."

The day after the accident, my sister took Bruce and me to Star of the Sea Church. The act of praying and lighting candles made me feel as if I were doing something to right the wrong. Nicky died four days later; he never regained consciousness.

After Nicky's death, many children were not allowed to play at our house. "No supervision," parents said. Ironically, the "no supervision" came later. My mother was home when Nicky got shot. She'd left the lanai for only a moment, but that was all it took for a disaster, one simple moment. Pieced together later, it seems that Norman actually pointed the gun at Buzzy and, playing on his last name, Lyon, shouted "Look, a lion." Bernard shoved Norman's arm out of position, and as he did, the gun discharged. Nicky happened to be in the way.

"It was an accident," Mother said to ease the ache. "No one's to blame."

The day after they buried Nicky, Mother took all of us to Maui, all except Norman. We arrived in shifts. Cynnie-Belle and two friends landed with Buzzy, Bernard, and Mickey. Bruce brought four more boys the next day. I flew in a few days later with Jeannie King. Jeannie wasn't a good friend, but she was the only one I could find who could come up with parental permission. Her father was a judge, maybe that was why she was allowed. He understood. In all, fourteen young people between the ages of 10 and 19 graced our home in Sprecklesville. Added to that were scores of kids who actually lived on the island. Kids of all ages and nationalities hung around Hale Ola at all hours of the day and night.

We amused ourselves playing Pig. It was a simple card game the object being to amass four of the same of each suit. Three tokens were placed in the circle of players and cards passed on call. If someone appeared to be winning, the dealer could reverse the course of the "pass." Ultimately, someone would scream "Pig," and the four players would dive in for the three tokens. The person slowest to grab became the pig and was ridiculed with oinks, snorts and finger pointing. While we younger kids played Pig, the older kids played poker or cribbage, but Pig was not beneath them. We also had fierce games of Monopoly that lasted for days.

Real pigs were a big deal on Maui. Kishaba, our caretaker, raised them. We had two cans in the laundry room—one for the garbage men, the other for the pigs. We had great times, after meals, emptying our plates into the trash, deciding what the pigs would like. Many an evening, we'd pile into Kishaba's pick-up truck, and holding on, brace ourselves for the wild ride to Happy Valley where he slopped his hogs.

During the day we often went to the Country Club. The boys played golf while the girls drove the carts. We'd eat steak sandwiches and lie by the pool. "You have nice legs," Buzzy told me one afternoon. My first compliment. I loved him for it. Well, I thought, whatever happens, I have nice legs. I was as porky as Kishaba's pigs, but I had nice legs.

Haleakala, a mountain so large it took up the entire sky, loomed above the club. We drove to the top and marveled at the rare silver sword plants that grew only there. At the summit, we watched the craters from the lookout house. The craters were supposed to be like those on the moon. In the distance lay the island of Hawaii. After frolicking in the thin air, we went to Kula Lodge for steak dinners.

We took picnics to Kaanapali Beach. It lay beyond the little town of Lahaina. Lahaina wasn't much. There was one hotel for the sailors who docked their boats along the wharf en route to or from another South Seas island. Kaanapali Beach was on the edge of a cane field. All of Maui was cane fields. The dirt road we took to reach the shore ended behind a large open hut which, at least, had a roof to shelter us from rain squalls. There were a few donkeys that we rode if the owners appeared.

The beach, a cove really, was isolated and wide. I was too chicken, but the other kids spent hours diving off Black Rock.

The Maui Palms Hotel, the first new hotel to rival the old Maui Grand in Wailuku, was another place we haunted. My mother knew the owner. She'd get a hotel room for the day to use for changing clothes even though our house was only 15 minutes by car. "It's a treat for you," she'd tell us.

She lost her ankle bracelet during one of our visits. It was quite a crisis. We all scrambled to retrace her steps in an effort to find it, but our efforts were in vain. The next day a life guard removed it from the filter. We all breathed a sigh of relief.

We returned to Honolulu in time to start Punahou. Cynnie-Belle decided to stay home rather than return to boarding school. "Good idea," I told her.

Fifth graders were the kings and queens of the Winnie Units. We were the oldest in the school complex, leaders of the little ones. We had authority.

There were two new teachers from the mainland. Miss Fleck was flamboyant. She was tall, thin, and long in the limbs. She wore her dark hair short. Her class was filled with the beautiful students, the in-crowd brain-wise.

Miss Ensch was another Alice in Wonderland. She was more full-bodied that Miss Fleck, and quieter. She could hold her own, though, on any occasion.

I was in Miss Ensch's room. We had the personality kids, the cut ups who were bright, but not the brightest. The two teachers were best friends, which pretty much merged the two classrooms. I loved it!

"Roger called to ask if there were any chance of ever getting back together." Her back was to me as she spoke on the phone. "Said if not, he was going to marry Mary. Of course, I told him no. Then he had the nerve to ask me to the ceremony. Figured since Lib and Mary were my good friends, I'd want to come to the nuptials. Can you believe it? He just doesn't get it. I don't give a hoot about him, never have."

Then why did you have us? I thought as I eased away from the door.

Roger and Mary were married a week later. Cynnie-Belle, Bruce, and I attended. Mom opted, instead, to take Buzzy to the dentist.

We all went to see "Man with the Golden Arm." I was pretending to get a monkey off my back when the phone rang. I staggered to answer it, a fix, I thought.

"Mom, it's Dr. Johnson," I yelled, covering the mouthpiece and sobering up. A heated conversation ensued.

"I refuse to make him cut his hair anymore," she said in her most icy tones. "We've been to the barber shop three times trying to please you and Punahou. This is America, not Nazi Germany or Russia," she said and firmly hung up the phone.

"If Bruce wants long hair, he can' have long hair," she announced. "You know what that idiot said?" she continued. "Punahou is a private school. If we want the students to wear green, they will wear green."

I was sorry Dr. Johnson didn't have a better argument. Bruce was beginning to remind me of the hoods who danced on "American Bandstand." Not only did he sport a duck tail, he wore those long pants that flared at the cuff called "drapes." Only lowlifes, drop outs, wore drapes.

The principal in the matter ultimately won. After a few tries and lots of promises on Mother's part, Bruce was accepted at Iolani, a small boys' school. Bruce fit right in, picked up pidgin English in a flash.

My grandmother took Marilyn, Ellen, and me to see "Love Me Tender" starring Elvis Presley. I was underwhelmed. I preferred to belt out songs by Brenda Lee or Fats Domino, which I did with regularity off an entrance wall near the alley gate. I'd pretend the wall was a piano, and, perched on a large decorative rock, would sing songs featured in "Your Hit Parade" Magazine. My fingers would dance merrily back and forth while I sang for Marilyn. Marilyn could not carry a tune. It amused her no end. It amused me, too. Took my Brenda Lee impressions to school. I captured audiences singing "Dynamite."

I got a cork board for Christmas. I was hanging it in my bedroom when I realized I had no thumb tacks. The tide was high and the winds strong enough to stir up sand storms. Not wanting to fool with the beach, I hopped on my bike and headed up the alley to the avenue. I knew my grandmother would have some. She always had everything.

I trotted into the house, yelling "Bey, Bey?" Halfway up the stairs, she intercepted me. "Shhh," she said, holding her index finger to her lips. "Pappy's not well."

I had never seen my grandmother look so worried. Grandfather ailed for years. His being sick was a part of our lives. We, or at least I, never knew him differently. "What do you need," she asked.

"Thumbtacks."

She returned shortly with two packs, one white, the other yellow. I selected the yellow ones. After hanging my blue horse with a yellow mane on my wall, I knew yellow would look terrific. I mean, look what those eggs did for Buzzy's rod!

"Thank you," I whispered as I left. "I'm sorry if I disturbed Pappy."

Biking home was no fun.

1957

THE FIRST OF JANUARY was a day filled with whispers.

"He's very ill," said Mother, offering little else in the way of an explanation.

Pappy died the next day. I knew he was dead the moment Mother walked in the door. She was awash in tears.

"His last words," Mother told us before bursting into sobs, "were, 'I've had a good life, about all a man could wish for.'"

I think she thought relaying his final words would ease our pain. Bruce and Cynnie-Belle were visibly shaken. I didn't care. There were unknown reasons for the space between us. I didn't want to know why. I had my grandmother. I loved her, she loved me. That was the only thing that mattered.

Mother, Grandmother, and Duke left a few days later for the funeral in Lebanon, Kentucky. When Mother returned, she told us Bey's brother, who was my grandfather's best friend, had been killed in a train crash on his way to the funeral. They were buried next to each other, a day apart. I only met the man once. The fatal train wreck was more interesting than the two deaths. I was sorry for my mother and grandmother. I just hoped someone continued to keep the glass jar filled with Juicy Fruit gum. Who was going to keep us supplied with cigar boxes was another concern. I didn't give a hoot about the cigar bands.

My grandfather died and Mother cut loose. She bought Larry a bar and became head cheerleader for Buzzy, who was becoming an accomplished stock car driver.

They called the bar "Vincente's." It was located near the McCully Bridge spanning the Ala Wai Canal. Vincente's wasn't as popular as the McCully Chop Suey restaurant on the other side of the bridge, but it did okay. Mother had enough drinking buddies to keep it pretty full. Shortly after it opened, they bought a couple of appropriate ovens and began serving pizza. Soon Vincente's became both bar and restaurant.

I didn't mind Vincente's, but I did mind the stock-car crowd. I thought the mechanics and body shop workers at Island Fender were creeps who spoke pidgin English and bastardized the verb "to be," or left it out.

Every Friday night, without fail, Mother watched Buzzy race. I hated going with her. I couldn't stand the noise, dirt, and rowdy crowds. I began declining her invitations. She finally stopped asking if I wanted to join her.

Larry and Buzzy started playing golf; serious rounds of golf, competitive matches between the two. Mother watched them play. She called herself their caddy.

"Buzzy, Larry, and I are members of the Hawaiian Golfer's Association," Mom announced.

"Why the Hawaiian Golfer's Association?" I asked. "You're not Hawaiian and you don't play golf."

"They like me," she answered. "I've been made an honorary life member."

"What about Larry? You told me he was Italian and Filipino."

"Larry has Hawaiian blood, too. Isn't it obvious?"

I didn't answer.

Actually, I didn't mind the golfers. They were married and had jobs in the hotel or tourism industry. They spoke well and had manners. The golfers weren't like the men at Island Fender. "Buzzy's burning them up at the track, leaving the competition in smoke." Mother told the golfers. "The other night he bull-dozed a wall and spun out twice. He's a big success, you know."

"Yeah, Dottie? Good for the kid. We're proud of him."

I could tell by the tone of their voices, they didn't care.

In between socializing with the Hawaiian Golfers, the Surf Club, the grease balls at Island Fender, and the Institute, Mother helped Larry at Vincente's. She also took him to doctor's appointments and to an occasional movie. It didn't leave a whole lot of time for Cynnie-Belle, Bruce, and me, but we survived. We were pretty used to it by then.

I found glory in the form of being good. I played with the vicious and not so vicious offspring of Mother's friends, fathers who dropped by for a beer with youngsters in tow. I took care of my surroundings, but I worried constantly. Every night I'd check the stove, the faucets, and make sure the refrigerator door was closed.

I mopped up Mother's messes, nine-course Chinese dinners for her buddies who lost interest in eating after the pupus and went straight into intense drinking. She'd continue cooking for awhile, hoping to entice them with her culinary skills, which were admirable. But it really was a no-win situation, and she would soon abandon all hope and retreat to her brandy. I'd clean up the kitchen before going upstairs to bed. The laughter and the vibrations of the Victrola shook my room and kept me awake. Groggy, I'd grope my way downstairs in the wee hours of the morning.

"Could you please turn the record player down? Please," I begged. "I can't sleep."

"Don't be silly," she'd say to me from behind the screen door separating the lanai from the living room. "It's not loud. Go back to bed," and turn to begin or continue her own roaring rendition of the current song on the turntable. "Mack the Knife" was a favorite.

I'd go upstairs and wrap a pillow around my head. It only intensified the base. Once I tried making a bed in the bathtub, but that, too, was of no use. I finally gave up trying to get through those nights. It was no use. Instead, I'd grab a box of ginger snaps from the kitchen and head out into the darkness toward the tree in the front yard—my tree—my ginger snap tree. It seems I climbed into its branches a thousand times. I'd straddle the limbs, get comfortable, then lie down on a plane perpendicular to our house, on a level with the lanai. With the house still lit and loud with music, I'd watch her from a different perspective. I'd watch and eat the ginger snaps. I didn't like the way she acted since her divorce. I didn't understand any of it, the men, the music, my mother. What about me?

Mother added another group to her entourage. Musicians. She was wild about Stan Wilson, a black jazz singer. He played at The Clouds, a seedy, off-limits hotel. She thought musicians were so great that she hired the Heavenly Twins to play bongos at Vincente's. Often she'd attend all-night jam sessions, and it seemed as if I wouldn't see her for days. Sometimes I didn't.

One night she decided to bring the musicians home. They left the confines of Waikiki and brought their instruments to Kahala. They arrived in the early hours and left a little after dawn. I slept at Ellen's, so I wasn't aware of all the musical improvisations. As I helped Ellen empty ashtrays and carry dirty glasses to the kitchen, Mother went on and on about the musicians. It was all she could talk about, all day long. "Buzzy, weren't they swell? Man, could they walk out a tune. I've heard a lot of jazz before, but none as good as last night."

Since I wasn't in the house, I didn't hear the music and I took her words with a grain of salt. However, anticipating a repeat performance, I spent the night with my dad.

Early the next morning I walked over to the stables. I didn't see a soul. I was entering the tack room when the morning paper caught my eye. Banner headlines read "Swank Kahala Home Robbed." I picked it up to see whose swank Kahala home. It was ours.

So much for swell guys, I thought, while I skimmed the

article. She'd done it again, put us on the list of social misfits eight months after Nicky's death. She managed to drag home some of the dregs. The jammers were like all her other pals, they just had a different occupation.

The thief, who carried off $12,000 worth of gems, was caught a few days later.

"He was a drug addict," my mother explained.

"Like Frank Sinatra? Could you see the monkey on his back?" I asked. My intention was to tick her off.

"How could he be stupid enough to fence stolen goods in the Islands," she continued, totally ignoring my sarcasm.

How could you be so stupid to bring bums like that to our house, I thought angrily.

Without a hint of remorse for the reputation she was building, she watched with maternal concern as Buzzy raced the night after the robbery was solved. He had a fever of 102.

"Poor Buzzy," she said.

"Right, poor Buzzy."

After the robbery, my mother settled down a little. I think she realized it was safer to hang around with the local boys than those from New York.

It was spring and I was excited. A big polo match was scheduled for the stadium. Another team had come in from Maui to challenge Honolulu's. I was told that not only could I hot walk the ponies, but could also ride to the stadium! I couldn't believe my good fortune, things had been so dreadful of late. No longer was I to be relegated to the back of a pick-up truck.

Late in the afternoon we left in rows of two, plodding along the Ala Wai Canal and over the McCully Bridge to the stadium. Motorists slowed, people waved. It was great. We must have made quite a scene, sleek polo ponies accompanied by overweight and overaged horses ridden by an array of humans fitting the same physical descriptions.

The matches went well. I was doing a fine job, basking in the envious stares from kids watching me from the grandstands. Bathed in glory, I rode beneath the bright lights of the stadium and listened to the sounds. Mallets whacking together, the rub of wood against wood, the grunts emitted by players struggling to untangle mallets. The muted thud of horses hooves was music to me. I thought I'd died and gone to heaven.

Then it got confusing. One of the ponies got hurt. People were yelling, a commotion followed. Someone handed me the hurt horse's lead. "Keep him walking," said a voice. "Don't let him go down." At that, the pony pulled back with a strength I could not match. The rope slipped through my grasp, leaving burns in its wake. In what seemed like slow motion, I turned and the horse crumbled to the ground.

I was not included in the return to the stables. Instead, I sat in the back of the pick-up truck, quiet, stricken, "if only" pounding in my head. I felt so alone. There were no consolers. A shot rang out, it seemed to bounce off the walls in its intensity. One shot and the horse was dead, like Nicky.

I hurt my foot. B.J. and I had walked down to the lower pastures to retrieve Diane's and Denby's horses as a favor. I slid the halter over Diane's horse's head. B.J. gave me a leg up. She was thin and agile, could propel herself onto any bare back. I could not. Before returning to the stables, we decided to take a little ride around the wooded area.

I didn't see the tar barrel until it was too late. It was rusty, its jagged top looked as if someone had pried it off with a primitive can opener. By the time I saw it, my foot was wedged between it and my horse. Looking down, I saw only blood.

"I hurt myself," I yelled to B.J. and cantered off. I dismounted at the rain barrel and plunged my leg into the water. I looked down. The top of my foot was in shreds.

Mother was home. It was still early morning. She arrived in

a taxi to take me to Dr. Lam's. He stitched me up. In the middle
of the process, I heard him say, "I should have put her under."

I couldn't walk for a month. I hobbled around the stables, but
it wasn't the same. My class at school and Pepper offered some
comfort, but things were changing all around me. Tourists
seemed to multiply. I'd ride to the edge of Kapiolani Park and
watch them at the Kodak Hula Show. Every day the sponsors
would provide hula dancers and lessons for visitors. Tourists
with ghastly white skin and wearing bright floral prints jerked
their hips back and forth, their eyes glued to the smooth motions
of the instructors. Most wore coconut hats, the green kind. I
watched them from afar, joked about their silly gestures and
the way they looked, but a fear underscored my laughter. More
subdivisions were being built, as were hotels. Residents were
pushing for statehood. Being a territory was fine with me.

For awhile, I tried to conjure up images of being a buckaroo.
I'd ride into the Australian pine forest in Kapiolani Park, shut
my eyes, and try to recreate scenes I had created in yesterdays,
but I could not. Nothing was there, it was all gone. Either age
or events had destroyed my ability to pretend. Another death,
I thought.

Pepper developed a mean-looking tumor on his right front
leg. I put gentian violet on it twice a day to no avail. The
vet finally diagnosed it as a cancer. I could have it surgically
removed or sell Pepper to the glue factory, which was not a big
deal. My third option was to have him shot. Not wanting to be
responsible for another death, I opted for the glue factory. They
could do it. He was taken away. I stayed home. In the afternoon,
I called the glue factory to see if he was dead. "No, he's still
tied up here," said the voice on the phone. I hung up feeling no
remorse. It had to be.

Shortly after Pepper got canned, my mother let me buy
Niele. The name meant "inquisitive." She was a beauty, a three-

quarters thoroughbred, one-quarter Arabian, two-and-a-half year old mare, but too much for me to handle.

A red-headed kid with slightly bucked teeth started coming to the stables with her father. He'd ride and she'd wait for him. Since I sat around a lot, trying to avoid Niele, we became friends. Her name was Drudie, short for Andruscilla, she said. Drudie's parents had bought Queen Emma's home on the other side of the Pali. They were planning to move soon. Her father was looking for a horse to buy. He was a doctor.

I fell in love with Queen Emma's home the first time I spent the night. It was a beat-up old mansion with wide planked wood floors and a fireplace in the living room. Queen Emma's bathtub sat in a different building. It was made of rock and was the size of a small swimming pool.

Drudie's family had everything: white mice that gave birth daily, stray dogs and cats, horses, a monkey that would ride on Drudie's mother's shoulders, and a litter of Welsh Corgis. Drudie, her two sisters, and brother were adopted.

I spent most of the summer at Drudie's. We'd help with the chores and animals and take breaks to walk through the banana and papaya groves that surrounded their home. Her parents treated me as if I were part of the family. Her mother even kissed me goodnight at bedtime.

I celebrated my eleventh birthday with Drudie's family. We were having breakfast when one of the Welsh Corgi puppies came flying in wearing a big red bow. With that, everyone burst into a chorus of "Happy Birthday." I burst into tears.

Mother named the dog Megan. She was as enamored with the little fox-like creature as I. To compensate for Drudie's family being far too generous, we gave them Niele. Secretly, I was relieved. The gesture ended my relationship with the stables, and I never looked back. In August, arrangements were made for me to join the Outrigger Canoe Club. I was interviewed by a committee of six. Whatever morals meant, I guess they weren't bothered by mine. I was accepted as a Junior Member, which was cool as I now had a new place to play.

Marilyn moved. So did the Hueys. Marilyn's parents bought a new house on the slopes of KoKo Head, past the end of the bus line. The Hueys packed up and left for the mainland to be near Dorothy. They ate the chickens, sold the latest rooster, and gave the parakeets to a pet store.

The loss of the two neighbors was cushioned by Drudie and Gloria. Gloria's family had moved into Duke's rental house on Kahala. Her sister Vicky was a friend of Cynnie-Belle's. Vicky brought Gloria over one day. We played canasta. The end of the game marked the beginning of our friendship, even though Gloria was Bruce's age.

Gloria was quiet, unassuming, and nonjudgmental. She was what I needed. Gloria spent much of her free time at Makaha, where her parents owned some beach-front property. They were building a prefabricated house. At night, if it rained, they slept in an old ice house—in sleeping bags on the beach if it did not.

"Come with us," Gloria would ask, but I always declined. I wasn't much of a camper. I preferred running water, beds with sheets, a kitchen and bathroom. Sleeping bags were not my idea of fun. They ranked right up there with sleeping in trees.

"Call me when you get back," I'd say and phone Drudie or B.J. with hopes of soliciting an invitation. It felt good, being wanted by my friends and their families. It felt good being with families that were together, families that had dads who came home. Dads that drove them to school.

Cynnie-Belle drove us to school. She'd drop Bruce off at Iolani, located on the banks of the Ala Wai Canal, before stopping to pick up her friend Kehau. Kehau was never ready. I resented waiting for her every morning.

"Why can't she walk?" I'd ask.

"If you don't like it, you get out and you walk," Cynnie-Belle would say.

Kehau lived directly across the street from Punahou. We would leave if we heard the first bell, which wasn't often. It was usually ringing as Kehau came out her front door.

The sixth grade units were old army barracks converted into classrooms. They looked suspiciously like the ones I had in first grade, which disappeared to make way for the new upper school science building. Although we were contained in one small area, we weren't isolated. Bishop Hall, home of seventh and eighth grades, sat on top of a hill not far from our location. On mornings when I had a few moments to spare, I'd meet B.J. and Gloria before class. Often we'd catch the bus home together.

The first man-made satellite was launched by the Soviet Union and the race for space began. There was more talk than ever about man going to the moon, and people on the mainland started reporting UFOs. I tried to reassure myself by thinking the islands were too far away for flying saucers. It made no sense, my logic, but it worked.

I was terrified of spirits. I had read "The Search for Bridey Murphy," and was absolutely positive my grandfather's ghost was omnipresent, watching me always. Perhaps his death was significant after all?

An atmosphere of gloom and doom prevailed. There was talk of fall out, Communism and nuclear war. Mother, forever the optimist, said not to worry. She assured us that the Russians wouldn't go to war. If they blew us up, they'd blow themselves up, and they weren't about to risk their own annihilation.

The world situation was bad enough. To make matters worse, Buzzy started having lousy luck. Every weekend something went wrong with his car. Broken axles, and spark plugs, no clutch, and no transmission disqualified him from racing. Once when everything seemed perfect, the event was cancelled because of rain. Buzzy was gloomy, morose. I wasn't used to seeing him in such moods.

To cheer him up, Mom took Buzzy to the mainland. Her post cards home told what sights they had seen. She took him to Cape Cod where they visited whaling museums and historic houses. At night they dined in fancy restaurants. From Montclair they motored into New York to see plays, ballets, operas, and the Rockettes at Radio City Music Hall. On the way home they stopped in L.A. to see Disneyland. Although unspoken, Cynnie-Belle, Bruce, and I were furious.

"How come we get to watch the Mickey Mouse Club on television, and Buzzy gets to see the real thing?" I asked Bruce. I would have asked Cynnie-Belle, but I hardly ever saw her anymore. She had a new boy friend, one her own age.

"Dunno," Bruce answered while examining his reflection in the mirror. "What do you think? Do you like this curl on my forehead?"

"No, it makes you look like Elvis Presley!"

"Do you really think that?" He puffed up.

"It's not a compliment, Bruce. You seem to forget, I don't like Elvis Presley. He's a greasy creep. Now, tell me what you think, why did Mom take him and not us?"

"Guess she likes him better," Bruce replied.

Cynnie-Belle became a cheerleader. She was dating Henry. Henry was the star of the football team. I was so proud of her. She was so popular and beautiful. When she wasn't home, I'd sneak into her closet and gaze longingly at her clothes, wishing I could wear the white body-gripping piece with red stripes. Someday I'll borrow that from her, I would tell myself before loping down the stairs for a bowl of ice cream. I was not sure how to get serious about dieting. Maybe my growing boobs would make me look thinner. Another level of protrusion, bigger than my stomach, would help, I hoped. It was a thought.

Since Cynnie-Belle had practice everyday after school, I rode the bus home through Kaimuki. Coming down the hill into Waialae-Kahala, I could see more areas being cleared out and new houses begun. The shopping center, although surrounded by a sea of mud, was completed. It contained our local department store, Liberty House, a toy shop, and drug store. Piggly Wiggly had long since been completed. The center was directly across the street from the transfer station in front of the Star of the Sea Church.

At the stop, I'd race to the shaved ice stand. You could get other things, like rice cones wrapped with seaweed, or manapua, a sticky white dough with pink meat inside. I always bought ice, shaved by a machine that whirred delicate flakes into a bin. When enough accumulated, the shaved ice was scooped up, packed into thin cylinder-shaped paper cups, and doused with one or more varieties of colored flavors. A straw and wooden spoon were stuck into it before serving.

A number of these stands were located around the island. The most mysterious was in Portlock, the last bus stop before KoKo Head. We called the lady who owned it Tokyo Rose. We were positive she was a spy during the war. Sometimes, someone would dare call her Rose. Giggles would ensue and the darer became a hero for a short time. I don't think the little, oily-faced lady knew what we were laughing about. How could she? She didn't speak English.

My grandmother returned. I watched closely for signs of sadness. I saw none. The day after Christmas she took us to the Moana Surfrider Hotel for a snowball fight. Some radio station thought it was a great idea to ship in real snow for us to see, touch, and throw. A giant mound of it lay on the dance floor, which was on the beach overlooking the ocean. A large banyan tree kept the area shaded, but it didn't keep the ice from melting quickly. I didn't participate, but I watched the batting back and forth of what quickly turned to water. I thought it was magnanimous of the radio station to do such a thing as ship snow to the islands. Deep down inside I wondered if the "real snow" was anything more than shaved ice.

1958

IT STARTED TO RAIN. The showers began innocently enough, but never let up. "Torrential rains," said the forecasters on radio and television. "No end in sight."

Storms in the islands were usually mild. Heat lightning flashed in the sky like a giant light switched on then turned off. We'd count the seconds until we heard the sound of gently rolling thunder, smug in our knowledge of its distance. We had none of the violence of Montclair storms, terrifying, with jagged bolts of lightning and ferocious claps of thunder. Only the island winds were to be feared, but they, too, were mild compared to gale force hurricane winds we'd see on news reels. So when the rain didn't stop, we got uneasy.

The ocean was a mean, gray body of choppy white-capped waves that pounded the beach with brute force. School was cancelled. Punahou was reported to have turned into a waterfall. Soaked, everything was soaked. I had trotted into the dining room from the kitchen, bowl of ice cream in hand, when I noticed the rug was wet. I scanned the ceiling for leaks.

"Mom." I cried. "What's happening?"

She took one look before yelling, "The books, get the books out of the room."

The water was rising at an incredible rate, the rug completely under water by the time Bruce, Buzzy, and Mickey came to the rescue. Before the bookcases were completely emptied, the water had risen past the first step leading up to the living room. Megan thought it was wonderful and splashed around, interfering at times with our book brigade. Our old dog Frau, who didn't like the water, kept her distance. I took the bird cages to my room; the winds weren't strong enough to blow out my windows.

The rain became an adventure. The only thing we could do was watch the water rise, and rise it did. At one point, Buzzy and Mickey rushed outside, found shovels, and proceeded to dig a trench from the house to the beach. Wishful thinking. The ditch became a canal, then a rolling river. It was no use. Cynnie-Belle called from Kehau's. Mother told her to stay put until it was over.

The water was nearing the second step when the rain stopped. Just like that it stopped, and the sun came out and the sky turned its customary shade of deep blue. We waded up the alley to see the rest of the world. There were neighbors in canoes, boats, or on surfboards, floating up and down the avenue, looking for those who needed help. In all fairness, it was nothing more than high drama. Anyone could have waded, knee deep, to safety. But everyone seemed to think they needed to ride something, so they did. Buzzy and Mickey borrowed the Buscher's boat and Bruce got on his surfboard to join the fun.

"Something's hurting me," I said while Mother warmed dinner on the top burners of our gas stove. We'd formed the second brigade of the day. I was the first in line, and as I stepped from the kitchen to the dining room, I felt an odd sensation in my legs. Mother gave me one of her "Don't be silly" lines before a particularly jolting shock sent me onto a metal step ladder that had not made it to higher ground. I refused to get off, daring someone to take my place in line. Buzzy volunteered. He too felt the shock and that sent everyone into action. The culprit was an electrical outlet. Luckily, no one was hurt, but I was angry over their initial disbelief. I could have been electrocuted.

Twenty-four hours later, Mother realized the water was not going to recede. By the time she called the Red Cross to have it pumped out, they were backed up with similar requests. We had to wait our turn. Meanwhile, the water turned smelly and our furniture started to mildew. Ultimately, we got it cleaned up and things were restored to their proper positions. I decided Mother was right about the virtues of cooking with gas. I had nagged for a modern electric range, the kind found in new homes. I was tired of checking the stove every night to see if the pilot light was on. The gas flame bothered me because it didn't go out. Lord, I thought, if we had an electric stove, Mother wouldn't be able to cook. Shoot, all of us could have been electrocuted!

Vincente's was closed for two weeks. "We're going for a new look," Mother said. "A real Italian look. There will be Chianti bottles wrapped in rope to hold the candles," she explained. "There will be red and white checked table clothes and we'll serve a variety of Italian dishes, including Spumoni ice cream." Spumoni ice cream sounded terrible, but she was deep into description. I reminded myself to ask about spumoni later.

"And," she said, "and," this time making the word into two syllables, "we're going to have an accordion player to serenade the diners."

It's right out of "Three Coins in a Fountain," I thought, exactly how I envisioned restaurants in Italy. Mother's really clever! "Mom, what about the Heavenly Twins and their bongo playing in the bar? Don't you think it might be distracting?"

"The what?" she asked, looking at me. I sensed she was sort of angry at the interruption.

"The Heavenly Twins," I repeated.

"Where on earth have you been, Laurie? We fired them months ago." She returned to the description. "And," she continued, this time drawing the word out for about five seconds, "I'm making Buzzy assistant manager to Larry."

I looked around. Buzzy's face showed his usual crooked grin. Cynnie-Belle's showed fury. Bruce stood, hands sunk into pleated pockets, hair greasy as ever, acting cool.

"Congratulations," I told Buzzy, because I was honestly happy for him. "That's great."

"Beats working at the pineapple cannery," he said.

I bet it did. I hoped his new position would last longer than his few days at Dole.

I enrolled Megan in an obedience class. Every Saturday morning for six weeks my grandmother drove us to a field along the Ala Wai Canal. She'd wait and watch us heel and sit and stay for an hour. Megan was quite obedient. When the course ended, I decided to hit the show circuit. We came in second every time, but we always won "Best of Bitch." Megan's brother was the only other dog entered in our category. Hoping to one day beat him out, I pursued the shows with gusto. Even Mother got interested. She adored Megan.

"What fun," she said when I told her about the state championship to be held on Maui. The Kennel Club had chartered a plane and we were to fly with our dogs, which we did.

There were dogs all over the airplane. Dogs on laps, dogs on seats, dogs under seats, dogs in the aisle, dogs wanting to pick fights, dogs, especially the small ones, wanting to hump human legs. I was flattered by my mother's interest. I was proud of her presence. Mother wanted to be with me!

Mother's Maui pals came to the show. They brought a cooler fortified with refreshments. It was a long day and an even longer evening. The awards were presented at a dinner that night. It took four hours to acknowledge everyone. We didn't get back to Kahala until very late, but I didn't care. I had Mother all to myself. We could have stayed home with an assured knowledge that we would have won "Best of Bitch," but we didn't.

—

It was either someone's suggestion or my mother's idea to start a golf club, actually an off-shoot of the Hawaiian Golfer's Association. It was a golf club solely for musicians. They called it Kane-Ka-Pila which translated into "Strike Up the Band." Mother was made president. Not being a golfer and as the only female member, she was also in charge of entertainment. No problem. Since there was no club house, our home became the 19th hole. Needless to say, my mother was in seventh heaven— golfers and musicians, her two great loves. Well, two great loves after brandy.

It was too much. Herds of Kane-Ka-Pila-tions would repair to our bar at all hours of the day and night. It didn't take long for them to run off Buzzy's younger crowd. Everyone loved "Dottie." Members vied for her attention. She held center stage and reveled in it. Buzzy did not. I wanted to ask him how he felt, now that he was in our position, but the time was never right. A new guy started coming around. His name was Benny, and he played the steel guitar. He was another illiterate; maybe, not totally. He could read music. Buzzy did not like him at all.

Fierce golf matches ensued. Mother appeared to be in between. "Sometimes I honestly don't know who to root for," she said.

Personnel problems started at Vincente's, particularly between Larry and Buzzy. Mother did her best to mediate, but the battles intensified. She fought with Larry, Larry fought with Buzzy, and Buzzy fought with Mother. One night, Buzzy got clobbered in a barroom brawl. In another, two of his fingers were broken. As an escape, Mother turned her attention to us kids.

Mother took us to see "Peyton Place." It left me in shock, unmarried teenagers "doing it" by Crystal Lake, no less. Two days later I got the measles and had to stay home in the dark.

Mother telephoned Hal Lewis, a disc jockey who called himself J. Aku Head Pupule. He sympathized with my affliction and dedicated a song to me. A few years before, Aku tried to give me a ride home. I was waiting for a bus across the street from the stables when he stopped. I would not get in the car with him. Mother told me never to ride with men. Aku was so impressed with my adamant refusal, he called to tell her. When I got home, she was there at the door, smiling. "It's okay to ride with people you know," she said as I walked in. She had a great time with that story for a while. After seeing old Rodney so worked up in "Peyton Place," I decided that the no-man method of transportation was probably best.

We went to Honolulu's first Rock and Roll concert. I knew it might be a disaster when we walked in the door.

"What in the world are they doing?" Mother asked. "Looks like they're plugging guitars into a speaker. My God, I've never seen such an assortment of drums."

The musicians were a few songs into the set when Mother stood up and said, "Let's get out of here." She was almost screaming to make herself heard above the noise. "I can't stand this another minute." She grabbed me by the elbow, pushed aside our folding metal chairs, and pulled me out of the Civic Auditorium. Actually, I was relieved to be outside. The noise was excruciating, but I also was disappointed. I'd anticipated the concert, looked forward to hearing live "Rock and Roll." Why did it have to be so loud? Paul Anka was a star unto himself. He didn't need all that noise. You could barely hear him.

It took a few moments, sitting in the car, before my mother realized her mistake. I could have told her the others had no intention of leaving. The rapt expressions on their faces attested to the fact. No one was about to take us home. So there we sat, Mother and I, in the parking lot. I began to enjoy the concert, listening to the songs at a noise level made bearable by a building.

It was nice, my mother and I alone in the car. "Never again will I go to a rock and roll concert," she declared as we drove home.

"Now kids," Mother said not long after we rocked out of the auditorium. "I want to prove a point. I've got tickets to a folk concert. Folk singers address real issues, concerns about life, jobs, love, and death. They personalize lyrics, tell stories passed down from generation to generation. Their music makes you think. It's not mindless rock and roll. Folk songs can be understood, they're a reflection of culture. This man we're going to see co-wrote 'Goodnight Irene,' remember that song?"

I did. It was one of my favorites. But I said, "Sounds like folk singers are just country and western singers. Take Tennessee Ernie Ford and 'Sixteen Tons,' for example."

Bruce interrupted. "Folk songs sound like a history lessons."

"No wait, you guys," Cynnie-Belle kicked in. "The Kingston Trio are considered folk! We like them."

"We 'like' them because two of them graduated from Punahou," Bruce said sarcastically.

"Just because you never will," Cynnie-Belle snapped back.

"Cut it out, both of you," Mom scolded. "It will be fun."

This time, she made sure we were all with her when she marched out of the auditorium.

"Guy's only sung two songs," I whined.

"Doesn't matter. He's a communist, let's go!" she said.

"Guess his lyrics tell stories you don't want to hear," Cynnie-Belle chimed in. I could tell she was ecstatic over Mother's mistake.

If that mild-mannered man is a communist, I thought, maybe all those films at school, the ones on the Russians and how commies could infiltrate our country, were right.

Roger and Mary had a huge party to celebrate the house they built on Kaiko'o. The developers had exhausted Waialae-

Kahala and Henry J. Kaiser was making his mark with Hawaii Kai, located at the foot of KoKo Head. In search of new territory, builders landed on a dusty stretch of land on the other side of Black Point, where Diamond Head Road became Kahala Avenue. Building sites were laid out on the gentle sloping terrain that dropped off dramatically near the sea.

Where my father and Mary bought, the ocean view separated the expensive homes from the rest of the subdivision. When Dad first showed me the site, I thought he was crazy. It was on the side of a cliff, a vertical piece of land that shot straight up, but it turned out all right. The result was an A-frame house with three levels. The bad part of it was the walk from the street to the front door. But the steps from the garage to the front door serpentined enough to provide rest levels to catch your breath. The right stairway rose to the kitchen door with no breaks. Other than that, the house was magnificent and modern. Its large front patio lined with flower boxes provided a spectacular view of the Pacific.

So my father had a party. All the in-laws and out-laws showed up. "Everyone gets along and marries each other eventually," my mother liked to say. It was a success. Mother came with Larry and Buzzy. I rode with Cynnie-Belle, Henry, and Bruce. Although I didn't announce it aloud, my father told me one of the bedrooms was just for me. I helped show people through the house that evening. For awhile, it felt like a Chatham lifestyle in the tropics.

I attended cotillion on the grounds of the Royal Hawaiian Hotel. The studio, which backed up to the Outrigger's volley ball courts, was rented by Dan Wallace. He'd line us up, girls on one side, boys on the other, and call out the directions before he put on the music. "Step together, slide together," he'd say, and we would follow his instructions in a sort of disorganized unison. When he thought we had the basics, he'd ask the boys to take a partner. A mad dash across the floor would ensue, and when the shoving and scrambling ended, Dan was left with happy and not-so-happy couples. Then there was me, the one standing alone. I didn't feel that anyone disliked me. They were all my friends from school. The boys just didn't want to take the chance of getting hurt maneuvering me around the dance floor. I didn't blame them.

Once in a while, Dan would make sure I had a partner. We would proceed to step together and slide together and bend to the call of "dipsy-doodle," me leading a poor boy around at arms length the entire time. My only guarantee of a partner was the bunny hop, but that was okay. I enjoyed watching the others.

Mrs. Wallace was Dan's assistant. Their favorite demonstration song was an instrumental named "Patricia," which was terribly boring. My classmates would shuffle their feet and whisper to each other while whirling around the floor. The only fun one was the "Lindy" which we could put to tunes like "Rock Around the Clock." Our final dance of the season was formal, kind of. We were to come dressed as a celebrity. I sprayed my hair blond and wore a black shirtwaist dress and white gloves. I carried a sheet of paper in my hand that I patted periodically through the evening, a hint to those who couldn't guess that I was Patti Page.

Mother and Larry parted company. I came home one afternoon and found her in tears. "It's all over," she said.

"What?" I asked, alarmed, thinking something absolutely terrible had happened.

"Larry and I, we broke up—he's found another girlfriend, someone much younger," she continued, as if I needed to know the details. "I had Buzzy fire him last night."

She's talking like a teenager, I thought.

"I'm sorry Mom." I really was. I didn't mind Larry who was

always nice to me. I wondered how she found out about the girl friend, so I asked.

"Buzzy's seen them together. He thought I ought to know before Larry made a fool out of me."

She shed a few more tears and that was that. Mother merely changed the name of "Vincente's" to "Allegro," and made Buzzy, age twenty, the manager.

My brother taught Gloria to smoke in the parking lot of Allegro. Mother had taken us to dinner and we were in the car waiting for her.

"Take a drag, then inhale it down your throat," he instructed.

We were allowed to smoke at fifteen. "If you can drive, you can smoke," my mother told Cynnie-Belle when she first got her license.

Gloria did as she was told, moaned, and started to cough.

"Do it again," said Bruce. "It takes a few times before you get used to it."

She did, but with the same results. I sat in the back seat, watching with envy, but enjoying every minute of the ritual playing out before me. Mother came out and told us to "run along." She had to stay a while longer.

Gloria spent the ride home lying as best she could on the front seat, complaining of being dizzy. I didn't care how she felt. "Sit up Gloria, for God's sake. It looks like I'm being chauffeured."

"It will stop," said Bruce. "It only lasts for about fifteen minutes."

It took a few days to find time alone with Gloria so she could teach me to smoke, too. It was terrible. My head spun and I felt nauseated. The effects, however, did not deter me from doing it again. We got B.J. hooked a short time later.

Our smoking was discovered by Gloria's mother. I spent the night at her house, and when all were asleep, we smoked and flapped wet towels around to absorb the odor. No one woke up and caught us in the action. We were too sly for that to happen. But the next morning we were severely reprimanded. Her mom, while taking out the garbage, saw a pile of cigarette butts under Gloria's bedroom window. I never did find out what she thought about the wet towels.

The Jardines moved into the Huey's house. Their son, Billy, was a year older than I, and I had seen him at school. He was a knockout. I began my "be aware of me" campaign on moving day.

"Ellen," I yelled from the back door to the wash house, "I'm going to put the birds outside for awhile," which I did. Task accomplished, I sat in front of their cages. The position allowed a nice view of the Jardines' back yard. I watched, through the hedges dying to get a glimpse of "the boy next door." No go. "Ellen," I yelled awhile later, "I'm going to take the birds in now."

"Fine," she replied, waving a soapy hand to me from the window, and returning to her washboard.

"Ellen," I shouted after I put the birds back, "I'll help you hang the wash," which I did. "Everything is so clean," I said in a very loud voice. "Must be the Rinso Blue." Ellen looked at me strangely. I could hear voices in and around the Jardines' house but no other signs of life. Megan, I thought. I'll take Megan for a walk on the beach, which I did. I practiced obedience commands as if they were something new. Megan, also, looked at me strangely.

It went on like that almost all day. I would run out the back door as soon as I saw someone pulling into our driveway. Mickey, Buzzy, Bruce, Cynnie-Belle, it didn't matter. They were greeted with a boisterous hello and how are you. I babbled away, much to the confusion of everyone. In between, I made progress reports to B.J. and Gloria. "I can't believe there's going to be a boy next door, just like in the movies!"

"What about Robbie?" asked B.J.

"Robbie Israel doesn't count," I said. "He's been a neighbor all my life." Actually, I had never thought much about him. His family included four boys. They lived on the other side of the Buschers. The Israels stayed pretty much to themselves. "Got to go, B.J. A car is pulling into the driveway."

It was late afternoon when I decided to sacrifice my dog by giving her a bath in the front yard. Suspicious of my intentions, Megan rebelled. I was covered with water and dog shampoo, drenched, trying desperately to get her rinsed off when I heard a "hello." I looked up to see Billy, the most beautiful boy I'd ever seen, walking toward the Israel's. "Hi," I replied, swooning. From that moment on Robbie Israel counted. After all, he was a friend of Billy's.

"Wouldn't it have been easier to go over there?" Bruce asked at dinner.

"Dina Jardine goes to Dominican," Cynnie-Belle said. "She started with Barbara and me our freshman year. I'll introduce you tomorrow."

Eternally grateful for their help and understanding, I went to my room and listened to the sound track from "Oklahoma." I played "Out of My Dreams" over and over and over again.

I did not meet the Jardines the next day—I chickened out. Instead, I watched from my bedroom window, waiting for more boy-next-door trips to see Robbie. Sometimes I'd catch his approach and race downstairs, hoping to make it outside before he crossed the lawn. One weekend, I spent most of a night hiding in the bushes between our yards. His friends were visiting. I watched them at play. The girls, most of them cheerleaders, were lovely and slender; the boys, handsome. Billy was part of the in-crowd. There was no way I could compete. I vowed to diet. I had it that bad.

I began early evening walks with Megan. We'd make our way down the beach, settle into a spot underneath a coconut tree, and watch the sun disappear behind Black Point. We'd finish our walk in twilight. The routine of watching sunsets in the peace and serenity of the Pacific was a comfort. I was lonely, glad to have my dog with me.

Luckily, I wasn't talking to myself when Billy, at dusk one evening, jumped down from the coconut tree. It scared me to death when I heard the thud behind me. "Hi," he said, and sat down. The awkwardness between us quickly passed and we talked and walked up and down the beach until it grew dark. After that, we walked together every evening.

The first time he kissed me, he smelled like bacon. We were at my grandmother's house, but she was back in Montclair. We sat on the outside steps to the shower and watched the full moon. At some point, he put his arm around me. It grew chilly, so we resumed the position on the steps inside the lanai. Neither of us said a word. Having nothing to look at, I stared at his shirt pocket. After what seemed an eternity, we managed to move our faces into position. He kissed me and he smelled like bacon. Not wanting to break the spell, I stifled my desire to ask if that was what he'd had for dinner.

When I got home, I checked the mirror to see if I looked different. I didn't. Relieved, I brushed my teeth and went to bed. I was disappointed. It was not like what I'd read in "True Romance" magazines. Despite that, I became one with the Jardine family.

KPOI, our first rock and roll radio station, launched its debut by playing "Flying Purple People Eater" for 24 hours while daring the listeners to draw a likeness. Billy, Robbie, and I accepted the challenge. We spent an entire day in Billy's room, drawing and coloring our versions of the one-eyed, one-horned dragon. None of us won. It didn't matter.

Billy gave me a locket for my birthday. We were inseparable, with Robbie almost always at our side. It was okay; we were friends, the three of us against the world. We went to the 49th State Fair; we went swimming at Dukes; we tormented Whiz when we could. At night, when the tides were low, we'd watch the torch fishermen. Usually, we heard them before we saw them— the sounds of big flat sticks whacking against the surface of the sea. One hand held the paddles, the other carried the torches, lights to attract the fish. We could hear the fishermen talking to each other as they struck the water with what sounded like a enormous force. They were like cavemen using antique methods to herd the fish into nets they had cast before dusk.

We decided to try torch fishing. We spent an afternoon attempting to attach an old shirt to a broom handle. That night when it got dark, Robbie and Billy came to get me. I thought I was hot stuff being able to participate in such a masculine activity. I was a little apprehensive about walking out to the reef, but I didn't let on. I need not have worried. They threw me in the first canal and took off laughing hilariously. I was crushed. They had betrayed me. It seemed like they were gone hours before they pulled me out again. I charged home, furious and I didn't talk to either one of them for two days. When they came over, I told everyone to tell them I wasn't home.

Not long after Larry left, I got another bathroom chat. I sat down on the edge of the tub. Mother shut the door. "Cynnie-Belle and Henry got married. Not only that, they're going to have a baby."

"When?" I asked.

"When what?" asked Mother.

"When did she get married and when is she going to have the baby?"

"They got married last week at Roger and Mary's. The baby is due in February. Isn't it thrilling? You're going to be an aunt!"

Thrilling, I thought to myself. Thrilling to have my sister pregnant and married at seventeen? I nodded dumbly, astonished that Henry had actually "done it," like Rodney in "Peyton Place," had "done it" with my sister. One did not "do it" without being married, and my calculations told me they had "done it" before last week.

"She is going to Montclair to stay with Bey until Henry graduates next June. If Punahou finds out, he may lose his scholarship, so this has got to be a secret," Mother said. "If anyone asks where she's gone, tell them your grandmother's not well and Cynnie-Belle's gone to take care of her."

"Not well with what?" I asked, wanting a justification for the lie I was to tell.

"I don't know, just say she's not feeling well."

"What if someone asks why Bey didn't come out here? All her family lives here." I wanted all my bases covered.

"Stop!" said Mother, getting angry. "Congratulate your sister. She's in her room."

Dina Jardine became my surrogate sister. She took Billy and me everywhere. We would pile into her white Corvette convertible and head for Sandy Beach or Makapuu to body surf. On our way home, we'd stop for frozen chocolate-covered bananas or a large shaved ice at Tokyo Rose's.

Summer ended sadly. Billy and I realized we were much too good friends to be sweethearts. I watched him from my room one day. He, Henry, and Bruce had returned from fishing. They were anchoring the boat, waist deep in water. "All in the Game" was playing on the radio and I knew it was over, the going steady part of our lives. He confirmed it a few hours later. "I'll be away, going to school in Kamuela," he said. "It wouldn't be fair to you." I wanted to ask, "What is fair," but I didn't. There was nothing I could say.

Billy left for the Big Island of Hawaii and Dina left for Dominican, and my mother and sister left for Montclair. My mother broke the news to my grandmother after they arrived.

She returned from New Jersey in time to watch Buzzy's final race of the season.

My mother was on Maui when school started. This time I really didn't care. Seventh grade was great. I loved being in Bishop Hall with the eighth graders. B.J. and I were inseparable. Her cheerleader friends and the in-crowd Billy knew became my friends. Even though he and I were no longer an item, Billy had given me credibility. No doubt in my mind, I was cool.

My homeroom teacher also taught social studies. I called her the map dragon behind her back because we'd spend entire periods filling in names of cities on maps purchased at the book store. I hated the course and the countries that were so foreign to me.

I lasted in Latin for six weeks before changing to French, which was also awful. My cousin Stanton was in the class. He had a crew cut and wore his pants belted way above his waist. Worse, he carried a briefcase like a genuine jerk.

The one class, not subject, I liked was science. Our teacher was a big-time surfer and fun to be around. He was also very handsome. One day, shortly after school started, we participated in a movie. We were filmed looking studious in our seats. A messenger hurried into the room and handed the teacher a note. The camera zoomed onto the paper. "Surf's up," it read. He mouthed the words to us and we all made a mad dash to the door which caused a massive jam. He showed the film to us when it was completed. The scene after ours showed him paddling out to ride twenty-foot waves. The next frame, he was on shore, his board broken in two. He was carrying a piece under each arm and grinning.

By coincidence, both B.J. and I had lockers in the basement. We were together all the time, which proved not to be good. We were always looking for laughs, and one afternoon overdid it. We didn't mean to set off the fire extinguisher; we were just playing around, daring each other to dismount the red metal cylinder. B.J. grabbed it in jest and off it went. Not knowing what to do, she twirled around looking for a remedy. White foam shot everywhere, onto the lockers, walls, ceilings, floors, students, and Dr. Johnson who happened to be cruising the hall. The incident grew in proportion to the rumors. By the end of the day, B.J. and I were infamous in our audacity. We were hauled into Johnson's office, she first. Not having laid a hand on the hose, much less the extinguisher, I got off with a reprimand. B.J. was suspended for one day.

"Oh God, not you, too," said Mother when I got home.

"I guess Dr. Johnson called, huh?" I asked.

"You, my sweet little girl," she continued, looking totally betrayed. "How could you?"

It was easy, I thought.

Our notoriety brought us to my brother's attention. He thought it was great. "Pin Punahou," he told me.

"Ya, pin Punahou," I said in agreement, wondering if that were another way of saying "stick it."

Bruce declared I was now old enough to hang around the Outrigger, so I did. After school and on weekends, I was always there, as were B.J. and Gloria. The Club became my new home away from home.

Billy came back for Thanksgiving vacation so I put the Outrigger on hold for a few days. I was glad to see him. We resumed our walks up and down the beach. Robbie's living two houses away from me and three from Billy allowed us to sneak out without being followed. Our friendship was special, and while we liked Robbie a lot, we no longer always included him. Actually, Robbie's omnipresence drove me up the wall. But then, I'd remind myself that the two guys were friends and Robbie had known Billy first.

The Israels had a dog named Jeff. Like Blackie and Curly, Jeff was a cocker spaniel. Blackie was smart and personable. Curly, perhaps taunted once too often by Whiz, was mean. Jeff was just plain dumb. Adding to his lack of brains was a lack of beauty. He had droopy, red-rimmed eyes. Although he was black, for some unknown reason, perhaps a reaction to the elements or bad blood lines, his coat had patches of an outrageous shade of orange. Jeff was quite a sight, but we loved him.

Jeff would follow us up and down the beach, as would Megan. Unlike most of the dogs who liked to chase sticks thrown into the ocean, Jeff preferred to wade, head submerged, and search the ocean floor. Robbie, Billy, and I would watch the little bubbles of water rise to the surface as Jeff exhaled through his nose. When he found something of interest, the bubbles burst forth in rapid and frantic succession. "Jeff's got something," we would yell when a water frenzy started. We'd splash out to see what he'd discovered, our legs cutting through the water in loud thunks.

In time, we took Jeff for granted and dismissed his odd behavior with a shrug. Thanksgiving Day, however, he emerged with a fish flapping wildly between his clenched teeth. "Look at that," said Billy, who was the first to spot the dog. Jeff regarded us with some confusion. We began to whoop and holler. "Jeff caught a fish, Jeff caught a fish," we chanted, as we galloped down the beach to tell our siblings, neighbors, and maids. For a while after that, we watched Jeff like a hawk, but it never happened again.

The day before Billy returned to school, he and Robbie found a dead fisherman. The police and Coast Guard arrived mid-morning to search for a missing man. I was sitting in the front yard watching them fan out toward the reef, walking on the exposed coral beds because it was low tide. The water was crystal clear and displayed the sea below like a large looking glass. Only an occasional soft breeze ruffled its surface. Billy and Robbie appeared. I tried to stop them from helping the authorities. "We know the area better than anyone," said Billy. I couldn't argue the point. They went into the water and I went into my house. I was afraid they would find him, the fisherman who hadn't come home. And they did, not forty minutes later. He was wedged between two coral beds, his dead hands holding his fishing pole. Billy and Robbie were heroes. Their pictures were on the front page of the "Star Bulletin" that evening and the front page of "The Honolulu Advertiser" the next morning.

Neither of us said a word to each other, but Bruce and I noticed a change in the relationship between my mother and Buzzy. She started to call him "my baby boy." She bought him clothes, took him to night clubs, watched him play golf and race. He could do no wrong, forgiven immediately after his temper tantrums and a day or two's disappearance. "Bad Buzzy," she would scold. She blamed outbreaks of his hives on nerves. Watching her talk to him made me want to puke. She sounded like a dumb sixth grader. I was under a long-term impression that Buzzy and Diane, Mom's secretary, were sweethearts, but I began to wonder. Not quite knowing how to question the unquestionable, I shoved all thoughts of Mother and Buzzy out of my mind and comforted myself within the confines of the Club. All of us kids had problems, none of us said anything, but the unsaid knowledge of them left us loyal to each others feelings. I needed that, Bruce needed that, we all did.

"Let's stay home tonight, we'll build character," Mother would say on the rare occasions she had nothing else to do.

"Fine," I'd say.

"Sure," from Bruce.

We'd be gone before her second brandy. I didn't need her anymore. I assumed neither did Bruce; we had the Outrigger.

—

We didn't go to Maui over Christmas vacation. Mother was too busy keeping the restaurant afloat. I entered Megan in another dog show. Once again she came in second in the Best of Breed category and won Best of Bitch. I was tired of the same old results and decided that was it. I had other things to do, like hang out at the Outrigger. There, grown-ups left me alone.

1959

COMMERCIAL AIRLINES BEGAN flying jets in 1959. They cut travel time to the mainland in half and eradicated the need for a "point of no return." Bruce and I had not been out of the islands since 1953. Mother had the audacity to take Buzzy to Montclair for the birth of Cynnie-Belle's child in February.

"It's a girl," crackled her voice over the phone. "She named her Katherine." I knew where the name came from . . . it was the title of my sister's favorite book. One night she burst into tears while she was reading.

"What's wrong?" I asked, alarmed. Cynnie-Belle was not much for crying.

"It's sad, this book is so sad."

I guess it got better. I was kind of wishing she'd name the baby after me. I took a stab at a second chance.

"What's her middle name?" I asked Mother.

"Kuulei," she replied.

Oh well, I thought, maybe there will be a next time.

Bruce began to take me with him everywhere he went. He never said why, he just alluded to not wanting me home by myself. I didn't argue. It was neat. He even took me on his dates, me and Smitty, a goofy friend of his. If I spent the night out, he'd call to make sure I was all right. My brother became my father. His concern didn't bother me at first. It was nice having the attention.

—

Canteens were held once a month for the seventh and eighth graders who wanted to socialize on a Friday night. Teachers and parents would volunteer to chaperone and make sure no one got out of line while having fun. Fun consisted of swimming in Punahou's Olympic-size pool, playing the ball sport of the season, eating junk at the snack bar, dancing to records in the cafeteria, or merely cruising the entertainment spots of one's choice.

"Pal likes you," said B.J. "He told me he likes you."

"How could he like me, I've never even spoken to him."

"Believe me," she said, rolling her eyes toward the heavens and laughing. I watched her braces reflect the sun.

I'd never thought of Pal until that moment.

"Pal likes me, huh?"

"Yep. He wants to meet you at the flagpole during Canteen tomorrow night."

"Why?" I asked.

"Because he likes you, you dumb shit, haven't you listened to a word I've said?"

Dumb shit, God it was neat to be older and be able to use such words, I thought.

"Look, we'll go to the Canteen, then you can escape by going over the gate to Upper Field. From there, you walk to the flag pole on Middle Field and meet him. It's simple," said B.J.

So, I did. I went to the Canteen, had my hand stamped, signed in, and cruised with B.J. for awhile. At close to eight o'clock, she ushered me to the gate I was to scale.

"No way," I told her. "I'll never get over that."

"You can do it, come on, I'll help."

And she did, and I did, and I wended my way down the road. The moon was full, it helped me to see. Not wanting to appear four-eyed in front of my admirer, I stuffed my glasses into a pocket as I approached him.

I heard him say hello. I couldn't see him at first, but I heard him.

"Hi, yourself," I replied.

We walked to Bishop Hall listening to the sounds of rock and roll blasting from the cafeterias. He didn't say a whole lot. Neither did I. We sat on the steps outside the science room and watched traffic, then kissed until we realized it was late, too late. Canteen was over.

Pal got off scott-free. He'd never checked in. I put my glasses on and headed back to face the consequences. Buzzy was waiting for me along with all the teachers.

"I'll take care of it," he told them. Although perplexed, the authorities looked at him and let me go.

Bruce was at the wheel when we got to the car. "I'm not going to ask where the hell you've been, but don't you ever let me catch you doing something like this again," he snarled. In secret, I smiled. This is too much, I mused. Why didn't I rebel sooner. So much attention in so little time.

When I got to school Monday, Pal did not acknowledge me. In fact, he never did again. So much for being liked.

The Outrigger became my life. It hadn't taken long for me to be a part of the gang, a group of kids whose ages were within three years of each other. I was the youngest but no one seemed to care. Bruce arranged for me to take surfing lessons from a beachboy named Rabbit. I did and found my skills adequate, having my own board. Bruce and I would leave home at dawn to hit the waves before the tourists.

We spent most days playing cards, playing volleyball, sunning, swimming, surfing, and eating. On Saturdays my friends and I would kick down Kalakaua Avenue to see a matinee at the Waikiki or Kuhio Theaters. We'd sit in the very last row, throw our heads back against the wall, and wolf down Jujubes, Slim Mints, Malted Milk Balls, or Neccos. While waiting for the newsreels to start, the boys would take turns requesting songs from the live organist.

Drive-in movies found us in the front row. We'd sit on the hoods of cars, using the windshields as back rests. No one was ever sassy or destructive, but we were loud. We had to be. How else was the world to know how wonderful we were? It was our turn to make the rules; we just needed each other's vocal support to define our actions.

In March we became the 50th state and forgave Alaska for acing us out of the 49th position. I was in gym class when the sirens began to wail. We all ran outside wondering if we were under attack or being alerted to a tidal wave. Word spread quickly; Statehood! Residents could finally vote in the national elections.

School was dismissed. I ran down to Bishop Hall and found B.J. We headed straight for the Outrigger. The streets were wild. I think the entire population got to Waikiki before we did. People were lined up along Kalakaua, motorists were bumper to bumper, honking horns and madly waving to the crowds. It was a giant spontaneous parade in an atmosphere of total euphoria.

I don't know whose idea it was. We meant no viciousness in our actions. In our minds, we thought our enthusiasm and delight over statehood would best be exemplified by hurling water balloons, lovingly, into the mass of humanity outside the club.

So we did.

I swear I had no intention of hitting the lady square in the face. I froze when I realized the arc of water was on a collision course. It seemed to happen in slow motion. She was sitting, perched actually, on the front seat of a convertible. Her hair was beautifully styled, each strand in place. Her make up, although heavy, was applied to perfection.

It took a split second for the physical and mental transformation. The pretty woman became a raving shrew. Her hair, flattened by the impact, was sopping wet, water streaked down her face, leaving tracks in her make-up and eyelashes askew. She began screaming and sputtering like Bozo under the sea.

"Help me," she cried.

Out of nowhere came a policeman. I spotted him trying to get through the traffic jam before I turned tail and took off.

"You haven't seen me," I yelled to the ladies at the front desk as I sped past. I could make great time on foot when terrified. Alongside the volleyball courts, I considered my options. The beach was too obvious, what with me in a dress, I thought. The surfboard lockers, I'll hide there, which I did. I found an empty slot between two long, fat balsa boards, wedged myself in and waited for the coast to clear.

I never did get caught. B.J. said the lady and her boyfriend circled a few times in hopes I'd be dumb enough to reappear. The cop did ask the receptionists at the front desk if they had seen me. I assumed they told him no.

Our home became a playpen, the outdoors a giant sand box for the more-so-than-ever Baby Buzzy. He could do no wrong; he could want for nothing. Mother bought him a whale boat for serious fishing and an outboard for play. When he professed an interest in scuba diving, she bought him an aqua lung. He almost drowned in Duke's pool during a test run.

"Too bad he didn't," said Bruce when he heard the story.

I was beginning to agree. We had to speak in whispers so as not to wake him in the mornings. "Shhh," Mother would scold, "Buzzy's asleep." I'd swallow my rage over being kept awake by the sound of the bass and their nightly parties. It might have helped if Buzzy did something, but he didn't. "What about the restaurant," I asked her. "The restaurant runs itself," she replied.

To stomach the situation, I stayed away from home as much

as possible. I fled to the comforts of the Outrigger and the homes of B.J. and Gloria. If I couldn't experience a normal life, at least I could watch others!

Cynnie-Belle decided she'd had enough of the mainland and insisted on coming home. She arrived May first during the island celebration of Lei Day. Attired in Hawaiian garb, bedecked with garlands of leis and flowers, we went to the airport to greet her. Henry was king of the May Day festivities at Punahou. I was sorry I couldn't tell my friends that he was my brother-in-law. If Punahou officials knew he was married, Henry would have lost his scholarship and asked to leave the school.

"Here's your Aunt Laurie and Uncle Bruce," said my sister, the new mother. She ignored the presence of Buzzy.

The baby had dark hair, round brown eyes, and a pug nose. I held her for a few minutes before passing her on. I wasn't much on little kids, particularly infants. I lay low after they settled into the cottage attached to my grandmother's garage. Occasionally I'd watch Kathy for a short time, but I knew my actions would never be reciprocated.

I started paddling as a novice in June. Every afternoon we'd pile into cars and drive to a section on the Ala Wai Canal where the Outrigger Canoe Club trained. After warming up, we pulled tires attached to the end of the canoe for an hour or so. It was hard work and not a whole lot of fun. The canal smelled stagnant, its waters suspiciously murky. I always expected to see something dead floating past. I got in and out of the canoe with extreme caution, not wanting to get wet. Once in awhile, a misdirected oar would throw water in my face. I'd spend the next few minutes spitting and drying my mouth off with my shirt. When the races against other clubs began and we started to win, we got cooler and bolder.

One of our favorite pastimes was tormenting Richard.

Richard worked at the snack bar. Richard was queer and he loved being queer. When no adults were in earshot, he'd tell us stories about drag queens and how beautiful he was when he dressed as one. One afternoon he shocked us with a tale of an enema he'd given himself. "My intestines started coming out my ass," he said with fingers a-flutter. The girls left gagging, the boys egged him on. "Gross," we'd say. "Richard's just so gross!" But we loved to challenge him.

One day we got him. "Richard, knock, knock," said Willy, a somewhat thin boy. He was two years older than I and wore glasses. Aside from that, he was a scrapper, probably the most daring one in our group.

"Who's there?" asked Richard. He'd been wiping the table tops, but paused to flap his wrist as he replied.

"Me Ma," said Willy.

"Me Ma Who," said Richard before he realized he'd been duped.

We all screamed with laughter, slapped knees and applauded Willy's being so clever. Mahu was the Hawaiian term for homosexual.

"Well" said B.J. She was standing at the front desk as I entered the Club with Bruce. "Well," she repeated. "How did it go?"

"Okay," I answered through my tears. I was afraid to blink, sure the spanking new contact lenses would pop out.

"Can you see better?" B.J. continued.

"I don't know yet, right now everything looks watery. The doctor said it would take a few days."

It did. By the end of a few days, I was a pro. I could see better than ever. For the first time, I took a real look at myself. I liked what I saw. Large golden brown eyes, thick lashes and brows, shiny chestnut hair with red highlights, small ears, snug against my head. My chin was fairly large and my lips a little too thin, but altogether it worked. I'd lost some weight through the rigors of paddling and was no longer fat. I wasn't, by any means thin, but I wasn't fat, either. Buzzy was right, I thought, I do have nice legs. I'm okay, I said to myself. Not a knockout, but okay. The contacts were a great birthday present. Greater still, I became a woman.

My mother referred to it as the curse. I got the curse shortly after I got my contacts. I was in the girl's locker room with Judy, whom B.J. had introduced into our group. Judy's father was military. She lived out toward Makaha, which limited her visits to the rides she could catch into town. She and I were changing into bathing suits when I made my discovery. At first I was confused, probably because I was so unprepared. My knowledge of sex was limited to a movie shown to us when I was in sixth grade. I was not impressed by the charts and flow arrows that depicted the menstrual cycle. I was also ashamed because Cynnie-Belle was with me. All the other girls were accompanied by their mothers. Mine was on Maui.

"Judy," I said, "something is wrong with me." Judy, far more worldly than all of us, what with traveling all over the United States, assessed the situation in a glance. She assured me it was, indeed, the curse, and proceeded to fix me up with a Kotex pad purchased from a machine in the bathroom. Giggling, we left the locker room to whisper my secret to the other girls. I felt as if the entire club would spot the slight bulge between my legs. If they did, they never let on. When I got home, I called my sister. I had to let some family member know. My mother, again, was on Maui.

My cousin David got married in August. It was the social event of the summer. The reception was at the Oahu Country Club, located off the Pali Highway. The club was nestled into the mountains; its golf course, swimming pool, and dining areas overlooked the ocean-front expanse in the distance. You could see the docks for the large ocean liners and the Aloha

Tower, still the tallest building in the islands. To the right were the waters of Pearl Harbor. The ocean was stunning, as always, with its various shades of blue and green. The darker the blue, the deeper the sea, we were told. We had no reason to refute that piece of information. The air was always cool at the club and little rain showers came and went often. Usually you could see waterfalls cascading down the steep cliffs. The aroma of tropical flowers was constant.

The Oahu Country Club was known for its delicious iced tea. I don't know what their secret was, but one could drink buckets of it. There was always a frothy head on the liquid, and you didn't have to pour loads of sugar into the glass. You didn't have to put in any sugar at all.

Iced tea was farthest from my mind during the reception. Joining in the merriment and camaraderie of all the in-law/out-law relatives, I swiped the first glass of champagne I saw. Waiters were everywhere, weaving in and around the crowds with an agility to be admired. I felt daring and grown-up. After all, I was a teenager. I snatched a few more glasses of the bubbly before I started feeling light-headed. I realized I'd better eat something and was headed toward the buffet table when a waitress passed by carrying something that looked terrific. Blackberry jam on cheese and crackers, I thought to myself as I reached for one. Pleased to have something familiar and sweet, I shoved the affair into my mouth.

It took seconds before the little balls of jam started popping in my mouth and a terrible smell came through my nostrils. I felt as if I were going to throw up on the spot, but managed to make it, mouth closed, to the ladies room before I let fly the contents, caviar propelled by champagne. I was furious with myself for being such a hog and acting with a wisdom I did not possess. I waited in the car the rest of the evening. I didn't even get a piece of the wedding cake, not that I would have wanted it.

—

I started riding to school with Paul when school started. Paul, whom I knew from the Outrigger, had moved into the house behind the Jardine's. He bought my sister's '49 Ford after she and Henry left for his freshman year at the University of Oregon. Every morning I'd bring Paul an apple, which he'd eat on the way to school. I liked Paul a lot. Any other eleventh grader, especially a boy, would have made me ride in the back seat. It didn't take long for me to develop a wild crush on him.

I couldn't do anything about being separated from my older friends, who were attending the Upper School, so I decided to make the most of being in eighth grade. The dichotomy between the two main cliques that had started in the sixth grade still existed. We cut-ups spread out under the trees which bordered Middle Field before school and after lunch. The chic-and-smart sat on the side steps of Bishop Hall, probably to avoid grass stains. We all had classes together at some point and spoke to each other, particularly during class elections, but the differences remained. I did manage to lure one member from the rival group, however, and became a hero in the eyes of my girl friends.

His name was Geoff, another beauty in my book. Tall, dark-complexioned Geoff with gorgeous green eyes. He was walking back, alone, from lunch one day. I broke away from Wendy and Pat, two new friends, and caught up with him for a little chat. I did that for a few days. Finally I got him to come with me to our spot under the trees. The girls were incredulous.

My next move was to befriend Carol, who belonged to neither group. Carol was Geoff's cousin. She also lived next door to him. A week or so of scheming resulted in an invitation to spend the night at Carol's. I did. We made plans with Geoff to sneak out and meet after all parents were asleep. We did.

A few days later, Geoff asked me to go steady. I said yes. He gave me a St. Christopher medal as a symbol of his affection. It was lime green. I removed my gold medal and hung his around my neck. Geoff became a regular under our trees. So did Carol.

No single thing brought about the demise of Mother's relationship with Buzzy, but her frustrations with the YWCA might have helped. The YWCA cut off funds to the Institute and sold the building to raise money for more worthy causes. It seemed fair to me. After all, the members had over ten years to learn English. Mother, however, was really put out and tried desperately to keep the program going. Although her involvement had waned, she still participated in some of the luncheons. Her last-minute efforts to save the program failed. and the Institute became history. "Damn bureaucrats," said Mother when she heard the news.

Mother would say, "Allegro can run itself," as she fought for the Institute. Well it did. It ran itself into the ground, which left Buzzy with absolutely nothing constructive to do but play golf and drive stock cars. When he started getting drunk and losing races, Mother started to lose interest.

The physical evidence of Buzzy's fury and frustrations was minor—at first. Enamored by my social life at school, I paid little attention to the quarrels. But it got worse. Mornings found the lanai scattered with broken records, walls dented by flying ashtrays, smashed bottles, and glasses. Since he was too old to punish, my mother admonished him by going out with Benny, leaving and not returning until early morn. "Another thunderous dawn," she'd say. I didn't know whether she was describing the fights, her head, or if there was, indeed, thunder.

The crowning blow came when Buzzy destroyed most of the twelve pictures that hung on the dining room wall. "Cries of Charleston" they were called, each scene captioned by a sentence or two. He went after the sketches with an ashtray with Vincente's printed on it. I heard the crack and shattering of glass from my bedroom.

"Stop it," Mother screamed. "Stop it this instant!"

I sneaked down the stairs. Buzzy looked crazy, his eyes constricted into slits of malice.

"Fuck you, Dot. Fuck you and your fucking family. Fuck you and your fucking family and Benny."

I watched. I was scared to death, but I couldn't move.

"Buzzy, you are dead drunk. Get out of here, get out of my house."

"Your house? What happened to our house?"

Another picture shattered. There was silence, then noise from the piano. It sounded as if someone were standing on the key board. Buzzy's voice rang out again.

"You play this piano like shit," he slurred. "You only know chords, nothing about music. Is that what they taught you in finishing school? What does that mean, Dot, finishing school? That you can finish someone off, do away with them when they begin to bore you?"

"Buzzy, get down from there, immediately!"

"Shut up bitch," he yelled. "You and your fucking money, it's killing me. You're killing me."

"Buzzy, don't you dare," Mother screamed.

I backed up the stairs, closed the door as quietly as I could, got into bed and cried myself to sleep.

There was no sign of Buzzy the next morning. I found out Mom called the cops and had him arrested. He had pissed on her prized painting, a portrait of a spear fisherman poised on a cliff of coral, ready to strike. The painting, which she bought for a mere $150, was purported to be worth $1,500. The artist, now deceased, had done an incredible job capturing his subjects between each hair of black velvet. Luckily, it was the black velvet that kept the work from being ruined. It sort of acted as a buffer between urine and oil. When I got home from school, Bruce was gone. Ellen told me he'd moved in with Dad.

"Aren't you coming with me?" Bruce asked when he phoned that evening.

I really hadn't thought about it, but "Sure," I said, "come over, I'll be ready."

I packed up and explained to Ellen, who needed no explanations. "We'll be gone for awhile," I told her. "Take care of Megan," I added, wondering if my father would let me take my dog. I decided to see how it went first.

"Don't worry," said Ellen, "I understand." I gave her a big hug. "I'll call you," I yelled as I hurried out the door to meet Bruce.

Our departure was daring. Not one of us had ever been remotely so defiant. I believed it would make a difference, this physical statement of ours.

It did no such thing. Mother ignored the ordeal; didn't even phone to beg forgiveness or plead for us to return.

Bruce lasted a little more than a week at Kai-Ko. He didn't like the rules and regulations, the constant locking of doors, and inquiries as to his whereabouts. Restrictions weren't part of our lives, and Bruce couldn't and wouldn't cope with them. Me? I loved the rules and regulations. He left. I stayed. But I soon tired of their restrictions. At Mom's, I could stay out all night. I needed my freedom. I returned home about a week later.

Geoff and I broke up. It didn't bother me; there were too many other boys at the club on whom to lavish my attention. Everything was going fine. B.J. decided she was "in love" with Bruce. Why is it, I thought as we sat on the roof outside my bedroom window and smoked, why do all my friends end up liking my brother? First Calley, then Marilyn, Gloria, and now B.J. I wondered if their friendships with me were merely a shortcut to my brother.

"Well," I said aloud, "if you like Bruce, you had better break up with Peter, give him back his St. Christopher medal." Peter's was yellow whereas Geoff's was green. I liked the yellow ones better, although none of it mattered anymore.

"You know," said B.J. as she exhaled a lung full of smoke, "I'll call him right now," which she did. By evening, she and my brother were an item.

I had my first call-up-and-ask-me-out car date during Christmas vacation. To be honest, we rode in the back of a pick-up truck. I could hear "Come Softly Darling" playing up front as he kissed me goodnight. My mother didn't know about the date. I didn't tell her. She was too involved with Benny, who was now coming over to cook steaks on a regular basis.

"He's nuts," said Mother when she heard Buzzy married a girl from the roller derby.

The Dillinghams had their annual New Year's Eve party on their estate, located on the ocean slopes of Diamond Head. Our Outrigger group was invited, not only to attend the party, but to spend the night. B.J., Gloria, and I spent the entire day getting ready. B.J.'s dad, manager of the Princess Kaiulani Hotel, let us have a room "as a base" he said. In the morning we caught some sun at the club. We returned to the room, showered and changed, and left for Elizabeth Arden, which was located across the street. Our hair was washed and styled, our nails painted. On the way back, we stopped at every floor to check the ashtrays for cigarette butts. Once in the room, we wrapped the unlit ends in toilet paper so as not to get germs and we smoked. We talked in terms of "tug" which meant "great" and "bitching" which meant "greater." "Really bitching" was the ultimate. We told each other how "stoked" or excited we were about the party. In the meantime, we managed to dress ourselves and stuff our feet into high-heeled shoes.

The boys arrived at eight and we spent the last few hours of the old year mingling with the adults on a lawn aglow with torches. Men and women wore leis. The scent of ginger, tuberoses, carnations, and pikake melted into the salt breezes. Pupus were passed by maids wearing black dresses and starched white aprons. Above the quiet chatter we could hear the surf and the breaking waves. During the sit-down dinner, Hawaiian musicians played Hawaiian songs. As the night wore on, guests broke rank, kicked off their shoes, and hula danced to the words of the songs. All of us behaved. We were polite and felt honored to be attending such an event.

Just before midnight the fireworks started. Cherry bombs lit up the heavens, overwhelming our senses. We sat on the lawn and ushered in the New Year with a small glass of champagne. Word was that the world was going to end on January 1, 1960. But it didn't, did it?

TRANSITION YEARS
1964-1974

I HADN'T PLANNED ON LIVING IN KENTUCKY. I had planned on marrying Tommy. My brother Bruce landed in Louisville because we had roots in the state. My grandparents were born there as was my mother. Bruce was attending the University.

"Like hell you're going to live and work in New York," he shouted over the phone. I knew he was relieved over the cancelled nuptials. Ecstatic to be more precise.

I had told him of my post-high-school plans. I was in Montclair with my grandmother, trying to figure out what to do with my life. My mother married Benny, the musician, the week before I graduated from high school. She followed Benny to Japan the day after I left for the mainland. "Tommy was so kind," Mother told me later. "He put me on the plane to be with my honey."

Mother had been living with Benny for four years. Once in awhile she would come home, sort of token stays. Most nights I spent home alone. Home was my grandmother's old house two doors up from Duke's. She had given it to us. We moved in 1962.

"I've got you scheduled to meet the dean of the freshman class day after tomorrow. You better be here. You're not going to work in New York. You're going to college," Bruce said before he slammed down the phone. Unbeknownst to me at the time,

Bruce and Cynnie-Belle had spent six months arguing with my mother.

"They wanted me to interfere, put a stop to the marriage. You can't imagine how many letters Bruce wrote admonishing me. The fights with Cynnie-Belle were terrible," my mother told me later. "I'm surprised you didn't know." I was surprised I didn't know either.

"Why didn't you tell me?" I asked, secretly pleased to hear of their collective concern.

"I knew you would make the right decision. If I said anything, you might have married him."

I wasn't so sure. If she had said don't do that, I might have been rid of Tom much earlier. A guy who lived in his apartment building, someone who knew more than I, stopped me one day and said, "Hey, you'll make a great wife and mother, but not with him," as he gestured toward Tom's door. It was all he said, and all it took. I broke the engagement a few hours later. Tom, in anger, threw a glass salt shaker through our kitchen. It skipped across the stove, leaving spots of chipped enamel in its wake. I was frightened. My mother wasn't home, Ellen was in her cottage. I hoped Ellen couldn't hear.

"Look, maybe I'll change my mind. I just need to get away for awhile," I told him as I backed into the living room.

"You can't leave me," he yelled, then proceeded to punch out the hall wall, leaving his signature in knuckle prints.

"Please go," I said. "My mother will be furious if you do any more damage."

Surprisingly enough, he left. Tom liked my mother.

Tom. I met Tom through one of my Outrigger pals, Willie. Willie worked on a cruise ship that made its way to Diamond Head for sunsets. Tom was part of the crew. Willie asked me to go for the sail one night and backed out at the last minute. "I can't make it," he said, "but Tom can take you." Dressed and ready to go, I accepted the alternative.

At first it was wonderful. Both of us liked to write and shared our poems and short stories. It was nice to have a boyfriend. I had a lot of boy friends, but they were just friends. Tom was also older than I was and in the Coast Guard.

Tom lavished attention on me. When at sea, he sent messages through commercial pilots. I was flattered by those calls.

But then it was not fun anymore. I suspected that he was squiring a bunch of women around while I stayed home on school nights. When I questioned him about his whereabouts, he'd tell me it was none of my business.

"You're a scab, Laurie. You're damn lucky to have me."

I believed him. I believed him until that stranger in his building told me to leave.

Tom drove my mother to the airport the day I left. I rode with Wendy and Pat. Wendy and Pat were my closest friends the last two years of high school. Tom wept copiously at the departure gate. It embarrassed me. All I wanted was to get out of the islands. Once on board, I strapped on my headset for a little music. Peter, Paul and Mary were singing "Blowin in the Wind." I turned up the volume and smiled. Free at last, I thought as we roared down the runway.

Two days after my "You're not going to live in New York" conversation with Bruce, I was accepted at the university. I left Montclair and landed in Louisville, birthplace of my mother and city that launched my grandfather's rise from rags to riches.

Kentucky, where men walked on the outside of sidewalks, opened car doors, and rose when an older person walked into the room. People dressed up to go downtown. I had never seen snow nor the change of seasons much less driven across a bridge and into another state. Louisville wasn't Chatham, but close enough.

Flying in for the first time, I wondered if there really were a city. Our approach was pure pasture. I expected hoop skirts and parasols. My brother drove me to the university. He wanted to show me where he lived when he walked to class in temperatures of twenty degrees below zero. I thought the red brick three-story Victorian houses that lined the streets were hideous. My first night, Bruce took me to a bar on River Road called "The Pine Room." A brassy blond broad named Mabel played the piano while the crowd sang southern songs. I got a bit uneasy when everyone stood and belted out "The South Shall Rise Again." A friend of Bruce's who was engaged to be married offered to take me home, then proceeded to attack me in his car, parked on the banks of the Ohio.

"Cox Park," he said as he pulled off the road.

Right, I thought, as I watched him lunge across the seat. Fighting him off, I wondered if all that talk about southern gentlemen was for real.

I went to Cathy Riegler's home for Thanksgiving. We lived on the same floor in the dorm. Cathy was a true friend. She consoled me after I was rejected by a sorority. Seems the Pi Phi's felt I didn't have enough extra curricular activities during high school. At least that was what I was told. At the time I was relieved it had nothing to do with morals. I sure wasn't going to follow in Mother's footsteps!

"They don't know what they're missing," Cathy said, when told of my rejection. To raise my spirits, she fixed me up with a blind date. We went out a few times. I was grateful to have a date. Tom's "scab" descriptions still rang in my ears. When I went to Homecoming with someone else, my blind date stopped asking me out.

Cathy lived in Chagrin Falls, Ohio. Her parents were wonderful; her older sister, kind. She reminded me of Dorothy Huey. Chagrin Falls was cute and quaint. There was a gazebo in the heart of town. It reminded me of Chatham.

The day after Thanksgiving, Cathy took me to my first

enclosed mall. I bought a tight skirt and matching top. It had gold braided stripes across the front and gold epaulet shoulders. I wore it to a party. A boy named Russ asked me out for the next night. We went to a bar with a few other couples, drank 3.2 beer, played the jukebox, and danced. It was a perfect weekend. All of us had graduated in June, and being together made me feel a part of the entire class of 1964, United States of America. It was a feeling I never had at Punahou.

Russ wrote me a letter shortly after we met. I can't be that bad, I thought, but I didn't respond. He wrote again:

Laurie,

I think quite a bit about you, and I really want to hear from you. If you write we could probably figure out a way for me to get down there to see you. You are inside my limit and it wouldn't be too hard for me to get away for a weekend.

Did you get my picture? If not I will send you another one. You still haven't told me whether you have any of yourself.

Things aren't going too well for me. My grades are low and I really hate this place. All my life I have been on the move and doing things that have been exciting. I can't stand to sit around and study things I don't even have an interest for. I would do just about anything to get out of this field.

If you can bring yourself to write me, please do . . . a letter from you would mean quite a lot to me. You're a very wonderful girl and just getting a letter from you would really make me feel good.

Please write!
Love,
Russ

His letter came from the United States Naval Training Center, Great Lakes, Illinois. I wrote him a few times, then stopped. My blind date and I resumed our relationship. Later, Cathy told me

Russ was sent to a place called Vietnam. I never heard from Russ again, nor did I ever again wear my new outfit. My blind date told me I looked like a member of a marching band.

I lived in the dorm for two years. I loved college life. I ran for treasurer of the sophomore class and won, a first for someone with independent status. Our girl's dorm took first place in the Fryberger Sing, beating out all the sororities. I finally had a life of my own. I wasn't Dot's daughter, or Cynnie-Belle's sister. Bruce had cleaned up his act, was treasurer of his fraternity, spoke proper English, and wore normal clothes. He was even on the swim team. He continued his role of father figure. Having lost tons of weight in high school, I was noticed as I walked around campus wearing Villager outfits. I went home for a few weeks during the summer, but Hawaii was behind me. I had made it out in one piece, despite my childhood.

I moved into an apartment with two seniors my junior year. When they graduated and I was left on my own, my blind date, Barret, and I got married. It was perfect. He was perfect. Straight from the pages of "True Romance," a blond-haired, blue-eyed gentleman. Streets bore names of his ancestors. I finished my senior year, he attended law school. After I graduated, I taught school for a while, then surrendered to the Junior League and volunteer work. "You must do this, you must get involved with that," friends would say. So I did. I must-er-bated. I welcomed their suggestions with open arms, taking cooking courses and excelling to the point of becoming the gourmet instructor's assistant. Singer taught me to sew. I used my silver, crystal, and china, and gave sit-down dinner parties. I made pot-de-creme for dessert. My husband graduated from law school and joined the trust department of a bank. I got pregnant during our fourth year of marriage. I made my own maternity clothes. We had a son. We joined a club. I traded my Villagers for the Lily Pulitzer look. Never being fond of wooden, I carried needlepoint purses. My dream had come true. I lived in Kentucky and was married to a banker. It made my grandmother very proud.

But first there was our wedding. My mother was very much opposed to Roger giving me away.

"What has he done for you," she asked. "He's never paid your bills. Bruce has supported him for the past two years. Bruce has taken care of you, he should give you away."

"But Bruce is not my father," I said.

"When has Roger ever been a father to you? Has he ever told you what to do?"

"He spanked me once when I was little. He spanked me when Cynnie-Belle told him I was still sucking my fingers."

I didn't remember if I stopped after that or not. My thoughts drifted to the two fingers, middle and fourth on my right hand, that I washed carefully with soap every night before I went to bed. It never occurred to me that washing both hands at once would be faster. I'd run my two little fingers under the faucet, soap, rinse, and carefully dry them with a hand towel.

"Really, Laurie, what has he done for you? I'm paying for the wedding. I'd rather not have him give you away." Her voice shook my reverie.

"He's my father. Fathers, not brothers, give their daughters away." For a moment I thought she might come up with an alternative, like Benny, the idiot. We were sitting in a room at a Holiday Inn on Bardstown Road in Louisville. My mother had come to help me pick out a wedding dress, my china, silver, crystal, and other items for the bridal registry. It was June. The weather had been unbearably hot the entire time, but we enjoyed all the parties, luncheons, and showers. Mother was a hit. Luckily, she was still into wearing dresses and not pedal pushers and rubber slippers.

"Mom, I am the only one in the family who will have a

wedding like this. Please, I want to do it right. I want Dad to give me away."

"Okay," she said and hugged me. "We've done all we can here. Now I'll go home and find an Episcopal priest."

A few weeks later Mother called. "Episcopal ministers won't do home weddings. They only perform in churches. But not to worry, I found an almost-pure Hawaiian minister who heads the second oldest Hawaiian church in Honolulu," she said.

"Great," I replied, wondering what constituted an almost-pure Hawaiian minister.

Back in Hawaii, caution set in when we went to have a marriage talk with this almost-pure Hawaiian minister.

"Mom," I said as we were riding home from the church, "he smelled funny and really didn't say anything, not a word about getting married."

"Well, the Reverend has lost a wife and a lung this past year," she stated with emphasis on has. "It's probably the medication he's taking."

"In what order?" I asked.

"In what order what?"

"What went first, the wife or the lung?"

"I'm not sure," she said and burst out laughing.

The Reverend got so drunk at the rehearsal dinner that my father and Mary had to drive him home. Actually Mary drove, as my father, too, wasn't feeling much pain. I was mortified, embarrassed to death in front of my future in-laws. They turned out to be good sports, acted as if nothing went wrong.

"Mom," I said when we got home, "I don't think he's going to make it tomorrow." Fear rose in my throat. All I wanted to do was get married and it was about to get screwed up.

"I'll call a judge I know who lives down the street." She returned in a few minutes. "The judge is available. He even has a clean suit to wear and we're to call him if the Reverend doesn't show by 12:45.

The wedding was scheduled for 1:00; 12:45 was cutting it a little close. Oh well, I thought, at least he's in the general vicinity. Mother looked so pleased with herself, I let it slide.

We were married at 1:20 by the judge. The ceremony took awhile, I think it was a first for him. Either that or he wasn't too swift. It was a wonderful wedding and reception, attended mostly by my sister's friends. Cynnie-Belle was on her second husband. They had flown in from their farm in Bucks County, Pennsylvania. The Buschers, Mrs. Israel and Robbie, Mrs. Jardine and Dina, Billy and his bride of two weeks, most cousins, and their kids were there. My high school buddies had disappeared. Gloria was married and lived abroad. B.J. and Pat moved to the mainland. Neither left a trace. Only Wendy attended. My friends weren't there, but my sister's sure were. At one point, when I perused the crowd, I wondered who really made up the invitation list, but I didn't care. The absence of my friends was not important. I was starting a new life. I was ready to leave the old one in the dust.

My father escorted me down the stairs. Benny stayed out of the way. There were steel guitars and my eight-year-old niece danced the hula. Before we cut the cake, two local entertainers sang the Hawaiian Wedding Song. "Not a dry eye in the house," Mom said.

A limousine arrived and whisked us to the airport where we waited three hours for a flight that took 25 minutes. It never dawned on us to switch airlines. We were young and naive, didn't know any better and didn't care. Actually, I was preoccupied with the thought of "doing it."

A year and a half later, Mother called me in Louisville. "It's okay," she said.

"What's okay?" I asked.

"I checked with my lawyer. I even called the courthouse. Anything done before a conviction is still legal."

"Mother, what are you talking about?"

"The judge. You know the one who married you? Well, he's been disbarred for income tax evasion. Oh, and Laurie."

"Yes."

"I meant to tell you, his wife ran off with Uncle Duke shortly before your wedding."

IN THE END
1974-1984

I ADMIT, I STARTED IT. Eddie Dinkel had died. His widow had come for dinner. We were visiting my grandmother in Montclair.

"You know," I said to Mother, "I always thought that Eddie Dinkel might have been my father."

"No," she said. "As a matter of fact, Eddie Dinkel wasn't your father, but then, neither was Roger Ames.

It took a few minutes to absorb the information. I stared at her in disbelief. I thought of Ellen. Ellen who helped ease my childhood pains. Where was she now when I so desperately need her.

"This is right out of a soap opera." My voice seemed to be coming in echoes. A long silence followed. The horror must have shown on my face.

"I thought you would be thrilled, happy to hear Roger Ames isn't your father."

Great, I thought, here she is shattering my world and she rattles on about how I should be delighted. I'm grown and married. I have a child of my own.

"Happy? Mom, I've just spent the last ten years of my life being perfect and here you are flipping me into the twilight zone."

"Laurie," she said in a somewhat whiny voice that wasn't like her, but what else was new? "You were a love child; my love child like that song by Diana Ross."

Yeah, and "Papa Was a Rolling Stone," I wanted to scream. Temptations, 1972. Instead, I stood staring at her. I didn't know what to say. I didn't know what to do. Moments passed. It seemed like an eternity. Finally she came across the room and reached out to hug me. I froze and stepped back. She put down her arms. Now I'm the one swimming in slow motion, I thought.

"Oh, Laurie, if I knew you were going to take it so hard I never would have told you. Please, please don't be angry." Mother's voice snapped me back into reality.

"Who was he?" I asked. "What was his name?"

"De, DeForest Romain, not spelled with an e on the end. I met him in a bar, Pal's Cabin, actually."

"Where was Dad?" Dad. Dad is not my father, he's really not my father, there is no connection between the two of us, none. Not even our limp, mine from a confrontation with a tar barrel, his from a childhood bout with polio. I'd been so proud of limping like him. There were so few similarities between us.

"Your father . . . Roger was never home," she caught herself. "He was always in New York taking classes or looking for some business deal to get into. I went to Pal's a lot. I was lonely."

I wondered if Cynnie-Belle and Bruce were lonely too. Maybe they were in bed by the time she left.

"We lasted a few years. After you were born, the three of us went to Florida. I still have a few photographs we took together."

I knew I had been to Florida when I was a baby. It was a source of pride, particularly when other children boasted about places they visited. My repertoire consisted of California, New York, New Jersey, and Florida. I also threw in Illinois because we changed planes in Chicago. It felt funny to know she'd been in Florida with her lover . . . my father.

"When De realized I wasn't going to leave Roger, he got ugly about it, tried to make trouble with your grandfather. He finally gave up. I washed my hands of him. We moved to Hawaii and the rest is history."

She did it back then, I thought. She did it with De like she would do it with Soupy, Larry, and Buzzy. I had always been a little intimidated by her. I think, deep down, I was terrified she'd wash her hands of me.

"Laurie Romain," I whispered the next morning. "Laurie Romain," I tested another way of pronunciation. Romain without an "e" on the end.

A brief relief washed over me. I'm glad I'm still Johnston related, I thought. Our family stayed heavy into heritage after my grandfather died. We had all sorts of crests, family trees, stately oils of ancestors, even a Scotch plaid. A Johnston, I was told, married Sir Robert the Bruce, who hid in a cave after losing a battle twice. He watched a spider make three tries at a web before succeeding. Sir Robert was so impressed with the arachnid that he, too, made a third attempt and won the war or whatever it was he was fighting. My mother must have liked the story a lot. I mean, she named my brother after him. I wondered what "the Bruce" meant, though—"of Bruce" or "brute." I let the train of thought go. I had other things to worry about.

I heard Mother down the hall. She was singing "The Sloop John B" to my three year old son. I named him John because I had never known a bad John. Maybe it was a subconscious attempt at Johnston, an attempt to fit into the clan.

"Who do I look like?" I'd ask my grandmother. I wanted a reason for my dark complexion, large chin, long slender limbs. Johnstons were blond and blue-eyed like my siblings and cousins.

"You look just like Laurie," she would reply. Every time I asked, that was her answer. The only aspect I could rationalize was my height. My grandfather was 6'4", my cousin Diane 6'. My grandmother was the world's greatest diplomat. She could see DeForest through DeTrees.

My mother had sung "The Sloop John B" to my son since day one. The first time I took him to Mother's Day Out, he told the teachers his name was John B. Sails.

"Laurie, are you up?" Mother called. "We're going over to the big house in about an hour. Resin on the ball," she said, pronouncing resin, rozen. Her cheerfulness irritated me. We left John with Madge, who seemed the only symbol of continuity. Madge, into her third generation. I bet Madge knew about this father business, I thought.

The big house. The big house where my mother grew up and into her rebellion. It was now a nursing home, the pool filled in with dirt. The big house had been part of the family vocabulary. Trips to Montclair were highlighted by pouring over old photographs of the big house. Its grounds were even documented by using a device called a "stereopticon," forerunner to a Viewmaster. The big house entertained celebrities such as Brenda Frazier, debutante and briefly the wife of "Shipwreck" Kelly, Uncle Duke's best friend. It's doors were darkened by such greats as J. C. Penny, whom my grandfather helped get started, I was told. When my mother spoke of the big house, she preferred stories of their great danes or the two bear cubs my grandfather brought back from a hunting expedition.

I was sorry I saw the big house. Images of grandeur and Gatsby were dashed the moment I walked in the front door.

"Mom, I'll wait outside," I said shortly after our arrival. I'd seen enough partitioned rooms and sprinklers stretched across ceilings. The magnificent staircase was painted institutional green, woodwork and all. The third floor, where she and Duke entertained their friends, was like a cavern. So much for her childhood memories, I thought. And so much for my identity, I whispered to myself.

I was standing on the front porch when it dawned on me. "Hawaii? We liked it so much we moved." Bull! I flashed onto a scene. I pictured him, this father, this DeForest Romain, pounding on the door of this big house, madly running from window to window while beating his chest like King Kong. He can't get in. He leaves. Later, Grandfather pushes Mother out the front door. She stumbles into drifts of snow, clutching me in her arms. Grandfather points, "Go," he says.

"Go where." Mother asks in a trembling voice.

"To Hawaii," he replies. "It's far enough away. I'll have no scandal around here!"

"We liked it so much we moved" sure wasn't very creative. She could have come up with a better reason, I thought. Well, the obvious is the inconspicuous. Mother never did let the truth interfere with a good story. I started feeling somewhat depressed as I walked down the steps and into the yard. This is where it all began, I thought looking at my surroundings. Mom was married but the decisions affecting our family happened here. Her big-time father banker didn't want anything to upset his big-time reputation in New York. Mom had already given him fits when she married my father. Well, I always thought he was my father.

Suddenly, everything changed. Montclair, always a safe, sane haven, took on tones and textures of mystery. Later as I drove into town, I wondered if DeForest cruised the same streets. Maybe he still did. When I got to Nishuane Park, John and I threw bread to the ducks. As I watched them glide across the pond, I wondered if Mr. Romain lived nearby. After dinner, Mother's trust officer took me for a drink. We went to Pal's Cabin. While he talked, I scanned the bar and conjured up silent scenes in my mind. Scenes of DeForest and Mother sharing stolen moments, so happy together. When I got home, I pumped her for more information.

"He loved hypnosis and ham radios," she said. "I remember his call numbers. At the time he worked for the United Nations."

I perked up. Maybe it wasn't going to be so bad, a cut above her usual boyfriends. Anyone had to be better than Benny.

"I wired him at sea when you were born," she continued. "He lived on ships, off three months, on three months, probably why we lasted as long as we did."

"Probably," I echoed. Beachboys, bartenders, and sailors, I groaned, thinking about Tommy, the sailor I almost married.

I flew home. Home to build character. Home from Montclair to Louisville with absolutely no idea about what to do with my new-found knowledge. All this father stuff I told no one, it was too hideous. Who would understand? "Should I or shouldn't I" raged through my psyche. I was not one to keep quiet. "Laurie lives her life out loud," my mother would say. Super, I thought. But Mom, I had nothing to hide until now.

I never was a flower child. Hippies came in while I was preparing to graduate from college. Their long hair and free love philosophy did not fit the image I created for myself. Had I been a hippie, I would have referred to my mother's affair as an outrageous piece of information. I wasn't hip, but neither was I square. I listened to Crosby, Stills and Nash. I knew what it was like to look in my rear view mirror and see a po-lice car.

My silence lasted a week. Mother was right, I never could keep my mouth shut. I told my husband first. We'd gone to a neighbor's for a Mexican dinner. I drank a load of marguerites. It didn't take long to realize that I was barely able to walk. "We've got to go," I said. Dinner had not been served. "I can't stand straight." We left.

"My mother told me my father was not my father." We were standing at our front door.

"What? Your mother told you what?"

Say it slowly, I thought. I was having a hard time getting my mouth in gear. "My mother told me my father was not my father. Does this mean you will leave me?"

"No," he said. "No, of course not. What are you talking about?" He pushed open the door.

The dog shot out as if there were no tomorrow, a red blur.

Leaping, lapping, and grinning, she spun around in ecstasy, raced toward the street, then raced back. She looked as if to say "walk," or "let's walk," or "you've left me alone long enough, I deserve to be walked."

I ignored her imploring eyes. "Go wee-wee, Maile," I said. Maile stopped, and trotted obediently into the front yard and squatted.

"Good girl," I yelled. "What a good girl."

"Laurie, what is it?"

"The full moon, it's got something to do with the full moon," I said before I burst into tears. I was a wreck, glad our son John was spending the night with my in-laws.

"I don't know what to do."

"I don't know what to tell you. Do what you think is best," he said.

I threw a dog biscuit down the basement stairs. Maile went after it. I could hear her twirling around in her bed, looking for a comfortable position. I longed to be my dog.

I awoke the next morning begging for a big voice to come from the sky and tell me what to do next. I waited, my head spun, I knew my eyes were swollen. Bet I looked like one of Kishaba's old Maui pigs.

"Boys and girls, bring a picture of yourself as a child and put a caption to it," said my seventh grade teacher years ago. It was around the time B.J. set off the fire extinguisher.

I had chosen a picture of myself clutching a kitten. Behind me sat the wash house and the clothes lines once suspended over the septic tank. I had no idea who owned the kitten. It didn't matter. I chose the picture and attached a phrase I lifted from "True Confessions." "Mommy, why am I different." Brother, if I had known then what I know now, I thought.

Two days later we flew to California. I was too busy making arrangements to dwell or grieve over the loss of me before we departed.

California, Disneyland and Fantasy World, Tinker Bell images, life-size cartoon characters walking, talking stuffed replicas of Mickey and Minnie Mouse, Pluto, and Donald Duck. They spoke to me. I spoke back. I wanted to stay, play, and pretend, skip around, be a kid. I wanted old Walt to make things right, but Walt was dead and so was a part of me. We stayed in California for five days, then left for Honolulu.

Mother's home was jam-packed with children. My sister's five, my brother's three, and all their friends. By then, Cynnie-Belle had been married three times. She should have stayed with her first, but she thought there had to be more out there. Apparently, there were. Her second marriage was to a con man from New York whom Mother hated, said the only good thing he ever accomplished was Leslie, Cynnie-Belle's fifth child. Leslie was a gem. Her father was not. In fact, we believe he made off with much of Mother's jewelry and her Leeteg painting, the one Buzzy peed on. Cynnie-Belle dumped her third husband, a Mexican tennis pro, when he started moving his non-English speaking family into their newly built Kahala home. No, it was more than that, he was also having mucho affairs. "Three times charm," said Mother before she forbade Cynnie-Belle to marry again. It was getting too expensive. Husbands two and three went through most of Cynnie-Belle's trust fund. Mother paid all her bills, tuitions to private schools and colleges, Outrigger tabs, Liberty House charges, utilities, mortgage payments, everything. I didn't realize how extensive her support was until I saw my sister flip a pile of bills on Mom's kitchen table. "Here, I can't pay any of these," she said.

"Why do you bail her out?" I asked. "She'll never take responsibility if you keep paying for everything."

Mother's answer astonished me. "She might not let me see the children if I didn't."

"You can't be serious!" I was incredulous. "How utterly ridiculous." I was angry with her absurd logic. What about me? I wanted to ask. You've never helped me. We did borrow some money to buy our home, but we paid you back with interest. To date, Cynnie-Belle has lived in seven houses and owned a farm in Bucks County, Pennsylvania. Every piece of property was financed by Bey or you.

I kept quiet and, in a silent rage, left the room. I didn't want to start an argument.

Do what you think is best, I thought when we returned to Louisville two weeks later. I hauled out the dictionary. Best: "Most excellent, most suitable, most desirable, surpassing all others." Was it best for my mother to tell me? The news sure surpassed everything else. Where "most suitable, most desirable" fit in terms of my reputation was another matter, not that anyone need know. "Do what you think is best," I said out loud. "I think it's best to see a doctor, the tightness in my chest is killing me." Although I had quit smoking in 1968, I was convinced I had lung cancer. It gave me something to worry about.

"I'm tired a lot, and I sleep a lot, and my chest hurts when I cough," I said, holding my fist to my mouth. I emitted a few choking sounds for the stethoscope.

"Laurie, your lungs sound crystal clear, but I'll send you over to X-ray to be sure."

I left for another floor, another office, another form to fill out.

"I was right," he said upon my return.

And I was wrong, I thought.

"Your lungs look terrific."

I passed on the opportunity for a cute comeback and went for the really big one.

"Doctor, a few weeks ago my mother told me my father wasn't my father."

He paused, I could see he was somewhat taken back. "You were adopted?" he asked.

"I wish," I said. "No, my mother had a boyfriend while she was married."

"Laurie, you can't be certain the boyfriend's your father."

"Oh, yes I can. My mother sent me pictures. There's no doubt, this father and I, we look exactly alike." I wanted to add that I once hoped she'd made a mistake by screwing up calculating her screwing dates, and that the rhythm method had, indeed, worked. But, I knew, no matter how lousy she was in math, she'd told the truth.

"It doesn't matter who your father is," he said. "You're you."

"You look just like Laurie," passed through my mind. I wondered if he knew my grandmother.

"John," he called into the waiting room. John trotted in. "Take your Mother for a martini."

"I knew it," I muttered as I marched across the parking lot. "I should have gone for a comment on terrific lungs. It would have gotten a better reaction." So much for forms and medical histories. They were only half correct now.

On the ride home, Gladys Knight and the Pips sang "You're The Best Thing That Ever Happened To Me." I threw my head back and sang along with them.

I phoned the previous owner of our house. He, too, was a ham radio operator. A sign?

"Is there a directory? I mean, if I have someone's call letters, can I find out where they live."

"I don't have one," he said. "But there is such a thing. Call an electronics store, they should have the information."

I did.

They did.

"Call letters belong to a DeForest Romain, Pompton Lakes, New Jersey. Here's his telephone number." I hung up. How easy. Two tries and I find him. Now what?

I called twice after I got his number. Both times a kid answered the phone. He would be back in a few minutes, I was told. I replaced the receiver, terrified. I had no idea what I was going to say and was still not sure I was doing the right thing.

"Is Mr. Romain there?" I asked on the second try.

"Just a moment," he or she said.

"Yes?"

I hesitated, then stated, "I don't know whether you want to talk to me or not, but my name is Laurie."

Twenty-eight years of silence seemed to stretch between us before he said, "Yes, my God, yes. I never married, never got over your mother. Yes I want to talk to you." His voice choked, I sensed the tears. "I never stopped thinking about you, but after '64 I figured you were out of high school and on your own."

We played catch-up for the next hour.

"It's amazing," he told me. "I've just returned from Florida. I was there taking care of my mother. She died so I came back here. I have my own home in Pompton Lakes. My relatives are here."

I had new relatives. I wondered what they were like.

"I've never gotten over your mother," he repeated.

Nor I.

June 6th, 1974

Dear Laurie,

There are so many, many years to live and make up for and so many things to talk of. Now I already understand your likes and dislikes, identical in many ways to mine, your love of music, books, on which I've let myself down somewhat during recent years, it will take forever to catch up with one another.

In this old photo of myself, taken at the time you were born, how much we look alike. I was then about the same age you are now. And, getting your letter this morning, I thank God for so many things . . . that you didn't panic and hang up the phone when the kid answered, that I happened to be home on vacation, that I had moved back here to the hometown from Fla., where I'd lived for a few years. The kid who answered is just one of several who come over quite frequently. None of them have anything and I try to help them out a little. Got five of them seasonal passes to a swimming pool a few days ago and was just bringing a couple back the second time you called.

The photos you sent me are really beautiful and I am so proud of you, Laurie. You are everything I knew you would be. In the pictures of you leaving for school I can see both your Mother and myself in your face. Your voice is very much like your mother's. I'll never ask for anything else or want anyone else in the world or the rest of my life. Thank you for the photo of John. What a beautiful child. His father can be so proud of him. And thank his father for his understanding and complete devotion to you for letting you find me. For as much as I wanted to, I knew I never would have or could. Now my whole past life seems of nothing and after all these years I have something to live for.

I was going to send you a picture of my home, which I'm sure you'll like. But I think it's better to have you see it in person.

I understand the terrible strain you went through during those past two weeks and I am so proud to have a daughter with such strength of conviction.

I'm going over to mail this now so it goes out in the afternoon mail and you get it by Saturday. Then tonight I'm going to call once more to let you know I received your letter and that I've mailed this.

Again, thank Barret for everything he has done for the two of us.

From now on,

"Love, Dad" he hand wrote. "It's De for Deforest."
But I knew that all along.

—

Had I known he would not be a knight in shining armor, I'd never have called. After a couple of frantic weeks phoning back and forth, I made plans to visit. He sounded decent enough, but I wasn't prepared for his appearance. He looked like his pictures, but the frozen reflections didn't hint at the slob he was to become. Tall, with bull dog jowls, rotten teeth that cut a jagged path across his smile. What have I done, I thought, as I rode the moving ramp down the middle of the concourse. He was leaning against a window. The pedestrian walk lay between us, streams of bodies sliced between our stares, cutting off the full impact of our total selves. Behind him I could see planes pulling in, parking, pulling out, vehicles to transport people from here to there, from there to here.

"Okay, I've arrived," I said under my breath.

He came rushing over, blubbering something. He was so nervous I felt sorry for him, me in my Izod dress, prim and proper, an older female version of "Little Lord Fauntleroy."

"Oh Laurie, you're so lovely. I'm so happy, I'm so proud. Oh, Laurie, you're really here" he said and swooped down to hug me. He smelled musty. I tensed.

Crazy Guggenheim, I thought. He reminds me of Crazy Guggenheim from the Jackie Gleason Show. Crazy Guggenheim, the spastic, the guy who talked like he'd had a stroke.

"I just can't believe you're here." De's voice broke into my memories. "Everyone is so excited to meet you. I can't wait to show you the town and my house."

He was oblivious.

We piled into his beat-up old white Ford Falcon and hit the ramp heading north. "Montclair," a sign read. My heart fell. This is all wrong, I shouldn't be here, this is not where I belong. My grandmother is a half hour away, and here I am, speeding up a highway in search of a life I never had. A life I never experienced, nor wanted, I realized. But, I was stuck, at least for a few days. Damn you, Mother, I thought, before I realized De had asked me a question.

"This is it," he said proudly as he pulled into the carport about fifty minutes later. "I own it, it's all paid for."

"You own a carport?" I asked. "Great."

De paused, then laughed. "You're too funny," he said, "No, I own the house and carport."

"Nice," I replied, and it was. A stone cape cod situated on a large lot. He showed me through the downstairs—two bedrooms, two full baths, a huge fireplace in the living room. He paused to point out a number of paintings he had brought back from China. They reminded me of motel pictures. Maybe that's why he likes them, I thought. Maybe they remind him of my mother, that is, if they "did it" in motels.

The ham radio was on the second floor.

"Same one that's in the picture?" I asked. Mom had sent me an old business card of his. It showed De posed in front of a ham radio. Across the top were sprawled his call letters.

"Same one," he said with reverence. "Here, I'll show you how it works."

Before I could tell him that later would do, he'd tracked down one of his cronies. "It's my daughter," he said to the voice.

It didn't take long to learn about "over" and "out" and "Roger." Roger. How ironic!

I met Aunts Grace, Blanche, and Alice. We visited the family cemetery where I acquainted myself with new last names. Bob, Pompton Lake's Chief of Police, dropped by, as did De's friend Jeanette, her three daughters, and boyfriend, Smokey. "Jeanette hasn't any money," he told me after they left. "I help her and the kids out when I can."

Saint, I thought.

"I have one sister," he said. "We don't speak. She thinks she's too good for me. She has a daughter."

He showed me a picture of his niece, a new first cousin. "She is very pretty." I told him. It was true. The only other picture I saw was of his mother. She was about seventeen when it was taken. We looked exactly alike.

At night, after a few drinks, he'd get maudlin. "I've been so lonely, all these years, so lonely. I often sailed into Honolulu, but I didn't want to disrupt your life."

Thanks, I thought, you didn't. The disruption was my doing.

"Why didn't you marry?" I asked. "You could have gotten married."

"No, no," he said, and shook his head, brushing the thought away with a wave of his hand. "Your mother, I've always loved your mother. I also enjoy the solitude of being at sea. Being by myself is satisfying."

Then you chose your loneliness, you chose to be lonely and isolated, I thought. He seemed so sad I hadn't the heart to interrupt his misery. I was not about to create waves around a fragile raft.

The three days passed. I was more than ready to leave. "I'll call you," I said, pulling quickly away from his embrace. His shirt wasn't tucked in right. Skin from a pot belly peeked out between the buttons.

Now what, I thought. Telling might have been best for her but it sure wasn't best for me. The anger began on the flight home. Why did she do this to me? It was all so simple and now it's all so complicated. I realized I had opened a can of worms, worms I should have kept buried in the past among the layers of yesteryears. Now what? Now what? Now what!

THOUGHTS, 1974

You look just like your aunt, they say.
Curtsy, bow, Laurie, take it away.
But you know now
You cannot escape.

Veil the identity Put on the cape
Dad, I hope you're feeling well.
Everything here is simply swell.
But it is not, nor can it be.
You are gone Father,
You are not he.

He must have hurt
So very much.
And now I know
I fear to touch.
A game I play with him
With you
How to act
What to do

I call both Dad now,
My siblings don't know.
And Christ, I'm scared
To tell them so.

An outcast, a freak
I no longer belong.
Will they say that?
Tell me so long?
My child, my life
What to do?
Face the reality
See it through!

"Well?" asked Mother. The connection was crystal-clear, like my lungs, I smiled to myself. A joke between me and me.

"His teeth are rotten. A couple of front ones even wiggle back and forth when sounds involve his lower lip."

Silence on her end.

"He has a nice house, he owns it, it's all paid for," I added. "Mom," I paused for a deep breath. "Why did you do this to me? You messed me up." I felt anger sweeping through my body. "You messed me up, I don't belong with him in Pompton Lakes. The only thing those people care about is baseball. I've put in a lot of time making my life the way I wanted it. A life totally unlike yours, and you go and mess it up."

The novelty of a new identity was gone. The surprise in the box of Cracker Jacks was a dud. I should have heeded the warnings on expectations long ago when I failed to win one of Lassie's puppies. I waited by the mailbox for months. No one ever explained the regulations concerning animals brought into the islands. They had to spend six months in quarantine to avoid the possibility of rabies. I should have known that, like I should have known this was not going to be a piece of cake.

I could hear her sniffling through the wire; emitting a moan. "Don't cry!" I told her, my voice stern. "Crying is not going to help me. You need to help me. Why did you do this to me?" The sobs began.

"Don't be angry, I never meant to hurt you. I wouldn't hurt you for the world. I love you, Laurie. I've always loved you. You're my baby girl."

I used the same words when I spoke to my dog. You're my baby dog, Maile. My baby girl, my baby bitch. We're both bitches, my dog and I, I thought.

I wasn't going to have any of Mother's defense. "How would you know what hurts me?" My voice started to rise. "You were never home while I was growing up. You were never there to see, even know, what hurt me. I hurt every night you didn't come home until I stopped caring anymore. I hurt every time you lavished attention on your boyfriends, Buzzy and all his buddies. You bought and gave them everything, you left nothing for Cynnie-Belle, Bruce, and me. Don't you dare talk to me about knowing my hurts." I slammed down the phone. I was so mad I kicked the kitchen door.

A few minutes after I slammed down the phone, she called back. "Laurie, I'm sorry. You're upset. I know this has been hard on you, get some sleep. I'll call you in the morning."

"Right," I replied. My tone was docile. I replaced the receiver. I'd make like Susan Hayward in that movie Mom and I loved. Remember, Mom? The one about that lady's fight to overcome an addiction. Remember, Mom? We both read the book and saw the movie, "I'll Cry Tomorrow." For you, I'll get some sleep. Then tomorrow, I will cry.

Then I did what I always had done in the face of adversity . . . I went to work on a bigger and better me.

In all honesty, I could never say my mother didn't care. She stayed with me for six weeks when my son John was born. She cooked, cleaned, and fed him in the wee small hours of the morning. She showed me the art of taking care of a baby, from bathing to burping. She also told Maile it was all right to jump up on her bed. I caught them together one morning. "Mom, the dog's not allowed on the furniture."

My statement fell on deaf ears.

I had John too quickly. The labor got away from me.

"Bear down during the contraction," the doctor said.

"I have no desire to do that," I told him between clenched teeth. "None. I'll push when the pain subsides."

"It doesn't work that way, push," he commanded.

So I pushed with the pain and out popped my son and out popped a whopper of a hemorrhoid.

I couldn't pee in anything but a tub full of warm water for two weeks. I faked an "I am just fine" release from the hospital.

During the fourteen days I was tied to a tub, I made two runs to the emergency room. Numerous trips to my gynecologist proved futile. No one knew what was wrong. No one could explain the pain I was in, a pain and pressure so great I could not stand straight.

"You've got blood clots," my mother said. "I know that's what it is, I get them when I have polyps trouble."

Once every few years she'd call to say some polyps had been surgically removed. She always called after the operations. Didn't want to worry you, she would tell me.

"That's what it is, Laurie."

The pain and pressure increased. I finally called a surgeon one evening. "I've been sitting in a bath tub drinking brandy and trying to pee for the past two hours. What shall I do?"

"Drink more brandy," he said. "If that doesn't work, call me back."

An hour and a half later, I was in for my third and final visit to the hospital. He extracted the clot and the pain disappeared immediately.

"What did I tell you," said Mother when I got home. "Now it's time I got back to my Benny."

She left six weeks after her arrival. After her departure, the dog continued to jump on the furniture.

CHRISTMAS 1974

Ring it out!
For all the years,
For all the sadness,
For all the tears,
For all the times,
I did not know.
It's not my fault.
Don't tell me so.
Don't tell me I'm not who I am.
Don't tell me, Mother, for I can't stand.

I am not strong,
My will is weak,
I need strong liquor to make me sleep.
I need just someone to tell me why
I want to live. I want to die.
Wallowing? Yes I am indeed
In total self pity but total need.
Where to turn?
Whom to call?
Echoes bounce from wall to wall.
Games I play from day to day.
"She's just neat," I hear them say.
But neat I'm not nor can I be
When father thought is no longer he.
Ring it out!
The old year.
Deck the halls
And all that cheer.
Ring it out!
Raise the roofs.
Santa's reindeer
Stomp your hooves.
Ring it out!
Christmas past.
All's not well
It will not last.
Yesteryears of deck the halls,
Days long ago
Resounding walls
Stop the music!
I can't stand.
Hush my child,
You're in too deep.

Long ago I asked why?
Different, yes, no matter, sigh.
And now facts known,
I am so sad.
It's not my fault
Santa
I am not bad.

We went to the Pine Room for New Year's. Mabel was still there, and the songs about the South were the same.

1975

"I'LL MEET YOU IN NISHUANE PARK," I told De in July. I was in New Jersey, this time tucked safely in the arms of Montclair. I was apprehensive. John was too young to be curious about the stranger he would meet. I hoped he wouldn't mention it to my grandmother or Madge. I could just hear him saying, "We met a nice man in the park."

"Oh really, who was that?" my grandmother might ask.

"Just someone who calls himself my dad," I'd reply, answering for John. "You might have met or heard about him, say maybe twenty-six, twenty-seven years ago. No big deal."

But it was a big deal, a big ordeal sneaking off to meet him. I felt as if I were cheating. I hated the deceit.

He was there when we arrived, standing at the entrance. Behind him I could see a large boulder. Someone had spray painted the word "rock" on its surface. The word was white.

"What a beautiful little boy," said De when we reached him.

He pronounced beautiful, "beeyoutiful." It irritated me.

"He looks like me but he has his dad's coloring, the blond hair and blue eyes." The Johnston's coloring, I thought, the Romain chin, I realized. Not eager to discuss heritage, I changed the subject. "Let's go ride the twirl-around."

We parted a half hour later. Selfishly, I didn't feel any guilt. "John needs to have lunch and a nap," I told him. Reason enough. "You do know how to get to the Montclair Art Museum?" I asked. He was picking me up in two days for another visit to

Pompton Lakes. He assured me he knew the location. I watched the Falcon pull away, then took a picture of the white rock-rock.

"I'm going to visit some friends today," I told my grandmother. If she suspected anything, she did not let on, nor did she ask who these friends were. I had a story made up if she did question me, but I was spared that lie. I left for the parking lot of the Montclair Art Museum.

Another day in northern New Jersey. I saw Grace and Blanche and Alice again. Everyone was still watching baseball. Bob came by shortly before lunch, Jeanette and the girls a little later. I assumed Smokey was at work. I didn't ask, I didn't care, I wanted to leave. Around two, I told De that I needed to go.

"I didn't give a number where I could be reached. If something happens to John, they won't know where I am."

"Call if you're worried." He motioned toward the phone.

"No, I'd rather just go." I pictured someone spotting my grandmother's car in the museum parking lot. I felt nervous, paranoid.

No one asked questions upon my return. The day was over. I had met my obligation. I was still the dutiful daughter.

"Madge, can I talk to you?" I asked later that night.

"Sure, Sugar," she said. "Something's bothering you, I can always tell."

It took only those words for me to dissolve once more. It took awhile, but I finally got the story out. "Did you know anything about what was going on?"

"Oh Laurie, oh my baby, I'm so sorry."

Madge looked terribly sad. I started crying again. She put her arms around me. "My baby, my poor baby, you poor child," she said over and over. "No, no, I didn't know anything. I knew there was trouble with Miss Dorothy, but nothing about the trouble. They left for Honolulu. No one told me what was going on. Seems one day they lived in Montclair, the next, they didn't."

Trouble . . . took trouble to paradise.

"Is there anything I can do?" Madge asked.

"No, no, there's nothing you can do, nothing anyone can do." The damage has been done, I thought.

In October, I spent another day in Pompton Lakes, another half hour in Nishuane Park. My sister called during my visit to say that Roger was very ill. "You need to come home," she told me. "He's in intensive care." I took John back to Louisville and left the next day for Honolulu.

I spent more time sitting in the sun than sitting at the hospital. It was hard to sort out my feelings toward Bruce and Cynnie-Belle. My biological bloodlines had been severed. Where did I fit in? What were they to me? I strained to watch for similarities among the three of us. My sister and I sounded exactly alike, that was about it. When I answered her phone, people would talk to me as if I were she. When set straight, I'd hear, "Sister? I didn't know CB had a sister." The response left me livid. Did she not care enough to let my existence be known? Or were there, simply, too many newcomers on the island too many who moved in after 1964?

My dad, my father, Roger, whoever he was, stayed hooked to monitors for a few days. The monitors reminded me of the Relax-a-cizor. I hoped it worked better. Four days after I arrived, I left. He was fine. A cyst was found and removed.

I thought about death on the long flight back to Louisville. Roger, although not physically, had died as far I was concerned. I felt he used me over the years to get back at Mother. I remembered the phonograph record he brought for her birthday. His first appearance after the divorce. From that point on, I became his little girl. I was too happy to question why, just accepted the many dinner invitations. Often we'd eat at the Tropics, a lovely open restaurant in the heart of Waikiki. He knew the owners, Peaches and Tony. I'd never met anyone with a name like Peaches. It was neat. Every time we went to the Tropics, he'd have our picture taken. I'd carry a copy home to show Mom.

As I got older, he made sure his apartment was stocked with Spam and treats for me and the members of "The Sly Ones." The ultimate was "my own room" in his Kaiko'o house. Me, me, me . . . I thought he did it all for me, the baby. I realized, now, the baby bastard was the best way of getting to my mother.

Roger had not worked in ten years. My brother bought him a bar on the island of Molokai, but Mary ran it. When I was a junior in college, Mary wrote and asked me to send money each month. I was nineteen years old. I responded by writing Roger. "I didn't know Mary wrote you," he replied. "Of course, I don't expect you to supplement my income." I wondered if that were true.

He used me, he used me, he used me. All these years he knew I wasn't his child and he used me. Disconnected, enraged, I slowly passed the point of no return. Wish they still had that stupid old contest, I thought . . . could stand a bottle of champagne, could use it in celebration of the new me!

Mother was right. Roger was a very self-centered man. "Every time I'd try to leave him, he'd have a nervous breakdown. Finally, Dr. Lam said someone was going to be hurt, might as well not be me," she told me over the years.

It wasn't you, I thought. "It wasn't you, Mom, it was all your money. It was your money, not you," I whispered. Roger had been successful at first. He had his own company after the divorce. The success, however, didn't last. A proxy fight rendered his stock worthless.

Dawn was breaking as I landed in Chicago. Dawn was breaking in more ways than one.

1977

WE ARRIVED IN TIME to give Benny his Christmas present, a six pack of "Billy Beer" I hand-carried on the plane. I thought he'd get a kick out of the hops. It was presidential stuff, and since Benny told everyone in Kahala that he was President of the Kahala Beach Association, the gift seemed appropriate. My sister and brother hit the roof when they heard what he was telling people. I didn't care. I didn't live there. I stayed away from the continual conflicts between Benny, Bruce, and Cynnie-Belle. The latest scandal they uncovered involved a woman he had stashed away at a local establishment.

"Dot showed me her phone bills. This one number kept appearing, so Bruce and I called," Cynnie-Belle told me the night we arrived. "It was the Pagoda Hotel. I asked for Mrs. Kaneaiakala. And damn, if there wasn't one registered. We phoned the room, a woman answered. We asked to speak to Benny. He just left, she told me.

"Tell him Cynnie-Belle and Bruce called to say hello."

"Then what?" I asked.

"Told Dot. She didn't seem surprised."

I watched Benny unwrap the beer.

"Hey, my honey," he said to Mother, "Look dis, dis great stuff. I went red about dis. Tank you, tank you, Laurie," he said, smiling, and nodding.

Benny liked me. I didn't live there, I was not a threat. If he knew about my mother and De, I wondered how he would feel.

I was sorry I couldn't justify Mother's nonchalance over his affair. "Hey, not to worry," I wanted to tell my semi-siblings. "Mom, like Benny, has been there, certainly not in the Pagoda Hotel, but places similar." But then, who am I kidding? They knew her as well as I. Well, almost.

"Hey, my honey, I go hide da beer. No like no one to drink it," he said and headed up the stairs to his room, the room which was my grandfather's before it became mine when we moved in '62. A few minutes later, Benny headed out the door to spend the holidays at Hale Ola. I watched him lumber off and into his Lincoln Continental.

"He wanted to leave us in peace."

Right Mom, he left us in peace for a piece, I thought.

Benny had always been a point of contention and conflict. Ellen quit the first year Mom was married to him. I was away at school. I assumed from information gathered that she'd slipped on the porch steps and suffered a bad fall. I suspected he shoved her. Although she never let on to the fact, she alluded to it. Benny, a man not to be trusted, a man like the husband Ellen left over twenty-five years before. No wonder her silence.

Benny shoved my mother around, too, but she didn't quit or complain. The extent of his abuse was not known. "She blames her bruises on falling," my sister told me. It made sense. My mother did fall a lot. She'd party hard, then crash. On her refrigerator door she hung a sign that read, "I don't have a drinking problem. I drink; I get drunk; I fall down, no problem." And that was, honestly, the way she felt. When she called to tell me she had three broken ribs, I believed her story.

"I was chasing Skoshi in the back room and fell," she said. Skoshi was her obnoxious miniature dachshund. Mother had gone from great Danes to dachshunds to miniature dachshunds. From Peter Balls, the Nazi Mother almost married when she attended the University of Munich, to Roger to DeForest, to Benny. In between there were Soupy, Larry, Buzzy, and more than a few other affairs. All the same animals, I thought. Of course I couldn't speak for Peter Balls, but I felt safe in the assumption. They were all pricks, but Benny was the biggest one of all. He was a mean SOB, an illiterate, a liar, and Mother worshipped the ground he walked on. I couldn't figure it out, so I stopped trying. After all, as I said, I no longer lived there.

Benny went to Maui and flew back on December 29. He was loading a bag of Maui onions, a treat for us all on Oahu, into the Continental's trunk when he keeled over in the airport parking lot. Cynnie-Belle called around ten. Barret, John, and I were staying with my grandmother who rented our old house next door to the Buschers after she gave us her home in 1962. Everyone was asleep when the phone rang.

"Benny's had a heart attack," Cynnie-Belle said. "I think he's dead. Bruce's gone to get Dot. He'll pick you up, then me."

The four of us drove to Tripler Army Hospital, the night's silence broken only by Mother's voice.

"He called me before he left. He called to say he'd be home before midnight. Usually he doesn't call, but he called tonight. Maybe he knew something was wrong. 'My honey, I love you,' he told me before he hung up."

I wondered if Benny knew it was Mom and not his lover at the Pagoda Hotel he was calling. My honey could be anyone. I wondered if Bruce and Cynnie-Belle were wondering the same thing as we sped down the freeway.

(I rode to school with the Glessners when the first mile stretch of that freeway was completed. Mr. Glessner was so excited about it he failed to see the dog run onto the highway. I saw the dog. I saw the dog launched by the impact of Mr. Glessner's front bumper. I turned quickly toward the rear window and caught the dog in its descent. The sun was rising, the sky a brilliant glow. Mr. Glessner kept going, left the animal to die in the middle of a brand new highway. I sat back and stared at his neck. I didn't realize I could hate anyone so much.)

"We're here," said Bruce as he pulled up in front of the hospital. CB jumped out and ran in. I followed. Mother went with Bruce to park the car. "I want to compose myself," she said.

"Take the tubes out of him," Cynnie-Belle hissed. "I don't want my mother to remember him like this."

Benny was on a gurney and Benny was very dead. Moments later my mother arrived. I watched in silence. My brother helped her into the room, gently.

"On no, my honey, not you my honey, oh no," she cried.

I fled into the hallway and fell apart. An intern quickly rushed over and led me into a waiting room. I realized the move was not one of sympathy. He wanted me out of the corridor. Too much, it was all too much.

Benny's funeral lasted three entire days, from 9:00 to 5:00, from 7:00 until 10:00. We helped choose a casket. Three birds, soaring off in formation, were imprinted on the exposed satin of the lid. Benny lay there in a dark suit. We helped Mother pick out an appropriate shirt, shoes, and socks. It seemed so dumb.

On the third day the casket was closed. We drove to Punchbowl National Cemetery where he was interred. Then we partied. A continual barrage of relatives and friends came by to offer condolences. His kids by the first Mrs. Kaneaiakala played Hawaiian music. There was much singing and dancing and many tears.

I have to say again, in all fairness, that I'd never seen Mother so devastated. She would rally for awhile, then sink back into a sea of tears.

Benny's funeral was a lot different from Judy's funeral. It was 1963, the end of my junior year of high school when she died.

"Come ti leaf sliding with us," said B.J. It was a Friday. The rains had finally let up. It had poured all week.

"I can't, my car's ready to be picked up at the gas station. Mark's giving me a ride." Mark was my latest crush and the thought of mudsliding was not as tempting as being with him. I opted for the seven minute ride from school to the Chevron station rather than the few hours they would spend careening down Mt. Tantalus and hiking back up the trail they created.

"Come on Frizzy, it will be fun. We haven't gone for a long time," B.J. argued. Frizzy was a name I picked up in my freshman year. I had a permanent, it was a disaster.

"No, I'll catch you later B.J." Although I knew it would never happen, I hoped Mark just might ask me out, it being Friday and all.

"Suit yourself," she said and walked away.

Mark did not ask me out. He dropped me off at the gas station and left. I thought briefly of going home, changing into blue jeans, and hooking up with the mud sliders. The thought left as quickly as it came. It seemed too much trouble. Besides, I probably wouldn't find them. Tantalus had too many sliding places. Seeing their parked cars on the road as a clue didn't occur to me. I spent the evening home, alone.

Barbi, a long, lanky friend of mine, came rushing up to me the next day. I was at the Outrigger, sitting on the steps outside the lobby, waiting for the troops to trickle in. Barbi was the one who had taught me to wear Tampax. She yelled instructions while standing outside the stall in the locker room. For Christmas she gave me a box of them, not ten tubes, but forty. She had unwrapped each one, removed the hard cylinders of cotton, and replaced them with sticks of candy. I discovered the contents of the gift before I inserted one. Another thanks-to-God-for-small-favors.

"Judy's dead," she said.

Nothing registered in my brain.

"Judy who?"

"Judy, Judy Brooks is dead. She got hurt in an automobile accident on the way back from ti leaf sliding yesterday."

"Judy Brooks is dead?"

"Yes, I can't believe it, can you?"

"No, I can't Who is Judy Brooks?" I asked before realizing what was being said.

Barbi's dad was a doctor. He was in the emergency room when they brought Judy in. He told Barbi that they didn't think she was badly hurt. There was only a spot of blood on her right arm. He told her Judy kept saying, "I don't want to die. Please don't let me die." But she did. The impact caused massive internal bleeding.

I rode to Judy's funeral with B.J. and her mom. Under ordinary circumstances, B.J. would have insisted on driving. This time she did not. I had never seen my friend in such anguish, her grief inconsolable. I had to hold her up when we reached Judy's coffin.

"Look. She has her graduation muu-muu on and she's wearing her class ring," said Mrs. Brooks, raising Judy's hand toward us so we could see. "The only things I ever wanted were for her to graduate from high school and for her to get married."

B.J. fell apart. I felt as if I were someone else observing the rituals of death. Mrs. Brooks started screaming, "Don't you touch her, don't you dare touch her!" when the funeral director tried to close the coffin. Mr. Brooks had to hold her back.

"I didn't feel anything," I told my mother later. "It didn't even look like Judy."

"The Judy you know is gone. She lives in your memories now. What you saw was only a symbol of the Judy you knew."

Mrs. Brooks got one of her wishes. Judy received her diploma posthumously. The year book was dedicated in her memory.

Benny received a total of $1,445, gifts given to his memory.

"What a tribute," said my mother when the funds were totaled.

What a tribute? I wondered if it would cover the final expenses at the Pagoda Hotel.

1978

I CALLED MOTHER A LOT after Benny's death. I was concerned about her, but my real reason had to do with the bitch of a winter we were having. It started snowing the day I got back. The air was frigid, the Ohio River frozen, and I couldn't get out of my driveway. Food was in short supply, as transportation routes— the river and railroads were having the same problems with ice as the truckers. I called my mother for "poor baby" sympathy. Secretly, I think she liked the calls. No matter what happened, she didn't have to live on the mainland. Our problems were not her problems, which suited Mom just fine.

"Laurie," she said. It was late afternoon. "I hear you've got a blizzard going on in Louisville. My poor baby, lashings of snow and now this."

Outside, gale winds licked every available space between windows and doors. My house was being played. It sounded like a symphony of kazoos.

"Well," she continued, "at least you can walk to the liquor store."

"No, I can't. The entire town is closed down."

"Oh dear," I heard her say before she muffled the receiving end with her hand.

And then it began, a batch of individual "poor babies" came over the wire. I smiled and listened to the voices of Madge, my sister, Stanton, my grandmother, and a few others. The message was topped off with one unified roar of "Pooooooor Baaaby".

Why am I living here when I could be out there with them? I thought. I could be with all those crazies, having fun, lying in the sun, listening to the latest loves, loves lost, hearing about pranks pulled on one another. I hung up feeling good. Maybe moving back wouldn't be so bad. Eventually the snow melted, as did my fantasy about returning home. Well, half home. The part in Pompton Lakes did not interest me at all.

Mother called me on the twenty-second of April. "I have some distressing news," she told me. "I put Bey in the hospital this afternoon. Dr. Lam wants to do some tests."

I knew my grandmother had had a nasty fall a few days before. "Did she hurt herself more than you thought?"

"No," Mother replied. "It's more than that. I haven't said anything because I didn't want to upset you."

Since when has not upsetting me been a concern of yours? I wanted to ask. "Go on," I said instead.

"She has no appetite, hasn't since shortly after New Year's. In fact, she spends most of her time feeling nauseated. Lately, her vision blurs to the point of blindness. Sometimes it lasts for hours."

Abject terror shot through me.

My grandmother didn't eat Christmas supper with us at the table. She insisted on staying in the living room, on the couch by the window—the window I had tied my horse under many years before. For an instant I rationalized. Mom, I wanted to say, that's the problem, sitting under the window in the living room, that's it. Why, the first time I sensed a loss of appetite was right there, in a chair under that window. Wasn't that I was sick. I was simply worried about my horse. That's it Mom, that's what's wrong. I felt as if I were Bozo the Clown desperately trying to get someone to turn the page. Help me, please help me, the words echoed in my brain. My grandmother had no horse to worry about, that was I, back then, way back when.

I had watched her throughout the meal Christmas day. In retrospect I realized she knew, and in her own regal way, was telling us she'd no longer be around. We were going to have to survive without her. For the moment, though, she was still alive and denial was so much easier.

"Laurie? Laurie are you still there?"

"Yes, Mom. Listen, call me as soon as you know something. I can't talk anymore."

I hung up, poured a glass of white wine, and walked outside. Daffodils hugged the edge of our driveway, a pink and white dogwood, in its final flourish of color, graced the front yard. Grass, an almost deep lime green, stretched before me. "This can't be," I said aloud. "This can't be! It's spring, my time of year, a time for rejuvenation, rebirth, suntans, and all the stuff that makes winter worth going through. My grandmother can't be ill. She could never die, could she?"

Uncle Duke took John and me to the airport after Benny died. Bey rode with him. She had never ridden to or from an airport with me, never, ever. "Last look," she'd say playfully as I got into a car. "Last look." We played "last look" every time I left Montclair. She'd stand at her front door, within the confines of her walker, and we'd yell "last look," each hoping to get the last look before speeding out the driveway.

I sat down on our front stoop. "I have absolutely no idea how I will exist without her," I said. "I have absolutely no earthly idea."

My grandmother, since 1964, saw that I attended and understood the operas and plays featured in *The New Yorker*, and *Cue* magazines. *Cue*, an almost biblical guide and reference to restaurants, cafes, bars, the theater, everything. I'd go to my grandmother's for all significant holidays. In between, I flew up for long weekends, weekends during which I licked the wounds obtained in tough courses, or wounds that belonged to a girl 5,000 miles away from a home she didn't want. School problems, friend problems, alone-with-no-home problems, Montclair was always there. Nothing's happened yet, I thought. I'll cry tomorrow.

Tomorrow began five days later.

FROM THE DESK OF LAURIE BIRNSTEEL

Laurie, your mother called, said your grandmother will be operated on 9:30 am tomorrow, Hawaii time. Dot won't be home until about 7:00 tonight, Hawaii time (12:00) but if you want to call her, go ahead. 4:00 — CS

The "C" stood for Carol. Carol was a kid I brought home to live with us until she turned the magical age of eighteen. At eighteen, she couldn't be locked up for running away from home. That was two years ago. Carol had long since moved out, but was over often.

Runaways. For the past three years, I had championed their plight. "Red flag," I'd say. "Runaways are children waving a red flag, something was wrong in their homes; help, they're asking for help." It was a perfect cause. I related to their sense of loss. I had done well. I appeared on TV talk shows; taped radio programs; spoke to civic groups; and trained volunteers to work at Shelter House, a YMCA program, focal point of my involvement. I conducted workshops around the country. I'd been appointed by the governor to a seat on the State Crime Commission. People looked to me for advice. I had arrived. I wasn't prepared for more trauma, I'd had enough.

Carol's message came five days after they hospitalized Bey. I stayed up until midnight, then phoned Mother.

"Operated on for what?" I asked.

"They're not sure. They think she's got some sort of growth in her stomach."

"Think? They don't know? They just think?"

"Guess not."

"Think? Guess? Mom, this is 1978. Leaches are a thing of the past. I mean, doctors should be able to do more than think and guess!"

"Laurie, I'm tired. I don't know anymore than what I've told you. I'll call you as soon as I hear something."

Thinking, guessing, not knowing? Great, I thought. Paul Simon was singing "Slip Sliddin' Away" on the radio as I hung up.

"The doctors did what?" I yelled twenty-four hours later.

"They took out her stomach, the entire stomach." Mother's voice sounded strangled through the wires. I could barely hear her.

"Mom, I'm getting echoes, I'm hearing myself say what I think I'm saying."

"Hold on," she said, her voice receding into the cables crossing the Pacific. "Hold on. I'll get an operator to connect us. This direct dialing is for the birds."

An operator to handle what? Operator, operation. My grandmother went in for a simple exploratory operation and came out minus a stomach. "How could you let them do that?" I blurted into the receiver when the second call came through. "She's 95 years old. How could you let them take out her entire stomach?"

"Please," my mother begged. "I didn't know what to do, the doctors said it had to be done to avoid the chance of a second surgery."

Well I'll say! I thought. "Did you get another opinion?"

"No, there wasn't any time, they told me her stomach needed to be removed immediately. They felt she wasn't strong enough to come out of one anesthetic and go into another a few days later."

I clasped my forehead between by thumb and middle finger. My mind is still within the confines of this skull, I thought. My reasoning is intact, but my emotions are not. I realized my grandmother, my idol, my saint, was going to die and there was absolutely not one thing I could do about it, but wait for that final, final moment. "Fuck you, Mother," I wanted to scream, "Fuck you. You allowed the invasion and the enemy will win."

"Should I come out?"

"No, no there's nothing you can do, just pray."

Sixty-three days later, my grandmother died. She never left the hospital. Mother kept me informed throughout. "Don't come," she'd tell me. "You don't want to see her this way. You need to remember our Bey the way she was." So I didn't. On June 29 Mother called. "Our lovely lady left us at about 8:25," she said. "Cynnie-Belle and I got there about ten minutes before to tell her good-bye. Please call those on the mainland who need to know," she said, her voice choking.

The phone calls managed to mask my feelings of absolute despair and emptiness. I felt like a sleepwalker, going through the motions of day-to-day life. I wanted to scream, but there was no place to go. Wherever I went, someone would hear. "You need to let go," said one of the social workers at Shelter House. "Just let go. Right now, it's all sitting inside of you, making you feel more miserable."

I was in my car when it began, softly at first, little mews that eventually evolved into wrenching screams. I scared myself. I couldn't stop the screams. When they finally subsided, I couldn't stop shaking. I managed to pull over, the street seemed deserted.

"I never got a last look, I never got a last look," I whispered. The pain, the pain was so personal, a sorrow too deep to describe. "Come back. Come back. What will I do without you," I moaned, echoing the words of the funeral I experienced on the slopes of Diamond Head so very long ago.

My grandmother was to be buried in Lebanon, Kentucky. Her family's plot adjoined my grandfather's family plot. It was a coincidence. My Great Uncle Billy, Bey's brother, still lived in Louisville. His next door neighbor, a Baptist minister, was chosen to conduct the service. Relatives arrived to pay their last respects. I made all the arrangements. My mother and sister, woozy from the long twelve-hour flight, had arrived first. My brother chose not to attend.

"We were plied with champagne," said Cynnie-Belle. She giggled, then belched as if I needed proof. "In here," she said, pointing to her flight bag. "Her ashes are in here."

I pictured a mound of soot piled on its bottom. I stepped back in expectation of ashes acting like ashes, swirling up and out into the open air. Cynnie-Belle loosened the zipper. "Isn't this pretty?" she asked as she pulled out an urn. "We picked it out, didn't we, Dot?"

"Yes," said Mother. "It was easy to choose an urn, easier than a coffin. Those coffins look so much alike."

I stared at my mother. She looked tired and defeated. "You've been through so much, Mom." I gave her a hug.

"Do you realize it was six months to the day of Benny's death? Six months exactly." She took off her glasses, wiped her eyes with her right fist, before giving in to weeping.

Arrivals are supposed to be happy, I thought. This was like no arrival I had ever experienced. A final approach, so to speak. "Let's go," I said, "It's going to be a long two days." Tears sprang to my eyes; it happens when I see other people cry.

Relatives trickled in throughout the day. I put them up at the Holiday Inn on River Road, the one across from Cox Park. The next morning, the procession left for Ryder Cemetery in Lebanon.

Butterflies, my grandmother loved butterflies. She collected them, not real ones but things symbolic. Not symbols, like casketed bodies, but knick-knacks having to do with butterflies.

My grandmother loved butterflies. We all knew it and knocked ourselves out to find perfect butterfly gifts for her.

We brought her coasters, dress pins, scarves, mobiles, whatever pertained to butterflies. She received nothing gaudy or tacky. As children, with a metal strip box of water colors, we'd try to out-do each other in our personal renditions of the insect. Maybe she chose to love butterflies because they were an easy subject for kids to draw or paint. Probably she chose them for their simple beauty and sense of freedom. Up until her death, my grandmother kept a bag packed under her bed. "In case anyone asks me to go anywhere. I'm always ready," she would say with a twinkle in her China-blue eyes. Butterflies, beauties that alight on flowers during the rebirth time of year.

We drove to Ryder Cemetery, gathered around my grandmother's urn, which sat on a table. Next to it was the headstone for my grandfather's grave. Her urn was draped and surrounded with leis personally brought or sent from the islands. Larger bouquets encircled the area where we stood. The day was beautiful, clear skies, a warm sun, a gentle breeze. Birds were twittering. God gave her a good one, I thought.

The Baptist minister gave a moving service. He did a magnificent job having never met the lady. "Cynnie-Belle," he said when he was through, "has written something she'd like to share with us."

Cynnie-Belle stood up and faced the crowd. "You can't leave us," she read. "We'll know you're still around, perhaps in someone else's smile, and sure—we'll miss you, that won't stop. You may not be here now, but since you're gone we'll know your beauty on our paths. We bathe you now in tears to send you on your way. Tiny prisms on a shining shroud. We'll know the sameness of the dust, and you will be locked into our hearts forever. So much beauty cannot ever fade away. We don't believe in good-byes, just changing shapes. We'll be looking toward you, gentle lady, and for a sign from time to time."

At that very moment, two large monarch butterflies alighted on the urn and paused for a brief second before ascending into the blue skies. A unified gasp rang out, then there was silence, a silence so reverent, so spiritual that minutes passed before the minister simply said "Amen."

Each of us believed the pause and passing of the butterflies was an individual experience. No one said anything until later. Notes compared, we breathed a collective sigh of relief. It was going to be okay. We were all going to get through the loss. The entourage returned to my house for food and spirits of another sort. Of the immediate family, only Bruce didn't make the trip. It was the last time most of us would be together. Once my grandmother died, so did the networking of relatives, scads of whom were not at her funeral, but appeared to pay homage when we returned to Montclair.

Dot, my mother and sticky little dots, a variety of colors I used to mark the contents of the house on High Street. My mother and I flew up the day after the funeral. Everyone else went home.

I labeled my grandmother's possessions, room by room. Mother held court with the stream of sympathizers. When I would ask her to help, she suffered twirling indecision. She spun around the room, distraught and in grief. I took charge. She fell apart. Petty arguments began. Mother would start crying. I stifled the rage I felt, grabbed the circles of color, and continued cataloging the final destinations of my grandmother's possessions. I got real tired of it all very quickly. Montclair was breaking down, as was my relationship with my mother. By the time I left two weeks later, the cold war between us had begun. I had thought I was through cleaning up after her. I wasn't. I resented the responsibility laid on me. Mother was the child; I was the adult. Madge eased the rifts between us, took me aside, calmed me down. If that didn't cover particular points of contention, Madge would start crying and I'd back off.

Distant relatives appeared with requests for certain items.

Luckily, my grandmother kept a list of bequests in a large binder. Fights between Uncle Duke and Mother weren't so easily set aside. A silver water pitcher and a portrait of my grandmother and her three sisters, painted when they were young girls, were two particular items which caused a battle. Duke had made off with both items years before and he wasn't about to let my mother have them now. There was nothing she could do except hiss at him over the phone. He was in California. She was not.

I didn't know how to handle all the books. I went through them, chose those I thought were worth something. Most were of a sentimental nature. I called a few old book stores. "If they're not first editions, we're not interested," I was told. Finally, someone came out and carted all of them away. I think he gave us $500. Maybe it was $300.

Princeton officials arrived a few days before I left. Decent of them. Emery, Madge's brother who chauffeured my grandparents for almost fifty years, announced their arrival. My mother was gone. It was all too much for her. She fled, opting for a few days in Atlantic City. She went with her high school friends. "My Scouts," she called them. "My Scouts and I are going to play for a couple of days. I have to get out of here. I am exhausted."

My grandmother donated her 18 acre estate to Princeton. She gave it to them long before anyone could even remotely fathom her death. Officials came to claim the property, check out the perimeters, see if it would, indeed, qualify for the faculty retreat they guaranteed when the contribution was being sought. I marched the two men across the fields. We strode north, south, east, and west. They spent time admiring the gatehouse, a house built before the turn of the century, maybe way before the turn of the century. It reminded me of something Paul Revere would gallop past on his way to warn someone about something. I loved the way the gatehouse smelled, dank and musty and reeking of history. The men acted like they cared. They did not. They were doing a job. I was trying hard to keep myself intact. They came. They saw. They left. I hated those two men as much as I had hated Mr. Glessner when he hit and killed the dog.

Emery drove me to the airport. First he fixed a dress of mine. Emery put on a pair of my grandmother's glasses, sat in the chair she napped in, a recliner, and proceeded to sew an errant button in place.

Every time I visited, Emery would be there to "fetch me" at the airport. We rode in silence through Newark during the riots of the '60s. Sometimes his back-street routes were terrifying. During college, Emery encouraged me to persevere when I'd get discouraged over my blind date. "Be cool, Miss Laurie," he'd say. "That boy will come around and marry you. He's a mighty fine person." Emery would tell me this during the mini-weekend retreats I'd take to Montclair.

Emery, Emery was my rock of Gibraltar, a living, breathing, walking, talking bundle of trust. "Miss Dorothy," he said a few days before I left. "Miss Dorothy's had it rough. Baby, you need to take care of her not fight her. Miss Laurie, you're different, stronger than all of them. She needs all your help right now."

I thought, briefly, of telling him about the father business. But I was too tired, the story too long. It would hurt him to know, I thought. Emery loved Miss Dorothy. To him, my mother was still a little girl.

Drained. I was so drained and so sad when we pulled away. Inside the house, I left my mother groupings of furniture, piles identified by their colored dots, dinnerware, things relating to the necessities of existence. Emery and I drove off. Before we left, I had spent the entire morning walking the grounds, taking pictures. I documented the estate in detail. I made sure there was no need for a last look.

During the flight home, I conjured up all the injustices inflicted on me by my mother, now the slot machine queen of Atlantic City.

July 21st, 1978
Arriving Hong Kong

Dear Laurie,

I'm glad you wrote when you did because I didn't get the letter until just before we left Guam, over a week to get there. There have been delays in most places, 4 days in Honolulu and 3 in Guam but supposed to leave Hong Kong tomorrow night. We dock early tomorrow morning.

As I write this you may still be in Montclair and I think of all the burden you've been carrying these past few weeks. It makes me feel so helpless and I can understand all, about how heart breaking it is for you to close up the place in Montclair and all the memories which you are reliving from day to day. Some consoling thoughts are your work and accomplishments there in Louisville and knowing within yourself that you are strong enough to do what you've been called upon to do. It makes me feel proud and good when you tell me about your work and the satisfaction you get from it. I'm looking forward to our getting together again. If you are home I hope to get there after this trip. The trip is lasting so long I don't think I can take two, even should I get off on the west coast. The vacation would still overlap. So it looks like I will be home about Aug. 17th for one trip and then perhaps take two this winter. So am wondering if you think you might go to Honolulu in August. We are scheduled to sail directly to Panama from Yokohama and not stop there in the Canal either. The first stop will be Savannah. So I can't phone you until then unless I make some call over the ham set. I really don't care much about phone calls over that but I might call you in a few days just to find if you are going to Hawaii or not. Unless I do get a letter from you in Japan next week. If I do it (my call) may come from some other state than Ky.

That little set has been a source of pleasure for me here. I've been talking back to guys on the east coast most every night and tonight fulfilled my one ambition with it. I talked to two fellows on the east coast. It was 7.30 P.M. here and 7:30 A.M. there. One was in Ossening, N.Y. and the other in Fairfield, N.J. down near Montclair. We were only about 100 miles outside of Hong Kong Harbor. When I look at it, it seems impossible that that little thing could reach all way back to N.J. You remember how small it is. It would be fun to have John see it work.

Tomorrow in Hong Kong the heat and humidity will be overwhelming. That is one of the worse climates on earth during July and August. There is nothing special to do.

Talked to a fellow in Hilo tonight and was told the typhoon was about 170 miles south of him so no danger to the Honolulu area.

Called my neighbors from Guam and was told the guy is taking good care of the lawn and house OK so far. Neighbors just sold their house so will be gone to Fla when I get back and I'll miss them. They have certainly been good to me. The son has been superintendent of the Butler High School and last summer when the guy that mowed the lawn took off and disappeared this fellow did it for me all summer.

If I don't get a letter from you in Japan, Laurie, and I really don't expect any because of every thing I will get to you by radio just to find out if you still are in Louisville when I get back or have gone to Hawaii.

Love,
De

1979

THE PHONE RANG JUST BEFORE DINNER on January 2, 1979. It was my mother. "You'll never guess what happened this morning. Cousin Stephen came over, said Tony Orlando was on the beach. Well you know how I love Tony Orlando, so I called Skoshi and out we went for a look-and-see walk. I've gotten to be an expert, you know."

She had. She caught a glimpse of Elvis Presley through his bodyguards when he was renting our old home. Whenever "Hawaii Five-O" crews filmed in the area, my mother often managed split-second background appearances. Just before Christmas, a rescue squad and helicopter made a dramatic save. My mother wrapped the victim in a blanket and rendered first aid. "My blanket's picture is on the front page of this morning's paper," she had told me the day after it happened.

"Go on, then what."

"Tony was standing in front of Cecily's. I rushed up all smiles, holding Skoshi. He was so nice about the whole thing. He couldn't have been more gracious. Of course, I was dying of embarrassment."

"Wait, wait, Mom, I missed something."

"Skoshi bit him," Mother said in mock horror. "He went to pet her. 'What a cute dog,' he said, and Skoshi bit him. Luckily it was only his hand, but had he been any closer, it could have been his face."

I chuckled, picturing the scene. The subject changed. I

listened to her talk about Cynnie-Belle's latest boy friend, Pat. Pat was always moving in or out of Cynnie-Belle's home.

"I felt sorry for him." Mother said. "He came over last night at six and didn't leave until nine. I must say, I felt sorrier for him at six then I did at nine."

"I don't think Pat should be living with Cynnie-Belle at all. She has three kids still living at home, it's not right." I could feel my anger surfacing.

It was then she lit into me. "Don't be such a prude, Laurie. You're always acting holier-than-thou."

"I'm holier-than-thou," I said, "because I speak from experience. I know what it feels like to have an errant mother." It was out before I knew it. There was no turning back.

"How dare you say that to me. I was an excellent mother, so is Cynnie-Belle. Her kids are wonderful."

I agreed. "Her kids are wonderful, but she is so self-centered. She does what makes her happy, skiing trips to Utah, fun weekends away. When she is home, she parties. She's just like you." I wanted to add, "And has about the same taste in men," but did not. It wasn't a fair statement. Cynnie-Belle's men were good-looking and smart.

"Don't start," Mother warned. "All three of you kids think I was a bad mother. I was never a bad mother."

"If all three of us think so, can you entertain the notion that, perhaps, you just might have been? You were good to everyone else's kids, paid them loads of attention. You simply ignored your own."

The conversation deteriorated. I brought up the financial support she afforded my sister and her family.

"I do it for her kids. If I don't help, she may turn them against me."

"Don't give me that bullshit," I yelled. "You own her and, in return, she drives you around. Pretty expensive piece of equipment. Be cheaper to find Herman!" I was furious and slammed down the phone.

Herman, I thought. God, I had forgotten about Herman. Herman the taxi driver. Herman's car did not look like a taxi. It wasn't yellow. It was a green, somewhere between chartreuse and a dark green. Herman's daughter, Frauxy for Foxy, often came with him. She would stand up in the front seat and watch me thump in the back. I'd thump, bang my head against the back seat in time with the music. I could hear the Mills Brothers sing, "Glow Little Glow Worm." That was it, I realized, the color of Herman's car. A glow-worm green with fins in two tones. I wondered whatever happened to him.

My mother and I did not communicate for weeks. The weeks turned into months.

Madge, who moved in with Mom after my grandmother's death, spent two dollars on a special delivery stamp. She placed the stamp on a letter addressed to me, scotch taped the seal and put it in the mail. A butterfly on flowers was etched to the left of my address. Inside, this explanation:

> "The design on this note was drawn by Debbie, who prior to her paralysis, was an artist. Through perseverance, Debbie trained herself to draw by holding a pencil between her teeth. Each original drawing takes up to two months to complete."

Wow, that's really something. I pictured Debbie working away under adverse circumstances before I read the letter.

> "My dear Laurie thinking of you all so much these days. I hope fine with so much bad weather but I guess John had a good time. I am fine and so glad to be here. We miss you all. It seems so long since you call I hope you all are well. You know Laurie how I feel about you: so please write me. You know me

and my feeling . . . should I say more. We miss heareing from
you. Our weather has not been to good lots of rain. Like your
little cottage the big house is better for you all. I don't no what
is roung but I do no your mother misses your call we all do.
You know I love you all way did and all ways will. Kiss John
for me.

My love Madge."

I didn't think my mother put Madge up to writing the letter, but I wasn't sure. A few days later, I wrote Madge. I thanked her for her concerns and assured her of my love. Everyone is fine, I wrote, don't worry. I made no mention of my mother. I was still too angry.

My grandmother's brother, my Great Uncle Billy, was diagnosed with cancer in March. He lived in Louisville most of his life. When my brother entered college in 1961, he lived with Uncle Billy for awhile. But Uncle Billy married Frances and my brother moved out. Frances loved Billy Graham. Bruce loved Goldwater. It didn't take long for the two to detest each other. Bruce began calling her Black Frances. The nickname, unbeknownst to her, stuck.

I was with Uncle Billy when he received the diagnosis as was Billy's neighbor, the minister. We left the hospital together.

"I can't believe it," I said. We were in the elevator. "He was going to travel, enjoy the money my grandmother left him. What a rotten thing to happen."

"Life is a gift. You take it one day at a time."

"I guess," I replied. "My mother always said when the man upstairs calls, you go."

My mother. The silence remained between us. I'd also managed to keep phone calls with De to a minimum. I'm an accomplished isolationist, I thought proudly. Who needs them?

My pride got tested a few days later. "Your mother phoned," said Barret. "She wants you to call her back."

"Damn, just damn it," I whispered. I was furious. "Shit, she's making me reciprocate. Probably called when she knew I wouldn't be home." Her voice tape played in my head. "You will do as I say, and you will do it now." I waited a few hours before dialing. I had an unbelievable hope she wouldn't be home. Hopes were dashed on the second ring.

"Let's drop this Mexican stand-off. Uncle Billy called with his news. What do you know."

Uncle Billy's health became our neutral territory. I was cordial, although aloof. I'd call my mother and she would listen to my intense involvement with Billy and his disease. Then, as if tired of death, she'd change the subject. She talked of all the zany things happening among her many visitors. I never phoned to find her alone. "It's like Grand Central Station," she told me. "Hoards of humanity pass through all day and into the night." My mother was not complaining. She was letting me know that life goes on with or without my presence or my approval.

Uncle Billy was furious about his condition. His wife, Frances, received his wrath. The doctors gave him three months, he lived eight. I became his soul mate and saw it through until the end. We took trips to the family cemetery in Lebanon. "I want to be buried right here," he said and pointed to a place next to the grave of his first wife. "I want to be next to her, the mother of my two boys."

In helplessness, I watched Billy's deterioration. I took him books to read until he could no longer hold them. I prepared dishes to eat, morsels which wouldn't affect the chemotherapy sores in his mouth. I listened to the gurgling as he sucked strawberry soup. I watched him treat Frances like dirt. I tried my best to run interference. I didn't do much good. For consolation, I sneaked bottles of sherry to her. I'd sit and listen to

Frances while she drank and smoked and Billy lay beached in his bedroom.

One time he told me, "I don't feel comfortable in anything but a tub full of water. It's the only time my body feels somewhat normal."

"I know exactly what you mean," I sympathized, remembering the aftermath of John's birth.

Frances called November 6. It was election day. "I had him taken to the hospital last night, I couldn't get him out of the bath. EMS came. It was awful."

"How is he?"

"I don't know, I didn't go with him. He was saying terrible things to me. I can't take anymore, Laurie."

Billy's sons arrived. They moved him into a nursing home. Billy blamed the decision on Frances. "She's strong enough. She could have lifted me out. She didn't want to, that's all."

I did not blame her. He was too much for her to handle, physically and emotionally. He was also wearing on my nerves.

"I want to see my dog," he demanded.

I took his dog to the nursing home. I stood outside and held the dog up to the window. The dog was hyper. I was afraid it would try to dive through the glass. The visual contact, however, made no sense to the animal. I returned to the car covered with scratches. "What am I doing?" I asked aloud. What was I doing? Making up for missing the death of my grandmother?

One day I arrived in time to see a nurse drag Billy across the floor to a chair. His useless legs brushed the carpet. "Old granddaddies don't die, they just disintegrate," he said as I watched. My mother was right, I thought. I'm glad I didn't see my grandmother at the end.

On November 17, I wrote: "The following lists are suggestions as to the allocation of personal items of William C. Rogers recited to me in the presence of his wife Frances and grandson Steve."

Billy began to cry when he got to the disbursement of his beloved duck decoys.

"I'm really exhausted," I told my mother. I wanted her to know all I was doing. I wanted her to make me a saint, but she didn't. She is probably still mad at the Vatican for doing away with St. Christopher, I thought in justification. When Mom heard old Chris was no longer a saint, she personally deposed the pope.

The coma began late in the afternoon. "I'll be right back," I told Billy. "I've got to get John, feed him, then I'll come back."

His lips had shrunk away from his teeth. His skin, gray-green in color, pulled tight across his face.

"Don't go," he mouthed. "Don't go."

His eyes, wide with fright, looked to be bathed in milk. He reached his skeletal arms in my direction and mumbled something else. I didn't know what he was saying. I couldn't understand him. "What, what did you say?"

He tried again and failed. I started to panic. I looked to his nurse for help.

"I'm going off duty," she said, "In one hour."

My God. He'll be alone. He can't be alone. "Can the agency send someone over?"

"Call them," she replied.

I looked at Billy. He was mouthing more words, words I couldn't understand.

"Please, talk slowly, I don't know what you're saying." Indecipherable whispers fell into the confusion of my mind. Make me understand. Oh God, make me understand. But God did not. God left me alone to utter assurances, assurances of my return in, max, sixty minutes.

I backed out the door, blowing kisses and calling, "I'll be right there. I promise. Hang on. It will be all right." In my mind, I listed the things I had to do within the hour—find a nurse, call his sons, settle John somewhere. The dog's walk would have to wait.

I did manage to accomplish my tasks in less than an hour. I remembered Frances last, and called. "I think he might die tonight," I told her.

"I know," she said, "The nursing home called. I can't go there anymore. I can't. I just can't."

I returned to the scene. I inhaled sickening sweet smells, odors of the infirm, odors of antiseptic masking urine. I remembered the TB hospital in Kaimuki. Holding my breath is not going to work in here, I thought, as I headed toward Billy.

I passed an empty room. A few weeks earlier its occupant had stopped me. She seemed like a sweet old lady. "Come," she had said, gesturing for me to enter. I went in. Alone, she looked me straight in the eyes. "You are not who you say you are." She wagged her finger at me. "You are an impostor. You are pretend, a fake," she hissed.

"You are right," I answered. "I am." I left the room.

She was right, she was absolutely right. I am not a real me. I was supposed to be a cowgirl or singer. Hell, I'd still opt for mermaid, but they, too, aren't real. Figments of my imagination, that's what I am, a figment of the imagination. I felt guilt and relief in knowing it would soon be over. I was tired of the smells and staleness that engulfed me, clung to my clothes long after I left the place.

A new nurse had arrived and, to my sheer relief, the minister. Billy was a slim mound between white sheets. His breathing labored with thick bubbles. He sounded like Bozo. A Bozo no longer capable of asking me to turn the page.

"He's deeper into a coma," said the minister.

"He's going to die tomorrow," I replied.

"He may not, he could linger for awhile."

"No," I shook my head. "He'll die tomorrow."

"How do you know that?"

"Because, in a few hours it will be Thursday, the twenty-ninth. It comes in threes."

216

"Threes?"

"Yes," I said, weary beyond belief. "Benny, my mother's husband, died on the twenty-ninth. So did my grandmother. Tomorrow's the twenty-ninth."

The minister took me for some coffee. "My mother always warned me not to drown in middle-class America," I said. I had given him a capsule of my life.

"You'll never drown in middle-class America," the minister said, laughing. "You may tread water for a few days, but you'll never drown."

"You mean there will always be someone or something to turn a page for me?"

"Turn a page? What do you mean?"

"Nothing," I replied. "Right now it means nothing."

When we returned, Uncle Billy's breath had eased. He snoozed in child-like innocence.

"I shouldn't have left this afternoon. He was trying to tell me something. He didn't want me to leave. I need to help him now. I need to tell him that the man upstairs is calling," I said as I crawled on the hospital bed and wrapped myself around his fetal position. I whispered into his exposed ear, "Let go, it's OK to let go. It's all over now, all the pain, all the anger. Relax, give it up, let go. Please tell my grandmother, when you get there, that I'm sorry I didn't get the last look. Tell her I helped take you out, that I love and miss her as I love and will miss you."

"Come. Come with me, Laurie," said the minister. "Please, come with me." He tugged, then pulled me gently off the bed. "You're exhausted. You need to go home. You need to rest. I'll stay here, you go, get some sleep." It was 11:30 pm when he walked me to my car.

The phone rang an hour and fifty minutes later. There was never any doubt, it was not a "what now?" No, it was not a "what now," merely another "now what."

I called Mother two days after Billy died. "His funeral was lovely," I told her. "The minister did another wonderful job."

"Good, I knew he would. Hold on a minute." I could hear her say, "Look in the cabinet at the foot of the stairs."

"What's going on?" I asked.

"I'm getting my silver together, the house apes are here helping me."

The house apes were my nieces and nephews.

"Why?"

"I'm going to sell it."

"Why?"

"I never use it. And if I don't it will probably be stolen eventually. Besides, I could stand the extra cash."

"What about the silver punch bowl and goblets you use for the egg nog parties?"

"Laurie, I haven't had an egg nog party in years. Furthermore, I'm never again going to have one. They got so out of hand when you and Bruce were in high school."

She was right. They did get out of hand. Every teenager in town crashed. Still, I felt she could find another use for the sterling service.

"I had my emerald and sapphire rings appraised," Mother continued. "The emerald is worth $15,000 and the sapphires around $22,000 each. My father bought two sapphires in Ceylon. I'm giving Cynnie-Belle the ring and letting you have the pin. The emerald I think I'll sell."

"Why do you need the extra cash?" My voice steady, my emotions not. I buried Billy this morning. I buried your mother's brother and you don't care, I thought. Mad images of the past eight months flashed before me. I, who hated the circus, became a pro juggler, throwing one task into the air while I completed another. I cooked, I cleaned, I drove car pools, and walked the dog. I was involved in all aspects of Shelter House and its Board.

I created a public awareness campaign for the State Crime Commission. I entertained friends. I took care of Billy and I took care of Billy and I took care of Billy.

"Market's down. I've lost quite a bit of money." And, as if to goad, she added, "Cynnie-Belle's in Utah skiing. I need to go now, I've got the kids' dinner on the stove."

"I got $625.00 for the silver," she told me when I phoned New Year's Eve. "I also took some broken chains and stuff to Mr. Gold and netted $225.00. How about that?"

"How about that?" she asked. "How about that!" I answered.

1980

OTHER THAN THE ERUPTION of Mount St. Helens, 1980 was not an earth-shattering year. I enrolled in graduate school, aimed for a degree in Community Development. My classes were on Friday nights. I was in no hurry.

In July, Mom celebrated her 65th and I celebrated my 34th birthday. Cynnie-Belle gave the two of us a party. My sister actually located two of my old friends, Gloria and Wendy. They were my surprise. Big of my sister, I thought. The rest of the crowd consisted of relatives, neighbors, and my sister's gang which, in effect, was also Mother's.

Mom carried a sign that read "Makule Power." Translated, it meant "power to the elderly" or words to that effect. She carried it with her all evening. She paused and posed for pictures. Mother didn't need a sign, her power was visible enough.

Mom's surprise was a portrait of Skoshi. The same lady who did ours in the early 50s, did the dog. Actually, the artist's rendition of Skoshi was similar to her renditions of Cynnie-Belle, Bruce, and me. Our pictures looked as if our only differences were hair, eye, and dress. Mom hung Cynnie-Belle and Bruce next to each other. I was nailed on a lone wall in the dining room.

"Don't mention it to Mom," I whispered to my sister. "But the dog looks like us Ameses."

Cynnie-Belle snickered. "You're right."

I'd momentarily forgotten I was not an Ames.

The party-goers loved the painting as much as Mother did. "Sko-shi, Sko-shi, Sko-shi," they chanted after it was unveiled. "Makule Power," yelled Mom, pushing and pulling her sign into the air. The next morning, Skoshi's portrait was placed on an easel in the living room. No matter what door you came through, no one, I mean no one, could miss seeing it.

I stayed a month, during which time I let loose and learned to party with the rest of them. Them. I shall now call "them" kitchen additions, those who sat around my mother's kitchen table, sometimes from sundown to sundown. They came alone, in pairs, en masse. Party dolls, overgrown delinquents out for good fun. They were the in-crowd, spill-overs from the Out-rigger. Laughter was a given and, in spite of my resentment, I joined in the hilarity. It was a whole lot easier to laugh than keep up the continual criticism of my sister's lifestyle.

I did accomplish a few useful things during my stay. I took John to visit Ellen. The family she worked for lived on Diamond Head. Their house sat above the old stables. I stopped by the Jardines and saw Dina. She filled me in on Billy, who lived with his family on the big island of Hawaii. I saw the Buschers, but I saw them a lot. When the kitchen additions weren't at my mother's, they were usually sunning on the Buschers' front yard. I called on Mrs. Israel. Mr. Israel was dead. I did not see Robbie. I went to dinner with Roger and Mary. I paid. My mother and I took Aunt Libby to lunch.

One afternoon I was on the beach when I heard her call, "Laurie, look who's here." I turned to see her coming down the front steps. Larry Vincente was behind her. He looked pretty much as I remembered.

"Hey, Dottie," he said. "That's Laurie? Where went the fat kid? She's tall and skinny now, eh?" All his words were directed to Mom. It was as if I didn't exist.

"Isn't she something," Mother agreed.

I stood there, self conscious in my bikini. "I'm here folks" I wanted to say. I say "folks" when I'm in the islands, "you all" in Kentucky, and "you guys" when I'm up north. You-hoo, tell the Yahoo he can talk directly to me, I thought as I stood there. Actually, I could have said it out loud.

Mother and Larry continued their Chip-n-Dale conversation. "She has been thin a long time, baby fat when you last saw Laurie."

"Dottie, but when did she get beautiful?"

Beautiful? I never ever thought of myself as beautiful, much less getting beautiful. Being fat left me with a great sense of humor. But beautiful? I never entertained the notion. The summer we moved into Grandmother's house, Billy Jardine went to Europe. He sent me postcards. One was a picture of Bacchus, party god, straddling a turtle. Bacchus, nude and obese, rested one hand on his hip, the other reached out as if he were saying, "Wait a minute." Water pours from the turtle's mouth. Red flowers crawl upon the garden wall behind him. They look fake.

"This is our guide leading us through Italy. My turtle is very bouncy, thus I find this post card difficult to write. The weather is here. I wish you were beautiful," wrote Billy. Funny, I'd forgotten about that card. At the time, I wished I were beautiful too.

"Hey," I said to Larry. "I also have terrific legs!"

I returned to normal when Barret arrived. The American Bar Association was holding its annual meeting in Honolulu. We entertained, along with Bruce, lawyers we knew from Louisville.

1981

"I'm giving Cynnie-Belle a fortieth birthday party," Mother announced on New Years Day. I had called to wish her a happy. "It's going to be the biggest and best party ever! Bruce and I decided to go country. He's finding a band, Stanton's looking for a stagecoach." My cousin, Stanton, was in productions. If anyone could find a stagecoach, it would have to be he.

"We're going to have it at Cully's." Cully lived next door to Cynnie-Belle. He had a large yard. My sister's yard was taken up by a patio and pool. "Believe me," she continued, "it's going to be a first-class blast. You have got to come."

I don't got to do anything, I thought. I felt as if I were being turned inside out. I was not in an expansive mood. Mom had sent the Ceylon sapphire pin to me and I'd finally taken it to a jeweler over the holidays. I was told the stone was severely flawed, too flawed to use.

"Here," said the jeweler, "look at this." He held the stone up to a light. Nine-tenths of the five carats showed smudge. It looked as if someone had smeared vaseline in its middle. "The four little diamonds on the pin are worth more than this stone," he said. I had no desire to be out-shined by Cynnie-Belle again.

"Oh," Mother continued. "I got so caught up in the party, I forgot to tell you."

"Tell me what?" I asked.

"Tommy's dead,"

Good I thought, a subject other than Cynnie-Belle. "Tommy who?"

"Tommy, your old boyfriend. Bruce heard about it. Said he was shot in LA on his way to arraignment. He was in police custody, someone jumped out of a crowd and gunned him down."

"He was no good, Mom, we knew that."

"But he was so nice to me after you left."

"Mom, lest you forget, he was the prime suspect in Aunt Cecily's robbery." Tommy had appeared in the islands in 1976. Stanton let him stay with him. Tommy was there long enough to get the lay of the land. We all assumed he robbed Cecily's house. She had been out of town. When she got back, her silver and jewelry were missing. So was Tommy.

"Laurie, we can't be sure he did it."

"He did it, believe me he did it, tried to fence a gold necklace through me. He wrote a letter, asked me to sell the necklace. I sent it back with words to the effect of, "How dumb do you think I am?" Dumb enough to date him for a year, I thought. Dumb enough to put up with his verbal abuse.

"You know, Mom, he was often mean to me. He phoned once while he was at Stanton's. I asked him why. He said he was afraid I'd leave him. Maybe if he were nice, I would have stayed. Maybe he wouldn't have spent 18 months in a Pakistani jail for smuggling dope. Maybe he wouldn't have joined the Foreign Legion. Maybe he'd still be alive."

"Maybe if I had tried to break you two up, you'd have married him."

Maybe she was right.

I begged out of the invitation. I used school as my excuse and thanked her for offering to pay for my flight. "I'm working on my master's, Mom," I told her when she jumped on my case. "Classes are on Friday nights. Missing one would be like missing a month," I said, stretching the truth for a good story. There was no way in hell I would witness another display of lavish attention heaped on my sister. I was sick of hearing about her. I was sick of her boyfriends. I had had it. Besides, no one in my immediate family attended my "Dirty Thirty" party five years before. The only relative who came was Stanton. He flew in as a surprise. It was quite a party. The dirty tricks committee found a wooden cake that was large enough to conceal a three-hundred-pound, thirty-year-old virgin male who popped out of the structure at midnight. He wore a bonnet and a diaper, nothing else. I laughed so hard I wet my pants.

Mother sent me the newspaper articles on my sister's party. Photographs and copy described traffic being tied up for over an hour as the stagecoach made its way slowly down Kahala Avenue. In it rode Mother, my brother, his wife, Stanton, and Madge, all decked out as cool dudes. The stagecoach was a surprise to Cynnie-Belle. A note accompanying the clippings read, "Of course the part about the cow manure is, well, cow manure. We had bales of hay—but the columnists always have to get cute."

Cute? I wondered. Sounded like a lot of bullshit to me.

Shortly after my sister's birthday, Mom called. "My class from high school is having our Fiftieth Reunion. How about going to Montclair with me in June?"

I didn't hesitate. "Sure, that will be a hoot!"

Emery picked us up at the airport. His car sported a bumper sticker which read, M.H.S '31 REUNION June12 I AM BACK! Mother squealed with delight when she saw it.

"Old Man River! It's wonderful," she said. "I love it. Montclair High School, I am back!"

We drove through the town. Welcome home signs plastered many storefronts. Mom's class must have been something, I thought. We stayed at the newly renovated Marlboro Inn, a place we passed all the time when Bey was alive. The "Scouts," Mom's best friends, were on their feet cheering as we drove in.

"Here," said Gert Dinkel as we got out of the car. "Wear this." She pitched Mother a T-shirt. OURS IS THE FUTURE was stitched across the front. Underneath was written, IT'S HERE.

"God, our motto, and now it's here.

"Compliments of the publicity committee," Gert told her.

The first day, while the Scouts attended committee meetings, De picked me up and we drove to Pompton Lakes. It hadn't changed a bit, everything was the same, quiet and boring. Boring like De.

"How are you fixed for suitcases?" he asked. "The purser on my ship told me he could get some cheap. Shit, suitcases are about the last thing in life I need. I have a whole closet full. But I said, "Okay, get me a couple." I didn't want to offend him, we're good friends. He says they're blue and say 'Samsonite' on the tag. The trim's pretty nice. I guess Samsonite means plastic."

"Gee, that's nice of you to ask," I said, "but I, too, have more than my share of luggage." I pictured me in an airport toting plastic bags to the counter, as I had thirty years before.

The conversations went along like that all day. I had nothing to say to him, we had nothing in common. He was a chore. I wanted to be back in Montclair where I belonged. I did not want to be with him. I felt relieved when he dropped me off. I never saw or spoke to him again. Later he started phoning my mother. Actually, I think she called him first. Whatever, she told me he knew he didn't belong in my life. "He's going to leave you alone," she said.

"Thank goodness," I replied.

Before we left, Mother took me to Frances Rose's. Frances Rose's was a tradition between us when we met in Montclair. We'd go to the wonderful boutique and my mother would buy me an outfit. It always made me feel special.

In December Emery's wife, Ruth, died. "I want you to go to the funeral. I want you to represent the family," Mother said when she phoned with the news. It made me mad. It had been an exhausting fall with my taking a flurry of flights around the country attending conferences and workshops on juvenile justice. Then there was school. A trip to Montclair was an inconvenience, but I went. I left at six in the morning and spent fifty dollars on cab fare getting from the Newark Airport to Emery's. We did not go to the old home site during Mom's reunion. I was apprehensive, not knowing what I expected to see. Princeton finally sold the eighteen acres, which included the main and gate houses, to a developer for $250,000. So much for a faculty retreat.

My mother's Scouts and a few relatives attended Ruth's funeral. My cousin Diane came up from New York City and together we rode to the cemetery. We got hopelessly lost on the way and returned to Emery's to wait.

"Let's walk up to the house," I said.

"I can't," she replied, shaking her head. "I just can't."

I sensed tears. "Don't," I told her. "You'll make me start. If I start, I won't stop." I got out of the car. A blast of cold air hit me. "I'm going over there."

My grandmother's house was a mockery. It's tenant had store-bought electric lamp posts placed around the circular drive. They were connected by a string of extension cords that lay exposed on the ground. To the left of the front door stood a garage. It looked like a large packing crate. It might even have been one. All the blinds were drawn, as if there were something to hide. It was too ludicrous to make me sad. By the time I walked back, the mourners had arrived.

I left for the airport before it got dark. I didn't get to see the lamp posts light up. Probably just as well, I thought, thankful that my grandmother would never have to see such a sight. My grandfather started off as a lamplighter in Kentucky.

1982

"I CALLED TO SEE HOW CYNNIE-BELLE'S DOING." My sister had her eyes done. I wasn't sure what was wrong with them except a slight puffiness.

"She looks dreadful, all black and blue. It's as if someone punched her out."

You should know, I thought. My lower lip's getting pretty fat what with all the biting I do. Such a wimp, Laurie. Either you're terrified to confront her or you blurt it out.

"I thought the bags under her eyes were due to a lack of sleep. She does party a lot, Mom."

"You're right, but you know Cynnie-Belle. Remember that tummy tuck she had after the twins were born? Speaking of tired, I've been pretty tired myself lately. Probably cause Skoshi's got cystitis and she keeps me up all night. She either has to go or wets the bed, then I'm up changing sheets at 3 a.m."

"We've had wild weather," she continued, changing the subject abruptly. "The worst electrical storm I've ever seen, centered directly above the house. We've never had electrical storms, it's always been heat lightning. Remember how we'd count one, one thousand, two, one thousand, three, one thousand until we heard the thunder? This storm was like a Montclair storm."

"I sure do," I replied. "It sounded as if God were rolling a bowling ball across the sky." I pictured our old-fashioned storms. We'd stand in the front yard and watch them recede out to sea.

When they were over, we'd return to more important things in life, like existing, unaware of the rest of the world and other kinds of storms. Only we, we were the ones who counted. We were on an island in the middle of the Pacific Ocean.

"Well, give Cynnie-Belle my love," I said. "And you get some sleep!"

"I will, and I'm sure she'll be fine in a few days. Bob's been terrific to her. He's really a dear."

Bob was my sister's latest boyfriend. He was an undercover cop. It bothered Bruce. When told of the problems between my siblings, I made my mother clarify the term "undercover."

A few days later, I tracked down my brother. He was not an easy person to phone. I wanted to make sure Mom was all right. She sounded more tired than she was letting on.

"She seems tired, but I really do think it has something to do with Skoshi. By the way, your sister's eyes are so slanted, she looks like a Kabuki dancer," he said and hung up. My brother is a man of few words. I thought about Cynnie-Belle looking exotic, probably no more so than when I pulled my eyes into focus as a child. She just didn't have an index finger involved.

My brother loved to sail. He spent six months touring the South Seas. So when he planned a trip to Palmyra Island, no one gave it much thought. He was anxious to test his new 54-foot yawl, the Posidon. My mother called on May 18. It was John's eleventh birthday. "Bruce is three days overdue," she said. "If he doesn't come in soon, we're calling the Coast Guard."

A week passed. A search ensued. No sign of my brother and his wife was found. In fact, there was speculation of their never even reaching the island. The phone calls between my mother and me intensified. "Palmyra has such a bad reputation," she said. A couple had been killed on the island a few years back, it could have been twenty. At the moment it seemed like yesterday.

"Mom, I think if something were wrong, we'd know it. I just feel he's all right." She agreed with me.

Another week passed. The Coast Guard called off the search. My brother missed a court-appointed trial. His client, Jesse James Bates, was not a client my brother wanted. Jesse James and his buddies were bad news. When the case was first assigned, Bruce tried to get Jesse to change his name. He refused. Jesse did allow my sister to cut his hair. Bruce passed her off as a beautician and got her into his cell. We all thought it was pretty funny at first. As evidence grew against the man, my brother wanted no part of the case. His request to withdraw was refused. "Do you think he's hiding out until the trial is over?" I asked.

"That's an angle the reporters have taken," my mother replied. "I didn't want to upset you, but the newspapers are having a heyday with the story. I'm so worried." She sounded defeated. "If they only had a ham radio on board."

They could talk to De, I thought.

Another week passed. I called Cynnie-Belle. "What do you think?" I asked.

"I don't know. It's just so scary not knowing. I feel so helpless."

"How do you think I feel being so far away?" I retorted.

On June 8, my brother and his wife sailed into Ala Wai Yacht Harbor, totally astonished by the stir they had caused. "We weren't lost," Bruce told the press. "We were blown hundreds of miles off course by storms. We knew family and friends would be worried. On May 20, we entered an apology in the ship's log. It was everything we would have said on a ham radio if we had one."

I was so relieved I forgot to ask for a copy of the apology.

"Medical examinations cause disease," Mother explained.

"What in the world happened?" I cried. "One day I'm talking to you, and the next thing I know you're in the hospital." It was October.

"I thought the Honolulu Belly was coming from all the mangoes I ate and chutney I made and ate. Boy, did I have a bumper crop this year. When the nausea continued, I blamed it on bee pollen."

"Bee pollen?" I asked. "Where in the world did you come up with bee pollen?"

"Hush," she said. "I am allergic to everything under the sun except watercress and watermelon. Anyway, night before last I woke up in such pain. I almost called Cynnie-Belle to take me to the hospital. It got a little better. We went to Dr. Lam's yesterday morning, and he sent me to Straub Clinic. So, here I am. They removed some polyps which seem to be suspicious in nature. There's also talk of a tumor, but I'll know more about that after the surgery."

"Surgery? What sort of surgery?"

"Well, they think there might be some sort of tumor in me."

There's that word again, think, to be followed by guess, and then not sure. I shuddered. My ears played triangle. Be brave, be brave, I told myself. "Do you want me to come out?"

"No, no, come when we can visit and I'm healed. You'd just be sitting around the hospital, that's no fun. I want you here when we can have fun. How about Thanksgiving? You haven't been home for Thanksgiving in nineteen years."

"Great idea," I said with enthusiasm. I hoped it kept the alarm out of my voice.

My sister called after the operation. She was almost incoherent. "Mom has cancer. The doctor said maybe two years. They took what they could of the tumor and sewed her back up." As if to end on a positive note, Cynnie-Belle said, "The funny thing is, her liver is as clear and pure as can be."

"It has got to be the brandy," I told her.

They knew a hurricane was heading toward the islands when I left Chicago. Ewa, pronounced Eva. Mainland hype, I thought. There has never been a hurricane in Hawaii, not to my knowledge. I tucked the information away. When we left the California coast, heading southwest, I was sure everything would be fine. No airline would take that sort of risk, right?

Wrong.

"We should be seeing the outer islands soon," I said to my two new-found friends. We were only a handful of passengers seated in the tail section of the plane. Judy was a stewardess for the airline. Normally, she would have worked the trip, but this time was onboard, dead-heading with her husband for a few days of fun and relaxation.

As the minutes rolled by, the skies got darker. The aircraft began to jump and twitch, not a lot, but enough to make us to realize that there might, indeed, be trouble in paradise.

"We're heading into some turbulence," a voice announced. "Please extinguish all smoking materials and fasten your seat belts."

The weather got progressively worse. Subtle jolts became full-fledged bucks. It was like riding a roller coaster. I understood the term white-knuckling. My palms were drenched in sweat. I could hear my heart thumping wildly inside my chest.

Judy was sitting behind me. "It's okay," she said. "These planes can take a lot of abuse. Just be sure your seat belt is pulled as tight as you can stand. Slipping through them is the problem. And Laurie, we'll use the last exit door. It's not far at all, just follow me if something happens. We're lucky there are so few on board."

"Does that mean it's going to be a long and bumpy flight?" I asked. I couldn't remember what movie that was from.

"Could go either way."

Moments passed. I heard and felt a plunge of the wheels. I figured we were close to landing. Only the pitch of the engines warned of our final approach. Visibility was still zero. Clouds broke, the sea reached towards us in angry waves that crashed over the wings. Suddenly, there was a violent surge of air and we were pitched perpendicular to the runway. I banked my body in the opposite direction. It didn't help straighten the plane. I'm going to die, I thought, as I watched trees, buffeted by high winds, bend to the ground. Complete silence filled the cabin, humans suspended in a finite space between life and death.

I felt a surge of power. It seemed like a long, long time, but the mass of metal righted itself and ascended into the sky.

"We just aborted a landing," said Judy.

"No shit," was all I could say.

We did not try to land again. Instead, we flew to Hilo. Hilo had the only other 747 runway in the islands. Later, Judy, John and I sat in the hotel's bar with the flight attendants.

"Good thing we had the pilots we had today, and not the ones last week," said one of the stewards. He continued. "You know, if we had actually touched ground, we would not have had enough gas to get up again. And," he added, "if we had to abort another attempt to land, we wouldn't have had enough gas to make it to Hilo."

I got through to Mother around ten, five hours after our designated arrival time. "We were really worried," she said. "Cynnie-Belle and Leslie went to meet you. The announcement board kept flashing delay, delay, delay. When it changed to diverted, Cynnie-Belle freaked. Security wouldn't let her go to the gate area. Cynnie-Belle screamed at an official. Asked him what he thought she was going to do, hijack a plane. Out of nowhere, security came, took her and Leslie into custody, and interrogated them for quite awhile. She left a few minutes ago, took forever to drive home. There is no electricity, the streets are a mess, glass and power lines all over the place. Better you take a cab home. My poor baby, I'm glad you got the call through. I'm so grateful you're okay."

"I'm fine," I told her as I hung up. I'm fine and you're not. The weight of experience swirled around the confines of my mind.

I trudged back to the bar. Judy and John had left. I ordered a brandy, slugged it down, then went to my hotel room.

We cooked a couple of turkeys for Thanksgiving, once again thanks to our gas stove. Electricity was rationed throughout the island. Residents were allowed a few hours to use generated energy. A week passed before all power was restored.

Scads of people appeared for Thanksgiving. In-laws, out-laws, relatives, neighbors, and friends. I fetched Ellen for the occasion. Ellen looked no different. Her hair was thinner with a few wisps of gray, her voice a more pronounced sing-song, but Ellen was basically the same. "It's good to see you three children together, and, of course, your father and Mary," she said. We were in the kitchen piling food onto an assortment of trays.

"Ellen, you're a guest, scoot," I said. Her statement made me emotional. I thought of all the years she cooked our Thanksgiving dinner.

"No, no. I would rather be here. I've missed your mother, Laurie. We had many nice years together. I'm glad you left, though. Mr. Benny was not a nice man."

"I know, I understand. I'm glad I left, too." I wanted to continue, I wanted to say, Come back, live in the cottage, help us take care of her because I have to leave again, but I kept the fantasy to myself. There was no use resuming a doomed relationship; then again, they're all doomed, what difference would it make?

"I think Cynnie-Belle's about to have a nervous breakdown," I told Mother later that night. My sister seemed frantic, her mood swings scary. One moment she'd be laughing, the next in tears. I had witnessed two nervous breakdowns over the years. The first was a secretary who sat in my backyard threatening to blow up every mother fucker in the YMCA. The second was a misguided friend. "Mom, I mean it, Cynnie-Belle's out of control."

"Don't be silly, she's had too much to drink, that's all."

As if on cue, Cynnie-Belle waltzed into the room, dragging Roger and yelling, "Come on Bruce," to Bruce. "Pictures, let's get some pictures of the original family." Roger smiled sheepishly.

My brother, ignoring Cynnie-Belle, entered. "Hey Dot," he said, "let's sing Mack the Knife into my Heinekens." The mere mention of "Mack the Knife" made Mother ecstatic.

"All right!" she said with enthusiasm.

"Hey, do that later. I want to have our pictures taken," screamed Cynnie-Belle. It was too late. Mother's teeth were already exposed, her lips pulled back as she bared her pearly whites.

"Come on, take them anyway," said Cynnie-Belle as she shoved the camera into someone's hands.

Flash bulbs popped. Roger and I posed for the picture, while Mom and Bruce sang into his bottle of beer. Between the four of us stood Cynnie-Belle, grinning idiotically, her new eyes slightly shut and very slanted. Every snapshot showed my sister slinging the bird, middle finger erect, the rest not. I wanted to kick her fat ass. Instead, I cleaned up the kitchen as best I could, then drove Ellen home. The party continued well into the night. They sure don't need to roll any electricity into this house, it's wired enough, I thought before falling asleep.

It was as if the past twenty years never existed. We picked up where we had left off in high school. We were friends. There had been other friends, but for those hours, no one else counted.

"Billy's in town," said Dina, when I called with my regards.

"I'd love to see him," I told her. "I'm sure Mom would like that, too." My mother adored Billy. When he returned from boarding school for various holidays, he'd stop by our house before he went home. I liked to pretend it was I he had come to see, but it wasn't. He came to see Dot. Our paths had crossed over the years. If we were both in town, we'd manage a hello.

Once he and his wife, Cathie, helped make eggnog for Christmas. She was very pregnant.

"Here, drink this," Mother said and handed Cathie a glass from the last batch. "It's sure to bring on labor." Everyone in the room laughed. Cathie delivered that night.

"Eggnog seems to have the same effect as mint juleps," I said. "Must be the bourbon."

"Yup," Mother replied. "But brandy makes it easier."

I filed brandy away with bee pollen.

"Hi," said Billy when he called.

"Hey there," I replied. "Happy Birthday." It was the first of November.

"You remember?"

"Of course, it's not a hard date."

He laughed.

"Come over, my mother's dying; I've survived a near plane crash; I could use an old friend, one say around 38."

The night was picture perfect. A full moon left its reflection on the water, its brightness cast shadows on the beach, shadows of palm trees and people who strolled by drenched in moonlight. The sea was calm, the tides neither high nor low. Mini waves lapped the shore, while above, stars shone icy white. I beheld the beauty with reverence.

We drank wine and smoked cigarettes. We talked about our families, the original ones, not the ones we chose. Billy spoke of his father and his father's death. "I took his ashes out to the reef by myself. I opened the urn and threw them into the wind. Unfortunately, I didn't check the direction and I got a face full of him. No one wanted the responsibility of his disposal. Neither my sisters, brother, or mother wanted to help rid themselves of him once and for all. When I turned toward the beach, I could see my mother hiding in the bushes, watching me. It was like everyone was still scared."

I wasn't sure what Billy was trying to say. I suspected his

father hit him occasionally. But I was young then, too naive to think in terms of abuse. Besides, his family was my ideal family; bad things couldn't happen in their house. "Remember how we always thought your dad had another family stashed away in Japan? He was over there more than he was home."

"It was just as well," said Billy, partially buried in thought.

I told him about De in detail. "It was like finding the dead fisherman. Remember? You and Robbie rushed out and found him before the rescue squad. What did you do with the enormity of your situation? You spied a dead man wedged in the coral. You called the authorities. They came. Then what? You still had to live with your find even though it was body-bagged and taken away. My find is De. He is still among the living. I wish he would go away." Although De hadn't called since my mother's reunion, he was an ever-present guilt trip in my mind.

"Finding the dead fisherman was unimportant," said Billy. "Finding him was simple. It held absolutely no significance to those not involved. But the experience of finding the dead fisherman had elements of great significance to us children."

He continued, "I always thought the situation in your house was very important in a raw and forceful way. It was very damaging to your ability to recognize and have faith in a normal, stable family environment."

"That's why I practically lived in yours." I lit another Kool.

"Let me have one," he said. "I don't smoke, so I don't carry them with me."

Billy took a deep drag. "Normalcy is what you craved and needed above all else. You thought my family was normal. It wasn't. Shadows take the shapes of those things lit. Your mom was a passionate woman, still is. She wants it all. I don't think she ever had much respect for moderation, anymore than a racehorse or artist."

I sat and listened, mesmerized. Had he always been so full of insight? I could not remember.

Billy thought a moment. "I'll put you folks in nautical terms. Dot was the sail of the ship, but there was no keel to stay the course. You children stood on deck, often thrilled with speed and envied by us, your friends, for the freedom you enjoyed. It was clear to us, who genuinely cared, that you three lived in the grip of fear. Where are we going, will we crash into a hidden reef, and, most important, who will teach us to sail responsibly when the deck is no longer a support? We were terrified to think of living like you, but, at the same time, Dot had great significance to us on the outside looking in. Look where you are today. You've got a nice life; you experienced a lot in your childhood, but your survival skills paid off." And he added wistfully, "You've made it off the island, you got out of here."

"Perhaps physically," I replied. "Emotionally, I'm still beached."

I called Billy the next day. "An evening with you is equal to years of therapy. Thanks. Sometimes I can't help but wonder if I made up my childhood."

"You didn't make it up. I was there with you."

"You were there, your normal family was there."

"What's normal, Laurie? You know what they say about appearance and reality."

"Same thing they say about assuming . . . I suppose."

Three days after I returned to Louisville, Mother called.

"You should see the jazzy stairs Bruce made for Skoshi. It took a few lessons before she got the hang of them. Bruce solved her reluctance by placing a morsel of food on each step."

"What are you talking about?" I asked.

"I was having a hard time lifting her. Bruce made the stairs to fit at the foot of my bed. Now she can gallop up and down without bothering me. Neat huh? By the way, guess who received a proposal of marriage?"

Mom made "way" and "who" have two syllables. My alert

antenna shot up. "I can't imagine," I said. I really couldn't keep up with the relationships out there. They changed daily.

"Your sister."

"Cynnie-Belle is getting married? To whom?" I knew it wasn't the undercover cop. It had turned out he was already married.

"To a man she met in Kona last weekend." To give him credibility, Mother added, "He's from an old missionary family."

That means a WASP, I thought, and probably poor. She hasn't married one of those yet. "Mom, she needs a shrink, not a marriage. You're not going to let her do it are you? It's sheer impulse, like her second and third attempts at coupling."

"I'm thinking about it. She needs stability. My illness has made her very unstable, which makes me unstable."

"Cynnie-Belle needs to grow up and be responsible. I can't believe you'd let her do this! It makes no sense."

It made more sense when my niece Kathy moved into my, and then Benny's, old bedroom. Kathy, a college graduate back from California, had landed a job representing Esprit clothes. A perfect solution to my mother's situation. Kathy could take her mother's place as my mother's chauffeur and go-fer.

1983

CYNNIE-BELLE GOT MARRIED IN FEBRUARY and moved to Kona. The same month, a made-for-TV movie was filmed in and around Mom's house. They paid her $500 a day. The crews were there from ten until ten. It didn't bother Mother. She had a blast.

"I had no idea what was going on," she said when the filming first began. "People passing on the beach would stop to watch. Whenever the leading man appeared, they would start yelling obscenities at him. He'd just smile and wave back. Turns out he was one of the stars in the 'Rocky Horror Picture Show.' Seems there's quite a following of fans who recite all the dialogue while watching the movie."

"I've heard that," I said. "They usually run the show at midnight, too late for me, I'm afraid."

"Skoshi and I made our acting debut," she said during another phone conversation. "We were magnificent. The scene took place in an elevator. When the door opens, there I am holding Skoshi in my arms. Thank God she didn't bite anyone. I think she knew to be on her best behavior."

Mother and Skoshi were, indeed, in the film. I am sure they wouldn't have survived the cutting room if the cast and director hadn't liked her so much. Mom, not the dog. The scene itself was atrocious. My mother didn't know where to look or what to do with herself during the split seconds of her appearance. It was nice of them to keep her in, I thought, until I saw the show in its entirety. All of it should have been left on the cutting room floor. I cringed, thinking of the hype I'd given my friends. "There's going to be a great movie on TV," I told everyone. "Be sure not to miss it."

I called my mother the next morning. "Wasn't that the most awful movie you've ever seen?"

Silence ensued.

"I mean, other than the setting, it stank. The plot was dumb, the characters were unbelievable, and I felt violated watching our house on the screen. I felt exposed, even raped. What are you doing in my house, in my room, I wanted to say."

I realized I was babbling. I stopped to let my mother in for words of agreement. There weren't any.

"How can you say it was terrible. It was great. I had a house full of people to watch last night. Everyone thought the movie was terrific. We all loved it."

"Mom," I said, "I have nothing against the setting. The cast and script were lousy."

"Stop, I don't want to hear it. The movie was super."

She wasn't well. I decided to let her win.

A few days later my mother called. "Scouts for 'Magnum PI' came by today. They want to use this location for one of their shows. I told them I wanted a 'thou' a day. They said they'll think about it."

"The kids are going to love the tent," she declared over the phone.

"What tent," I asked.

"I went to Penny's and got a simply marvelous tent." She pronounced "marvelous" like an actress.

Her message began to sink in. "Wait a minute, are you telling me John and his friend are going to live in a tent?"

"Yes, they'll have loads of fun being outdoors by themselves."

Incredible, I thought. We were leaving in the morning to

spend four weeks in Honolulu. John was taking a friend. Plans had been made for months.

"Mom, John is twelve, his friend is fourteen. Staying in a tent, believe me, will not be considered a thrilling adventure. What's wrong with the cottage, maybe even a room in your house?"

"I've rented the cottage, and the twins are staying in the downstairs bedroom, Kathy has yours, which leaves one spare room for you and Barret."

I couldn't believe it, although it made sense. I was sorry I didn't figure it out sooner. My sister's children were home for the summer. Cynnie-Belle married the WASP and moved to Kona. Her kids had no place to stay. I was caught, couldn't do anything but get pissed off, which I did. It was easy.

"Fuck her," I said aloud after I hung up. "She's done it again."

My husband and the two boys were better sports. I watched them unfold and pitch the plastic tent. "The kids will be cooked as soon as the sun rises, that thing will be hot as hell," I said. Barret shot me a "watch what you say" glance. I trotted back into the house looking for trouble. It came in spades at bedtime.

I found John and his friend fast asleep in our room a few hours later. "What should I do?" I asked mother. "Wake them up, say it's time to go outside now?"

"We'll sleep in Kathy's room," I announced. "Kathy's in California, she won't mind." I had noticed her door was padlocked. It seemed sort of funny to me, but then, what else was new.

"You can't. I have strict orders to let no one into her room."
"Why?"

"Because the younger ones have taken some of her sample clothes. She needs her samples to make her sales."

Mom made the mistake of telling me she had the key. Had I thought the key was in California, I might not have reacted with such violence. Then again, I might have. "Give me the key," I said.

"No, I just told you I'm not to let anyone enter that room."

"Mother, I am not anyone. I am thirty-six years old; some even think I'm sort of responsible. Now give me the key."

I could tell she was searching for excuses. "The room is jammed full of racks," she said.

"I will move the racks aside. Be real. We're not going to hurt anything. Hey, lock us in if it makes you happy. I'm only asking to sleep in the bed. What do you think I'm going to do, cut up all the clothes? Are you telling me, in so many words, that you don't trust me being around Kathy's samples? I'm not going to give them away for Christ's sake."

"I'm not giving you the key," she said as she folded her arms across her chest.

"God damn you," I roared. "You don't care about me, you've never cared. Me the mistake—the mistake you've never controlled or owned. I've never been a Cynnie-Belle or Kathy to you. I have fought hard for my independence, and now you've decided to withhold a key. God damn you, I go away to college and the first summer I'm home, I find you've given all my clothes to Benny's asshole daughters. You allowed my grandmother's stomach to be removed. You killed her and you killed Megan. If you'd have used a leash on your way to the mailbox, she wouldn't have gotten hit by a car. My dog, my dog, I loved that dog more than anything in the world. I spent three entire days crying in the nurse's office at school. Three days. Could I have stayed home? Oh no, you were on Maui, there was no one to give me permission." I realized I was screaming. "Shit, you really know how to do it, don't you? If I had known the kids were going to sleep in a tent, I'd never have come."

Mother started to say something. "Shut up, just shut up," I yelled. "I don't want to hear one more fucking thing about anything. I'm getting out of here."

We left the kids asleep in our room. "I'm so mad I could have slugged her," I said to Barret. "She probably would have enjoyed it. I'm glad I didn't." I never realized I was capable of such rage.

We spent the night at the Outrigger Hotel, a monstrous structure that loomed over the site of our original club which moved to the slopes of Diamond Head in the early sixties. I could see the Royal Hawaiian Hotel from our balcony. The Pink Palace was dwarfed by high-rises.

We returned to Kahala mid-morn. Mom acted as if nothing had happened. I resigned myself to the fact that the boys had no choice but to become tent dwellers.

It wasn't even an hour before Mother said, "They're giving me a surprise birthday party this afternoon. God how I hate surprise parties, they should know that by now."

I knew about the party. My sister and her new husband were flying in from Kona for the celebration. A kitchen addition, who lived across the avenue, was in charge. She made all the arrangements. Her husband owned The Broiler. Well, the food will be great, I thought.

I wondered what response my mother wanted. I could say, "Hey, Mom, I'm only a visitor, I don't count. Have you forgotten? I am a nobody. I'm truly sorry about the surprise, but I, the nobody, had nothing to do with the decision. But, alas, I was told, which makes me a player in the performance. I don't want to be part of the act. I'd rather be a spectator. I'm better off watching dramas unfold. I'd rather stand back and applaud, laugh, and cry during the appropriate moments. But, but, but, here I am again, forced into a scene because I was given knowledge of something with which I had nothing to do. A surprise party's minor compared with all the shit you've shoved down my throat. Instead I said, "Excuse me," as I passed her presence going out to the beach.

"My mother is dying," I said to myself. "My mother is dying and she's gotten word there is to be a surprise party and she's pissed because she hates surprise parties. The real surprise would be if she had another birthday to live through."

I heard the entourage coming down the alley around four. Scads of her kitchen additions, neighbors, and relatives appeared blowing paper whistles and kazoos. Little cone hats perched on everyone's head were secured by rubber bands hooked under chins. T-shirts bore slogans such as "Eat Dead Fish." Mother's read "Caution, Falling Down Drunk." The troops were proud, and reveled in their success at pulling it off. Mom, naturally, played her astonishment to the hilt. Tons of cameras took tons of pictures; everyone wanted to pose with Dot. It was as if they needed proof of their participation.

I met my sister's husband. He seemed nice enough, soft spoken. Overwhelmed, I was sure, by the riotous revelers. After awhile, the party moved itself to the home of the hostess. Mother, deep in conversation, looked up to see her entourage marching toward the alley. "There they go," she said, "and I must be after them for I am their leader."

What a great line, I thought, as I followed across the lawn. I wondered why my brother wasn't there. He was less than wild over a lot of Cynnie-Belle's friends. He probably wouldn't have attended under any circumstances. He probably wasn't even invited. One down, twenty seven fun-packed days to go.

I told my sister about De.

"I've known all along," she said.

"You what?"

"I've known since the fourth grade. He sent me a letter, said he was your father. Mom tried to pass it off, told me it was written by some nut."

"Some nut? It was his nuts that put me on this planet."

Cynnie-Belle laughed. "I told Bruce about the letter and what Dot said."

"Was it around the time you two gave me such grief? When

your stares at breakfast were so awful I ate alone in the dining room?"

"No, that was due to that damn whistle of yours. Bruce and I didn't hate you. We felt sorry for you. When you got older, I envied your height and legs. I was even jealous."

"You, jealous? The teen queen? Miss popularity?"

"Yes, me," she replied.

"Did you ever plan on telling me?"

"What for? I never knew whether it was really true. What's he like?" she asked.

"Not much," I replied. I filled her in on the details, how I found him and all. Cynnie-Belle seemed relieved. I hadn't outdone her in the dad department. Later I discussed the matter with Bruce. He wasn't interested, so I let it drop. Their knowing, however, explained a lot of things. Why they were usually kind and considerate, more like parents. It also explained an experience I had at Central Union, if my math was correct. I was on a swing in the playground. Classmates were everywhere. Suddenly it was as if I were in a vacuum, voices muffled around me, I was totally alone. "Where would I be if I hadn't been born to my mother and father," I thought aloud. It was like an out-of-body experience for a five-year-old. As quickly as the moment came, it disappeared. Voices returned, my senses swept back into focus. I never forgot it, though, never.

Mother took us to Hilo. It was her way of making up for the tense tent situation, I was sure. We stayed at the Nani Loa, the same hotel that sheltered me from the unfriendly skies of Hurricane Ewa. It felt sort of deja vu.

We toured the volcano parks and had a picnic lunch at my brother's. He was building a get-away home above the volcano line. "I bought a bulldozer," he explained. His yard was cluttered with lumber and doors and sinks and toilets. It looked like the set of "Sanford and Son."

"I salvage old houses in Honolulu," he continued. "In return, I bulldoze them when I'm through. Then I put what I want into containers and barge them to Hilo." I pictured my brother, his long hair and beard blown back, destroying shacks and shanties. I was impressed.

It was a nice afternoon. Everyone got along. My sister, her husband, his two kids, and Leslie, Cynnie-Belle's youngest, drove over from Kona. Before we left, everyone had a chance to use Bruce's outhouse, a toilet seat perched on two pieces of wood, lid up, shaded by an umbrella that read, "Campari."

The next day we drove along the Hamakua Coast, our destination Kona. My sister spent the entire morning throwing up. "Must have been something I ate," she'd say just before yelling "Stop, I'm going to be sick." Her husband would pull over, and Cynnie-Belle would jump out, run in front of the Bronco, and puke. We adults tried not to watch, but it was kind of hard, her being right in front of us and all. The kids in the back were oblivious, all plugged into headsets, listening to various cuts from the "Synchronisity" album. The music, piped into their skulls, often came out in words. "Magic, magic, magic," one would sing. Another would boast, "I'll be watching you." Sting, making his mark but not strong enough to eradicate the retching sounds from outside. "Are we there yet?" a child inevitably would ask as we slowed down. "No," an adult would reply. Then, "How many more miles?" The scenic route punctuated by pull-overs was not fun.

We had lunch in the little ranch town of Kamuela. My mother arranged for John and his friend to go horseback riding. Billy's sister, Priscilla, owned the stable. Priscilla was older than Dina. I didn't really know her. I thought of calling Billy but I didn't. The kids rode. We sat in a bar and listened to the jokes of two local drunks. They were highly entertaining; sure beat the scenic route. We flew out of Kona two days later.

—

"Come see this," Mother shouted into the front door. My plane was to leave shortly. "I've never, in all my years, seen one this close."

I walked out to the beach. The winds were blowing so hard I felt my ears flapping. A rain squall was heading toward us, coming from the direction of Koko Head. Through the mist, I saw the end of a rainbow, its band of colors fused into the sand in front of Aunt Cecily's. The rainbow arched out to sea, and under its zenith stood my mother who had taken off in its direction. I stood there, listening to the very real roar in my ears. "This is it," I whispered. "This is the end of the rainbow." I needed no other sign.

John and I took a cab to the airport. No one was around to give us a lift. We were a little early. I noticed a plane was leaving for Chicago twenty minutes before our scheduled departure. I changed flights, then called Mother to let her know in case there was a crash. She wasn't home. One of Cynnie-Belle's twins answered the phone. I told him instead. He didn't seem to care.

I saw her as soon as I entered the cabin. My heart fell, I spun around, intent on getting off. "Laurie," she yelled and grabbed my arm, pulling me back to full circle. It was Judy, my hurricane friend. She was working the trip. "I'm not flying with you," I stated emphatically.

"Not to worry," she said.

"Judy, we defied death once. I'm not going to give it a second chance." I was thinking that maybe the rainbow was for me.

"Don't be silly," she said, pushing me down the aisle. "I'll take care of you. And is this your John?" she asked, reaching down to ruffle his hair.

Fall was full for me.

My mother called. "My boys lost, causing me to become intoxicated and call De. They lost again, yesterday, which caused me to become intoxicated and fall down. No harm," she said.

"I take it your boys are the Phillies," I asked, amazed I even knew who was playing in the World Series.

"You betcha."

"So how is De," I asked.

"He says he has no teeth and no prostate."

I was sorry I brought it up.

"Well, I really called to tell you that today's the anniversary of my operation. How about that? Dr. Ho says everything looks swell."

"That's terrific!" I meant every word I said.

In November she called to tell me about an earthquake. "I wasn't sure what it was at first, thought Skoshi was jiggling the bed. I sat up. Everything was rolling all over the place. I thought about making it to a doorway, then thought, to hell with that, Skoshi and I will just ride it down to the first floor."

She went on to describe watching Cynnie-Belle's first husband, Henry, in a baseball scene for "Magnum PI." "I had my picture taken with Tom Selleck," she said.

In December I called as soon as I received her Christmas card. "Mele Kalikamaka" it read on the outside. Inside was a color photograph of her and Tom. He has his arm around her shoulders. Both grin into the camera, his a better grin than hers. Under the picture, Mother had written in green ink, "How's this for chutzpah?" I didn't know what chutzpah meant, but it sounded as if it were something pretty funny.

"You are too much," I said when she answered the phone. It had been awhile since I talked to her.

"I got such a kick out of mailing those Christmas cards. Mainlanders, eat your hearts out."

"Are you all right?" I asked. "You sound terrible."

"I've had an awful time with the flu. I've been running a temperature of 102 for almost two weeks. I went to see Dr. Lam. He wants me to check into the hospital next week. I feel so lousy, I'm going in this afternoon. It's a good thing you called."

My mother AWOLed from Straub Clinic Christmas Day. "I demanded some valium then busted out," she told me.

1984

IN JANUARY, SHE BEGAN TO SUCCUMB to the disease. The tumor had resurfaced. They tried to operate, did the best they could, but the growth had attached itself to other organs. Although it was unsaid, I knew it was a matter of time.

I flew out for limited tomorrows, made three trips. In February I took on the doctors. There was no earthly reason for Mother to spend hours in waiting rooms, only to spend minutes with the physician. We began calling before we left the house. For five days we played Scrabble and listened to tapes from a "Prairie Home Companion," while a chemotherapist's concoction dripped into her veins. We also ate Oreo cookies, which Mom found hard to believe. "I've never liked sweets, never ate desserts, and look at me."

"I was the cookie monster, Mom. I still don't understand why you didn't stop my binge with desserts. Remember Bon Bons, those bell-shaped chocolates with vanilla ice cream inside? I could eat a couple of boxes and not bat an eye."

"I made it a policy," she said. "A policy of letting you children set parameters. If I jumped in, it would do no good. Life is to enjoy. You three had enough sense to quit when it was quitting time, sense enough to know when to let go."

My mother came home from the hospital. I had the refrigerator stuffed with various flavors of ice cream. I cooked meals that had some zing to them, meals like barbecued beef and carrots.

"Magic," my mother would say. "You're magic, Laurie. I haven't wanted to eat anything up until now."

"Duke's the magician, Mom. I'm simply cooking things I think interesting. Common sense dictates."

I flew back to Louisville. Two weeks later she called. "I went to check in for the second set of drips. They sent me home. Guess it didn't do any good."

I couldn't believe her doctors. Absolute idiots I thought.

I went out again in April. This time my cooking was not magic. Mother refused to leave her bedroom. "Just let me lie here," she told me.

"Mom," my voice stern. "You need to get up and get moving. You need to come downstairs, join the world. You give up by staying in your room. Please, for me?"

She did. She even managed to string some ribbons around the kitchen when she heard Bruce was appointed a judge. I knew my mother felt dreadful, but we ordered a cake and gave him a small congratulations party.

My twentieth reunion was in June. It was also Cynnie-Belle's twenty-fifth. Her class, which I liked better than mine, held its picnic at Mother's. Every five years, the class of '59 would meet in our front yard. I opted to stay home and enjoy Cynnie-Belle's colleagues. Mother made a brief appearance. She sat outside for a few minutes. She wore a blue baseball cap. On the visor was a replica of a hand slinging the bird. The hand was yellow. Blue and yellow were Punahou's colors.

I called on her birthday. I was in Canada with Barret and John. "I don't know," I told them after I hung up.

A few days before her death, she telephoned. We talked for one hour and twenty minutes. Before hanging up, she said, "I don't want to live if I have to live like this. I've told Bruce and Cynnie-Belle, now I'll tell you. I want Skoshi cremated, her ashes put into my urn. Bury her with me. Skoshi always lay at my feet, now she'll lie in my feet."

On August 7, Bruce phoned. It was mid-afternoon, Kentucky time. "It's over," he said. "Dot died in her sleep last night."

"I'll be there tomorrow," I told him, and I was. Once again I flew the friendly skies. This time, the ticket, which had held at a steady $525 rate, cost me $1,682. I tried to argue, to say that death kept me from an advanced booking. No one seemed to care, but then, no one knew my mother.

"Oh, Laurie," said my sister when she met me at the airport. "I wasn't there, I wasn't there!"

"It's okay Cynnie-Belle. She died in her sleep; no coma, no excruciating pain, she went peacefully."

As we drove toward Kahala, my sister related the incidents of the preceding day. "Kehau came to visit Dot and found her somewhat disoriented so she stayed the night. Around ten yesterday morning, she went upstairs to see how Dot was doing and found her dead. Kehau called Bruce, me, and the paramedics. I told her not to let anyone take the body until I got there. I needed to tell Mom good-bye."

I started to cry.

"Now I understand the term bag of bones," Cynnie-Belle continued. "Dot said that a lot. There was really not much left of her. It was so sad," said Cynnie-Belle before she fell silent.

I looked out the car window. We were at the top of Kaimuki. I could see the Pacific in the distance. The Pacific in its outrageous shades of blue. Part of a poem I wrote after my grandmother died flashed through my mind. I wrote it while vacationing on Hilton Head Island.

> *And I listen to the sea.*
> *And I think about me.*
> *And I long for the Pacific.*
> *And the times what were terrific.*

Because Montclair
Isn't there anymore.
Close the door.
Quoth "The Raven"
Nevermore.

Cynnie-Belle's subtle chuckles brought me out of my reverie. "What's so funny?" I asked.

"After I told Mom good-bye, I let the paramedics into the room. We were standing around her body when, all of a sudden, it looked as though she were moving her feet under the sheets. I thought this one medic was going to levitate, his hair about stood on end."

Cynnie-Belle's chuckles turned into air-gulping hysterics.

"It was Skoshi," she said between breaths. "Skoshi was sleeping under the covers. We'd forgotten all about the dog."

Her laughter was infectious. I joined the emotion. In moments, we were laughing so hard we were crying.

"I had a sign," Cynnie-Belle said as we passed the site of our first shopping center. It was now a huge mall, full of specialty shops, Liberty House, and a J.C. Penney's. The Piggly Wiggly grocery was gone, but another supermarket had taken its place. The Kahala Mall had everything. There was no need to go downtown anymore, much less to Waikiki.

"A sign?" I asked. "Like the butterflies?"

"Yes, like the butterflies," she replied and continued. "You remember her aquamarine jewelry? Remember how she lost it years ago? Dot thought she might have hidden it in an old box of Kotex that got thrown out long after menopause. Well, we looked everywhere for the necklace, ring, earrings, and a brooch to no avail. We finally gave up and forgot about it."

My grandmother collected butterflies. My sister collected owls. She had more owls than the law should allow.

"After they took the body, twin David and I remained in her

room. Somehow David accidentally knocked off this wooden owl I gave Dot ages ago. It was on top of her secretary. Anyway, the owl fell to the floor, its head came off and out spilled the jewelry. I started screaming "A sign, a sign, Dot's sent me a sign!"

My mother never sent me a sign. Well, there was a cardinal on her roof later on that afternoon. My cousins Stephen and David were sitting next to me. We were sprawled out on lawn chairs outside the front door. They had flown in from California for the funeral. The three of us were in a position to see the bird, but only I looked up. My sign? Our sign? We three Kentuck-ians. Theirs by birth, mine by choice. The cardinal, our state bird, perched on the highest point of the roof and looked down at me. I decided to keep quiet. Why stretch a concept, why try for a sign, why drink through glass straws? It was ground too dangerous to stand on.

Cynnie-Belle had already snuffed Skoshi by the time I arrived and taken her ashes to the funeral home. Everything was ready for the service the next day.

"Turn it up," said twin Bruce as we pulled into Punch Bowl National Cemetery. "What an appropriate song," From the radio came Marvin Gaye's "Mercy, Mercy." All of us started singing softly as we pulled into the area designated for outdoor memorial services.

My brother took charge. "Gather together," he said. Our entourage consisted of our immediate family, relatives, a few out-laws, and some close friends. "Gather together," Bruce repeated, "in a circle." His right hand clutched a bottle of Christian Brother's brandy. Once everyone was in position, he uncorked the bottle and poured a fair amount of the contents onto the flower-and lei-draped urn. When through, he raised the brandy to his lips and drank a shot. "For those who might need this, take a swig." The bottle passed through the crowd.

Here is some of what Bruce said between prayers, Psalms, and Biblical quotations:

"Boris Pasternack in Dr. Zhivago said what we, I'm sure, know and feel, in words I feel apply here.

"The stir is over, I step forth on boards, leaning against an upright at the entrance.

"I strain to make the far off echo yield a clue to the events that may come in my day.

"For Dot the stir of life is over. As we stand here this afternoon, we perhaps also, strain to catch her far off echo, so that it might yield a clue to the events which will come.

"As we stand here and listen, perhaps straining to hear an echo, Dot may be saying:

"Do not come to sit beside a low green mound or bring the first fragrant blossoms of plumeria or yellow ginger because I loved them so, for I shall not be there.

"I will look at you from the eyes of little children . . . I will bend to meet you in swaying hands of sun-drenched coconut trees and caress you with a passionate sweep of a good Kona storm blowing across the ocean in front of Kahala.

"I will give you strength in the trade winds and bring you peace in the tender shades of pink and gold when the evening shadows lengthen at sunset.

"All of these things that made me happy, they are a part of me . . . and now I shall become a part of them. Come celebrate life anew together."

Bruce continued,

"Do not stand at my grave and weep.
I am not there. I do not sleep.
I am a thousand winds that blow.
I am the diamond glint on snow.

I am the sunlight on ripened grain.
I am the gentle Autumn's rain.
When you awaken in the morning's hush
I am the swift uplifting rush
Of quiet birds in circular flight.
I am the soft stars that shine at night.
Do not stand at my grave and cry;
I am not there. I did not die.

"We all know Dot went out with joy and is now in peace. Dot used to say, 'I don't know where we are going, but I'm sure it will be the same place.'"

"Good-bye," Bruce concluded. "And now everyone of you, in your own way, silently or aloud, simply bid Dot, our mother, grandmother, aunt, cousin, or friend, farewell. We know in the sweet by-and-by, we'll meet her on that beautiful shore. Adieu." There was not a dry eye in the circle.

Later that evening, in the midst of a cast of thousands who had gathered to grieve and party, I caught Roger Ames looking at me with much sadness. Both fists were clenched together. I stared as he pointed to his heart before breaking his fists apart. My heart is broken, he said without words. So is mine, I thought pointing to my own heart before holding up two fingers for him to see. My heart is broken in more ways than one.

Three days later, I was gone. I salvaged every scrap of memorabilia I felt important. My school reports, pictures, letters I'd sent, poems, all the little things that symbolized our relationship. I left for the airport in a car already pointed toward the alley. I went down the back steps knowing I was headed for a final departure. In my hand, I clutched a carry-on bag. It was full of all my mother's day-by-day diaries dating back to 1931. I left holding her life in my hand, her world penned mostly in green ink. I had no idea what I was going to do with the information.

No earthly idea at all.

1991

I CALLED OUR OLD KAHALA NUMBER a few years after my mother's death. The number was one we had kept since 1948. Two extra digits were added in the late fifties to accommodate the growth in population. A kid answered the phone. I could not say, Can I speak to Mr. Romain?

I could not ask, Is my mother there?

Instead, I said, "I'm sorry, I have the wrong number," which I did and did not.

"It's OK," replied the voice. And it was.

It is.

EPILOGUE

IN THE UPSTAIRS HALL, in what was first my grandmother's house, there was a blackout bulb leftover from World War II. She explained its purpose to me when I was young. It seems that the bulb's shaft of light, turned on every night, cut a path of visible protection. It illuminated a fine line of safe familiarity. The same bulb shone for forty years. It is gone now. So too are the hedges and trees between many of the alleys. A series of brick walls line the Avenue. Almost all the old homes are gone, sold to foreigners to be razed for mansions. But in the late 80s, the foreigners' economy crashed and these properties, built to be dream homes, now lie neglected, empty, and boarded-up. Swimming pools stagnant. The foliage and flame trees stand dead. Brick walls, symbolic of being an American, you know, like entrances to subdivisions.

It's all gone. There are no more torch fishermen, the bay is dead. Often the first canal serves as a vehicle for raw sewage that spills into it during times of overload. Parents have passed as have all the dogs. Gone, gone, like the blackout bulb in our home. If I had known it was to be torn down, I might have tried to save it.

When I was first married, I met my mother in New York. I was waiting in the lobby of the St. Regis Hotel. I heard the sound of rubber slippers slapping on marbled floors. She appeared in pedal pushers. "Mother?" I said astounded, "You wore that to lunch with officers of the bank?"

"I sure did," she replied.

"Well, Mom, we're going to a fancy Italian restaurant tonight. I think you ought to wear a dress."

"Honey," she said slowly. "I hate to tell you this, but I didn't even bring a dress."

I sank into myself and wondered why God gave me this mother when there were so many from whom to choose.

No matter what my mother sprang on me, no matter what pieces of information she chose to impart at my expense, no matter what, when all was said and done, what was done was done. I had no power, no control to censor. Her realities became mine.

I realize now, I grew from my experiences with her. My mother trusted me to make my own choices and trust is love. She gave me humor and wit and a fierceness to succeed whatever the circumstances. She taught me to live with the rattling windows in my life. At an early age I learned to stuff cardboard between the screens to stop the noise.

I picture canoes going out to sea. The sun, about to slip over the horizon, looks like the yoke of a golden egg. I watch for the green flash which occurs after it's disappeared. Once I would have screamed, "The sun is gone, the earth is flat, there are no curves, no warmth, no bodies to burrow into, we have only ourselves, just us, you folks, you all, you guys." Not anymore. There will always be a new moon. I have howled at the moon. Bayed at all the wrongs befallen me. I could yell, "What have you done, Mother. How dare you leave?" But I will not. I know it is time to let her go. I'm just sorry I never got a chance to say, "Thank you."

THE END

ACKNOWLEDGMENTS

There are many people to whom I wish to extend my warmest thanks:

To Craig Childress, my creative writing teacher, whose belief in the beginning of this book enabled me to hele-on.

To my early readers whose enthusiasm led me to elaborate: Weda Riehm, Brenda Deemer, Jill Cooper, Nancy Opper Moser, Carol Peterson, Mary Lou Northern, Emily Kiesler, Shirley Wright, Mary Caldwell, and Pam Steward and Jonnie Vatter, may they rest in peace.

To those who suggested contacts in the publishing world: Carol Butler, Tom Noland, Bill Schuetze, Martha Neal Cooke, Ann Savarese, Sue Johnson, Sarah Gilbert, and Diane Johnston Patton.

To Dena Bentley, who first computerized this manuscript in 1991, and to Sammy Pope, my Macintosh man.

To Hope Hollenbeck, my editor and friend, who made me promise to resurrect this manuscript after it sat in a drawer for seven years.

To Diana Jardine and Priscilla Growney, who got *Kahala* into Eric Bollinger's hands at McKenna Publishing Group.

To Cynnie Belle Petersen and Bruce Ames, my siblings who shared my childhood experiences, and to my husband and son for their support.

To those I've overlooked, I apologize.

—*Laurie Ames Birnsteel*